Every Employee
a Manager

ABOUT THE AUTHOR

Scott Myers, an organizational psychologist, lives in Santa Barbara, California, with his wife, Susan—also an industrial psychologist. As co-managers of the Center for Applied Management, they conduct management research, write, and provide consultation services to organizations in both the private and public sectors. They are members of the American Psychological Association and the Santa Barbara Chamber of Commerce.

Dr. Myers' formal education was completed at Purdue University, where he received his bachelor's degree in 1948, master's in 1949, and Ph.D. in 1951. The same year, he joined Hughes Aircraft Company in Culver City, California, where he became supervisor of personnel planning, which included psychological testing, employee counseling, and personnel statistics.

In 1954, he was recruited by the University of Southern California to help establish the Public Affairs Institute and to direct the Personnel Management and Research Center, both at the University of Tehran in Iran. In these roles, he taught personnel management to graduate students at the University of Tehran (as Associate Professor of Public Administration) and directed Iranian researchers in the construction and validation of psychological tests for the Persian culture. His stay in Iran was extended to 5 years by an additional assignment for planning technical training programs and for translating textbooks into the Persian language.

From 1959 until 1973, he was a member of the corporate personnel staff of Texas Instruments in Dallas, Texas. He served as an internal consultant to TI and conducted research and published extensively on motivation, manpower development, and labor relations. His articles have appeared in the *Harvard Business Review* and *California Management Review*. While employed by Texas Instruments, he served two years as Visiting Professor of Organizational Psychology and Management at the Sloan School of Management, MIT.

Since 1973, he has been self-employed in roles that enable him to organize his life-style into three components: (1) tennis, gardening, sailing, and other recreational pursuits; (2) research and writing; and (3) consultation (which finances the other two).

His publications include the first edition of this book (McGraw-Hill, 1970), *Managing Without Unions,* and *Managing With Unions* (Addison-Wesley, 1976, 1978).

Every Employee a Manager

Second Edition

M. Scott Myers

McGraw-Hill Book Company

New York   St. Louis   San Francisco   Auckland   Bogotá
Hamburg   Johannesburg   London   Madrid   Mexico
Montreal   New Delhi   Panama   Paris   São Paulo
Singapore   Sydney   Tokyo   Toronto

Library of Congress Cataloging in Publication Data

Myers, Marvin Scott, date
   Every employee a manager.

   Includes index.
   1. Personal management.   2. Psychology, Industrial.
3. Job enrichment. I. Title.
HF5549.M93 1981   658.3   80-18858
ISBN 0-07-044269-X

   34567890   KPKP   898765432

The editors for this book were William R. Newton and Esther Gelatt, the
designer was Mark E. Safran, and the production supervisor was Paul A.
Malchow. It was set in Souvenir by Achorn Graphic Services.

Printed and bound by The Kingsport Press.

For Susan

A master in the art of living
   knows no sharp distinction
   between his work and his play,
   his labor and his leisure,
   his mind and his body,
   his education and his recreation.
He hardly knows which is which.
   He simply pursues his vision
   of excellence through whatever
   he is doing and leaves others
   to determine whether he is
   working or playing.
To himself he always seems to be
   doing both.*

*Author unknown, quoted by Peter T. McKinney, Exxon Chemical Company U.S.A., Houston, Tex., Aug. 11, 1977.

Contents

Foreword

The most important continuing challenge to industry in the years ahead will be to establish innovative programs that encourage the achievement of compatible employee and company goals. In a society that continues to change through the introduction of new technologies, a better-educated and more mature work force, and an increase of leisure time, it is necessary to know what these goals should be, what the measurable checkpoints are, and what has been and still needs to be accomplished. Management's role in attracting, challenging, and retaining the members of the coming generations is as vital to an organization's success as any breakthrough in technology or newly designed production equipment.

The truly successful growth organization of the future will require a marriage of industry's richest assets—the capabilities of human beings and the efficiency of operational systems. As high-volume, repetitive, and rigidly paced manufacturing systems place unyielding demands on people, management must show the same dedication to improving job satisfaction that it has given in the past to improving equipment design and satisfying people's pay requirements.

The "involvement" type of organizational climate is essential to successful management. Modern problems are too complex and diversified for one person or one approach. Therefore, we need a blending of skills and perspectives in the form of effective problem-sharing and problem-solving teams to achieve our goals. However, we need to remember that synergy through the effectiveness of people cannot be achieved instantaneously or through directives—that people require time and opportunity for the development of trust, communications, interaction, and commitment. Also, recognition of achievements is a vital motivational element of the "involved" management process.

The concept "every employee a manager" through meaningful work requires supervisory sophistication not common in today's organizations. Involvement of people in the planning and controlling as well as the doing of their work must be understood not as an act of good "human relations" or as a means of exploitation but, rather, as a sound business practice that benefits both the organization and its members. The supervisor of the future knows he or she is not managing a technique or a program, but a way of life at work that finds expression in all levels of the create, make, and market functions of the organization. Through this way of life, people gradually become more knowledgeable and competent, and migrate and polarize toward a total commitment which leads to continuing growth, success, and self-renewal for both the organization and its members.

A company's success depends on its ability to institutionalize innovation and thus make self-renewal an integral feature of its culture. Although a company's underlying philosophy may serve as a stablizing guide to organizational effectiveness, its objectives, strategies, and tactical action programs cannot be cast in concrete but must continuously anticipate and adapt to changing circumstances. During the decade since the first edition of *Every Employee a Manager* was published, Texas Instruments has continued to evolve under the guiding principles of its philosophy and unique culture. This second edition, in a similar manner, reflects adaptation to diverse work environments and illustrates the application of the same innovative principles in different types of organizations.

Mark Shepherd, Jr.
Chairman of the Board
Texas Instruments Incorporated

Preface

The first edition of *Every Employee a Manager* was completed in 1969, during my last years with Texas Instruments, and was illustrated with many of the strategies and practices that made TI the leader in its field. Because TI has no labor unions, the book was often perceived by readers as a blueprint for avoiding unionization. However, our subsequent experience and this second edition show that the philosophy and practices of the nonunion organization can be applied with equal success where unions are present.

During the past decade my wife, Susan, and I have continued to assist organizations in implementing the principles defined in this book. We have found employees in unionized organizations to be no less responsive to the opportunity to be responsible and self-reliant than members of nonunion companies. We have concluded that irresponsible and counterproductive behavior is but a symptom of the lack of opportunity to find constructive outlets for the expression of talent. The tarnished image of unionism often stems from its role in providing legitimacy to initiative not aligned with organizational goals.

Traditional managers and union leaders often perceive enlightened workers as disruptive and disrespectful of time-honored values and practices. While managers worry that their workers will unionize, union leaders are apprehensive of decentrifications. Both concerns are justified, as either action is but a symptom of rebellion against what workers feel to be arbitrary and oppressive constraints imposed by either company or union. Many employees smart from the implication that being referred to as a member of "labor" is tantamount to being classified as a second-class citizen. Although the concept "every employee a manager" remains to be defined to most workers, most of them are psychologically ready to implement it. All they need is an opportunity.

This book describes the conditions of the work place which provide such an opportunity. Examples are drawn from a variety of organizations—both union and nonunion. These conditions are not created full-blown from a single program or the efforts of a charismatic leader but, rather, from a network of systems which interactively compose a climate and way of life at work in which people can achieve personal goals through the attainment of organizational goals.

The masculine pronoun in this book refers to both men and women. It is used to avoid cumbersome language.

We continue to be indebted to Texas Instruments, as a primary source of examples presented herein, and to the late Pat Haggerty, whose rigorous and charismatic leadership has left indelible impressions on this author, Texas Instruments, and the managerial culture of America. The Goodyear Tire and Rubber Company, Eastman Kodak Company, QYX of Exxon Enterprises, Simon Engineering Company, Northwood Pulp and Timber Company, Molson's Western Breweries, PACCAR, Tektronix, The Eaton Corporation, Westinghouse, and the Tarrytown plant of General Motors have all in unique ways contributed to the mosaic that makes up this book.

Many individuals, too numerous to mention, deserve recognition for furthering the concepts mentioned herein. In terms of sheer numbers of people influenced, Phil Ensor (Goodyear), Dave Hunt (Kodak), Don Scobel (Eaton), John Paré (Canada Post Office), and Dutch Landon (General Motors) deserve special mention. Many individuals to whom we refer as "thought leaders" in company and union leadership roles deserve most of the credit for successes described herein because, like the soldier on the "firing line," these individuals are the primary risk-takers in this managerial revolution.

M. Scott Myers

1
Theories of Human Effectiveness

People's behavior stems from their interpretations of what they think they perceive. These perceptions influence and become crystallized or incorporated into their values or assumptions and, ultimately, their habits. Broadly speaking, then, individuals' values and assumptions may be thought of as their own personal theories.

The term "theory" implies a tentativeness which, if removed, would either invalidate the theory or establish it as a law. However, because ambiguity is uncomfortable for many people, they tend to defend their values and theories and act on them as though they were laws. The quality of human relationships is directly or indirectly a function of people's values or personal theories. Thus, harmony or conflict between individuals, groups, or nations results from compatible or incompatible perceptions and values.

This chapter deals with several theories of human effectiveness found to have relevance to the industrial organization. They are based at least in part on attempts by behavioral scientists to observe, measure, and interpret human behavior. That several theories exist to explain the same phenomena indicates that the observation, measurement, and interpretation processes have not been completely objective. However, upon examining these theories it becomes apparent that their commonality outweighs their uniqueness.

COMMONALITY OF THEORIES

Figure 1-1 portrays twelve theories of human effectiveness, selected more to reflect variety than to be comprehensive. Each of these theories is presented on a linear scale, the left end representing conditions conducive to ineffectiveness, and the right end conditions for greater effectiveness. These scales do not reflect the full complexity of these theories or their application, nor are they intended to define the scope or primary focus of

	INEFFECTIVENESS		EFFECTIVENESS	
ROBERT BLAKE	MANAGERIAL GRID			MANAGERIAL STYLES
	1, 1 Neutrality and Indecision	1, 9 Inadequate concern for production 5, 5 Compromise, middle-of-the-road 9, 1 Inadequate concern for people	9, 9 Integration of Resources	
JAY HALL	DECISION-MAKING GRID			
	1, 1 Decisions by default and precedent	1, 9 Inadequate concern for quality decision 5, 5 Decision through bargaining 9, 1 Inadequate concern for commitment	9, 9 Adequate concern for commitment and quality decisions	
RENSIS LIKERT	SYSTEM 1 Exploitive authoritative	SYSTEM 2 Benevolent authoritative	SYSTEM 3 Consultative	SYSTEM 4 Participative group	
DOUGLAS McGREGOR	THEORY X Reductive assumptions		THEORY Y Developmental assumptions	
CHRIS ARGYRIS	AUTOCRATIC RELATIONSHIPS Conflict and conformity, Alienation		AUTHENTIC RELATIONSHIPS Interpersonal and technical competence, Commitment	MANAGERIAL STYLES & SYSTEMS
WARREN BENNIS	BUREAUCRACY Authoritarian, restrictive management structure		DEMOCRACY Goal-oriented, adaptive management structure	
FREDERICK HERZBERG	ENVIRONMENTAL COMFORT ← — — — –Hygiene seeking— — — —		MEANINGFUL WORK — — — —Motivation seeking— — — →	
JOHN PARÉ	BOSS POWER -- Direction and control by authority SYSTEM POWER -- Bureaucratic controls PEER POWER -- Social pressure of group		GOAL POWER -- Self-alignment with organizational goals	
ERICH FROMM	ESCAPE FROM FREEDOM Conformity, domination, destructiveness		FREEDOM Self-reliance, spontaneity, responsible behavior	CONSEQUENCES OF STYLES & SYSTEMS
WILLIAM GLASSER	AVOIDANCE OF REALITY Maladjustment		COPING WITH REALITY Responsible behavior	
ABRAHAM MASLOW	LOWER-NEED FIXATION Halted growth		SELF-ACTUALIZATION Realizing potential	
DAVID McCLELLAND	LOW nACH More interested in things like affiliation, security money, possessions		HIGH nACH Achievement its own primary reward, high challenges, moderate risks, independence	

FIG. 1-1   Theories of human effectiveness.

their developers' professional competence. Rather, they are displayed as an aid in comprehending the commonality, as well as the uniqueness, of what might otherwise appear as a confusing and contradictory proliferation of theories. The top four theories place the focus on managerial styles or assumptions, the middle four are generally described as combinations of managerial style and management systems, and the lower four are predominantly descriptors of the impact of managerial styles and systems. The first four theories ultimately have as much impact as the middle four on systems, for managerial styles and values inevitably find expression in system design and administration.

Though the terminology and scope of these theories and their mechanisms for limiting or achieving effectiveness may differ, they have the common purpose of defining conditions which inhibit or enhance the expression of human talent. Applied in the business setting, these theories define conditions for improved goal orientation and for the reduced or more constructive use of authority. However, it should be noted that a descriptor on any given scale is not necessarily vertically aligned with synonymous terms on other scales. For example, Likert's System 1 refers to a style of management through exploitive use of authority, whereas Maslow's "lower-need fixation" represents a consequence of System 1 management or the environmental restrictions included in Bennis's "bureaucracy." Blake's 9,1 management style is similar to Likert's System 1 or Paré's "boss power," but is positioned to the right of these, as Blake sees 1,1 as a condition of lesser effectiveness—something of a syndrome of disengagement or security seeking similar to that described in Fromm's *Escape from Freedom*.[1]

Robert Blake and Jane Mouton[2] define organizational effectiveness in terms of two coordinates of a grid, numbered 1 to 9, showing the manager's concern for the human factor on the ordinate and his concern for production on the abscissa. The ideal 9,9 manager has strong and integrated concern for production and human needs. The 1,1 manager at the other extreme is disengaged from responsibility, and his behavior is typified by neutrality, conformity, and indecision. The 1,9 manager will subordinate organizational goals to human needs, while the 9,1 manager will drive for attainment of organization goals at the expense of human resources. The 5,5 manager compromises his position to balance the conflicting and fluctuating demands of commitment and authority.

Jay Hall,[3] with Vincent O'Leary and Martha Williams, describes group effectiveness as a function of the decision maker's concern for decision adequacy and his concern for commitment of others to the decision. The mix of the group leader's concern is plotted on a grid, the ordinate denoting concern with commitment and the abscissa concern with decision adequacy. Traditional decision making often presumes the pursuit of high commitment to be incompatible with decision excellence, requiring bargaining and compromise. Capitulation may take the form of a traditional 5,5 majority decision, a 1,9 good-neighbor decision, a 9,1 leader-knows-best decision or, at its worst, a 1,1 acquiescence-to-a-default decision. The ideal 9,9 decision maker assumes that better decisions can be reached if all resources available in the group are utilized, and strives for both high commitment and best decision.

Rensis Likert[4] describes managerial style in terms of four systems. System 1, *exploitive authoritative*, refers to the use of authority and coer-

[1]Erich Fromm, *Escape from Freedom*, Holt, New York, 1941.

[2]Robert Blake and Jane Mouton, *Corporate Excellence through Grid Organizational Development*, Gulf, Houston, 1968.

[3]Jay Hall, Vincent O'Leary, and Martha Williams, "The Decision-Making Grid: A Model of Decision-Making Styles," *California Management Review*, Winter 1964.

[4]Rensis Likert, *The Human Organization*, McGraw-Hill, New York, 1967.

cion with little concern for human needs. System 1 found common expression in the management prerogative era of the nineteenth century, and lingers on as the dominant style of some managers today. System 2, *benevolent authoritative*, found accelerated acceptance with the Hawthorne studies which revealed, among other things, that people responded well to attention and interest in their welfare. Early human relations training efforts put a veneer over System 1, resulting in System 2 with its paternalism and increased benefits. System 3, *consultative*, evolved gradually as managers learned that people were more likely to support what they helped create. Though participation sometimes emerged as manipulation, and management retained its prerogative of accepting or rejecting suggestions, at least people had increased opportunity to be heard. System 4, *participative group*, is presented as an ideal model in which the influence of talent or competence, rather than the influence of authority, provides the basis for achieving organizational goals. System 4 is based on assumptions that people's initiative, creativity, and responsibility find constructive expression if they have access to information and the opportunity to solve problems and set goals.

Douglas McGregor's[5] classic theory holds that a manager's style of managing reflects his assumptions about people. The *theory X*, or reductive, manager assumes that people need authority and coercion to motivate them, that satisfactory performance can be assured only through ordering and forbidding. He assumes that most people avoid work, shun responsibility, require definition of job goals, must be subjected to close control, and will misuse freedom. They should be rewarded for their successes and punished for their mistakes. The *theory Y*, or developmental, manager assumes that people prefer to discipline themselves through self-direction and self-control. He assumes that people respond better to challenges than to authority, that people seek responsibility, and that under the right conditions they can enjoy work. He assumes that high expectations, coupled with goal-setting opportunity by job incumbents, will result in higher goals and greater achievements. He assumes that freedom to exercise independence and to learn from mistakes are necessary conditions for responsible behavior and growth.

Chris Argyris[6] has defined *interpersonal* and *technical competence*, as well as *internal commitment*, as the key ingredients of organizational effectiveness. Technical and interpersonal competence are fostered by authentic relationships, high but realistic expectations, meaningful work, freedom to act, accountability, and goal-oriented team action. These conditions, in

---

[5]Douglas McGregor, *The Professional Manager*, McGraw-Hill, New York, 1967.
[6]Chris Argyris, *Integrating the Individual and the Organization*, Wiley, New York, 1964; Chris Argyris, *Organization and Innovation*, Irwin, Homewood, Ill., 1965.

turn, can be significantly influenced by organizational relationships and administrative control systems.

Warren Bennis[7] defines conditions for human effectiveness in terms of the organization's governing systems. *Bureaucracy* tends to quash initiative through its enmeshing network of complex, inflexible and restrictive rules and systems. *Democracy* is inevitable for the successful organization, as it enables people to give expression to their talents in defining and achieving synergistic organizational-personal goals in a climate of goal-oriented supervision and adaptive and flexible systems.

Frederick Herzberg[8] holds that man's lower-order needs and higher-order needs do not operate on a single continuum. The satisfaction of man's *hygiene*, or lower-order needs, has only fleeting motivational value and even then only up to a level of diminishing return. But man's motivational, or self-actualization, needs operate somewhat independently and have the potential for motivating a person beyond the level attainable by hygiene satisfiers. Meaningless work which offers limited opportunity for the expression of talent may result in hygiene seeking; on the other hand, meaningful work which offers opportunity for growth, advancement, responsibility, achievement, and recognition inspires motivation and tends to desensitize persons to their hygiene needs.

John Paré[9] shows source of power to be a key factor in limiting or enhancing human effectiveness. *Boss power* refers to the use of authority presumed to be associated with level or status in the organization, traditionally an expression of "management's prerogative." *System power* is expressed through controls imposed by management systems and procedures and, at its worst, represents networks of bureaucratic restrictions. *Peer power* is the influence of associates springing largely from affiliation needs which may emphasize the goals and needs of the group over the welfare of the organization. *Goal power* refers to the attraction of meaningful goals which offer opportunity for simultaneously satisfying individual and organizational needs.

Erich Fromm[10] describes man's effectiveness in terms of his ability to cope with freedom. If an individual during maturation is granted freedom, respect, and responsibility commensurate with his ability to handle it, he can emerge as a self-reliant, spontaneous, and responsible individual. If the severing of the apron string is coordinated with his naturally unfolding growth and independence needs, he is likely to attain autonomy and freedom. But the individual who has been conditioned into dependency

[7]Warren Bennis, *Changing Organizations*, McGraw-Hill, New York, 1966.
[8]Frederick Herzberg, *Work and the Nature of Man*, World Publishing, Cleveland, 1966.
[9]John Paré, "What's Your Power Structure?" *Canadian Business*, April 1968.
[10]Fromm, op. cit.

relationships and has learned to associate security and love with the use of authority, finds freedom frightening after leaving home and seeks substitute apron strings. His inability to cope constructively with authority and autonomy attracts him to patterns of conformity, manipulation, and destructiveness.

William Glasser's[11] reality therapy defines human effectiveness as a function of ability to get involved with others in responsible relationships and through this involvement to learn to cope effectively with reality. Persons in an environment where their talents can be used and where they are accountable for their conduct tend to develop patterns of responsible behavior. Maladjustment is a manifestation of escape from reality brought about by irresponsible social, authority, and work relationships. Unlike traditional psychoanalytic theory, reality therapy does not require the probing of the subconscious past; rather, it helps the individual face reality and accept responsibility for satisfying his needs through responsible role relationships that do not deprive others of need fulfillment.

Abraham Maslow[12] defines human effectiveness as a function of matching man's opportunities with the appropriate position on his *hierarchy of needs*, enabling him to progress upward. Primeval man, for example, was concerned with the lower-order needs of survival, reproduction, finding food and shelter, and escaping hazards of his environment. As he was able to satisfy these physical needs, his status and social needs assumed relatively greater importance. In modern societies of increasing affluence, man is increasingly concerned with prepotent higher-order needs for growth, achievement, responsibility, and recognition. Thwarted self-actualization needs result in lower-need fixation and halted growth, but opportunity to utilize talents enables a person to realize his potential mentally, emotionally and aesthetically.

David McClelland[13] has identified achievement motivation as a primary expression of human effectiveness. People who have a high need for achievement (n Ach) thrive on freedom to pursue challenging goals involving manageable risks, their primary reward being a job well done. People with low n Ach are more interested in other things such as peer acceptance, security, money, and material possessions, and are more inclined to avoid all risks or undertake unjustifiably high risks. Though n Ach varies among individuals, it is situational in that a person's n Ach may differ with his various roles. Also, n Ach can be developed and is often a function of cultural norms; the people of North America and northern Europe, for

[11]William Glasser, *Reality Therapy*, Harper & Row, New York, 1965.

[12]Abraham H. Maslow, *Toward a Psychology of Being*, 2d ed., Van Nostrand, New York, 1968.

[13]David McClelland, *The Achieving Society*, Van Nostrand, New York, 1961.

example, historically tend to have higher n Ach than people in some of the Middle Eastern cultures.

TRANSLATION OF THEORIES

Busy managers are understandably impatient with theory, expressing the view that their concern for practical applications leaves little time or energy for theorizing. They may fail to appreciate the late Kurt Lewin's viewpoint that there is nothing so practical as a good theory.

Theories are springboards to action and change. However, theories rarely lead to changed behavior, until deliberate and intensive efforts are made to apply them. The intellectual understanding of management theory has about the same impact on a manager's supervisory style that the intellectual study of snow skiing has on teaching him how to ski. In either case, his competence is developed primarily through application—through the actual practice of supervision or by actually skiing. If he is satisfied with his style of supervising or skiing, he will expend little effort in learning and applying theories for the purpose of changing his styles.

However, if he is dissatisfied with his performance to the point that his desire to improve exceeds his reluctance to accept assistance, he may approach the study of theory with a readiness to change. A theory will be useful to him if he can translate it into remedial action that will reward his efforts. It may begin acquiring relevance in the classroom if the learner believes it can help him be more effective.

Some theories find immediate relevance when introduced in response to appeals for help in solving pressing problems, such as an anticipated union organization drive, drops in productivity, or increased personnel turnover or absenteeism. Classroom experience is more relevant when actual problems are brought in for analysis and problem solving. This approach was followed in the Texas Instruments Motivation Seminar described on pages 15 to 17. Some theories serve a dual purpose, first as an instrument for identifying and diagnosing problems, and then as a method for prescribing remedial actions. Such theories are illustrated in the descriptions of Likert's four systems, Blake's managerial grid, and Paré's power structures on pages 17 to 22.

The Translation Process

The translation of managerial theory is accomplished when the application of a given theory leads to desired changes in managerial behavior. The application of theory generally requires a four-step process:

1. Awareness
2. Understanding
3. Commitment
4. New habits

Step 1:   *Awareness* may result from a convincing speech, reading a book, viewing an educational film, attending a public seminar, or simply shoptalk. This first step may occur for a manager when he gains at least a superficial insight into a new theory and the implied deficiency in his present style of managing.

Step 2:   *Understanding* may result from activity precipitated by his awareness of the possible need to change. He may read numerous books and articles on the theory and selectively choose training programs and attend lectures on the subject. This step may be thought of as an intellectual conditioning process. He may become an articulate spokesman for his newly acquired insight, but his managerial style may continue to follow old habit patterns.

Step 3:   *Commitment* to change occurs when he becomes aware of the discrepancy between his newly adopted theory and his everyday behavior, but only if he believes he will benefit personally through changing his style of management. Initial attempts are often discouraging and, if not reinforced by some type of rewarding feedback, may gradually be discontinued. Commitment and reinforcement must be strong and continuous to overcome established habit patterns. Moreover, his changed behavior is often viewed with suspicion by persons whose opinions about him have been crystallized by his previous style.

Step 4:   *New habits* are established when sustained deliberate applications of the new theory finally result in attitude changes and automatic and natural expressions of the desired changes in style of management. Attainment of the new habit-formation stage is a long and difficult process requiring perhaps 5 to 10 years of sustained reinforcement from steps 2 and 3. Some individuals never progress beyond step 2, particularly when others in the organization upon whom they depend for continuing opportunity do not encourage them through their language of action and words.

The application of management theory in a business organization generally begins with a step 2 intellectual conditioning experience to prepare managers for the step 3 translation process. The motivation seminar in Texas Instruments, described on pages 15 to 17, was based on an amalgamation of several theories, and it illustrates the nature and role of an intellectual conditioning process. Dubbed the "motivation-maintenance theory," it defines media in the typical industrial organization through which the needs of people at work are satisfied, as illustrated in Figure 1-2.

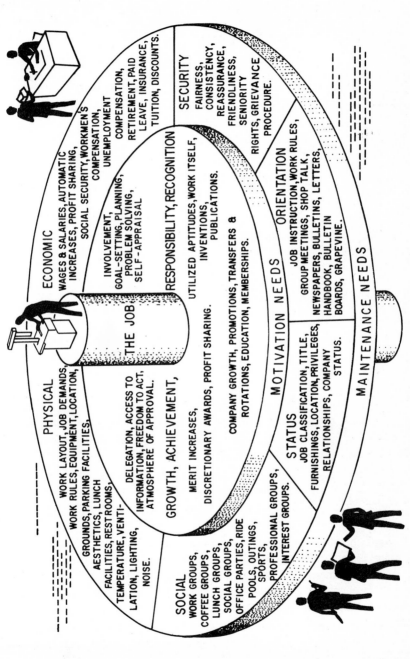

FIG. 1-2 Employee needs—maintenance and motivational. (M. Scott Myers, "Who Are Your Motivated Workers?" *Harvard Business Review*, Jan.-Feb. 1964, p. 86.)

The application of the motivation-maintenance theory in TI is presented in the following pages as a specimen intellectual message.

A Specimen Intellectual Message

Maintenance needs are synonymous with Maslow's lower-order needs or Herzberg's hygiene needs, and the term "maintenance" is used to denote the fact that people, like buildings and machines, must be maintained. Motivation needs, synonymous with Maslow's higher-order self-actualization needs, are being satisfied when man is developing his potential through the pursuit of meaningful goals.

Maintenance Needs The maintenance needs of people at work are quite similar whether the individual is a machine operator, as illustrated in the diagram, or the president, the vice president, the middle manager, the foreman, the technician, the secretary, or the floor sweeper. Though the maintenance of people is not the key to motivating them in the business organization, it is usually a prerequisite for fuller motivation. The same needs apply to people outside the industrial organization, such as housewives, policemen, clergymen, schoolteachers, and students. All require the satisfaction of their maintenance needs, defined here in terms of economic, security, orientation, status, social, and physical factors.

* *Economic* maintenance needs involve wages, salaries, and supplemental benefits received almost automatically by virtue of simply being on the job. Economic maintenance needs do not include forms of compensation stemming from meritorious performance, mentioned later as reinforcements of motivation.

* *Security* maintenance needs refer to feelings of people arising primarily from their perception of their supervisor as an impartial, consistent, reassuring, friendly type of person, and from the knowledge that justice prevails in the job situation.

* *Orientation* maintenance needs require the knowledge of the company and the job. This information is supplied by the supervisor, the printed media, such as newspapers and bulletins, or through the informal "grapevine" which exists in every organization.

* *Status* maintenance needs are generally satisfied through job classifications, titles, furnishings, privileges, relationships, and the company image or product image. The process of acquiring status is related to motivation factors of growth and achievement discussed later, but the possession of status or symbols of it is largely maintenance.

* *Social* maintenance needs are satisfied through formal or informal group activities in work groups, luncheon groups, coffee groups, ride pools, or after-hours recreational activities.

- *Physical* maintenance needs are satisfied by the work layout, parking facilities, air conditioning, lighting, rest rooms, eating facilities, regulation of noise levels, and other physical conditions.

When lower-order needs are maintained at adequate levels, dissatisfactions stemming from them are minimized. However, the maintenance factors in these six categories have only fleeting value as motivators. For example, when a plant manager air-conditioned one of his buildings that had not previously been air-conditioned, the enthusiastic response during the first week seemed like motivation. However, enthusiasm soon tapered off to a level that could only be called the absence of dissatisfaction with air conditioning. But when the air conditioning system failed, the response was immediate dissatisfaction, vociferous complaints, and lowered production. And when the system was repaired, building occupants were not motivated, they were merely returned to the level of absence of dissatisfaction. Their typical comments to the repairmen were: "What took you so long?" and "Why did you let the air conditioning go out?" Once employees have built air conditioning into their expectations, their feelings toward it can only go downward. Hence, maintenance factors are characterized by the fact that they customarily inspire little positive sentiment when added, but incite strong negative reaction when removed.

Maintenance factors are usually peripheral to the job, as they are more directly related to the environment than to work itself. For the most part they are group-administered, customarily by staff personnel, and their success usually depends upon their being applied uniformly and equitably throughout the organization.

Managers often fail to understand the ingratitude of employees toward maintenance factors such as the Christmas turkey, free coffee, and other expressions of well-intentioned paternalism. They are particularly disillusioned when these "jelly beans" (see page 182) become the subject of collective bargaining and become perpetuated as "rights of labor." Not all items in the outer circle are jelly beans. Jelly beans are unearned rewards such as the Christmas turkey or free coffee, and do not include earned rewards such as profit sharing or tuition refunds.

Since the turn of the century, supplemental benefits have increased in cost from less than 5 percent of the payroll budget to more than 30 percent. The more supplemental benefits are added as maintenance factors, the higher becomes their potential for dissatisfaction. However, it would be an oversimplification to conclude that maintenance factors are only increasing dissatisfactions, or that they are the primary source of dissatisfaction.

Maintenance factors serve a necessary function that can be appreciated only in historical perspective. In the era ending in the early decades of the twentieth century, the working man lived in a world of management prerogatives of arbitrary "hire and fire." He lived and worked in substandard conditions and received substandard wages. But over the years, four primary influences have brought about the "affluent society":[14] (1) the intervention of labor unions, which forced the sharing of company wealth; (2) labor legislation, which established standards for wages, hours and working conditions; (3) the mass-production technology, which priced automobiles, washing machines, refrigerators, and other consumer products within the reach of increasingly higher percentages of the population; and (4) legislation creating free and mandatory education for children of all Americans, including immigrants.

Maintenance factors embrace the wages, hours, and working conditions which have been the focus of collective bargaining for many years. The emphasis on maintenance factors by unions raises a question regarding the future role of labor unions and their ability to survive through a continuing strategy based on satisfying lower-order needs. Life in an affluent society where maintenance needs are satisfied would seem to preclude the need for unions. Because people's needs change, moving upward as lower needs are satisfied, employees in increasing numbers are failing to experience the satisfaction previously derived from improved maintenance factors, and are aimlessly seeking, with mingled hope and despair, something more meaningful than comfortable working conditions and routinized work. The union's role has gradually, subtly, and inadvertently shifted from "workers' defender" to a medium for displacing the aggression stemming from frustrations which it helped create. In short, traditional union strategy tends to develop "maintenance seekers."

Motivation Needs   The most constructive outlet for these frustrations in the business organization is upward through Maslow's hierarchy of needs to opportunities for satisfying self-actualization or motivation needs in terms of such factors as growth, achievement, responsibility, and recognition, illustrated in the inner circle of Figure 1-2.

- Growth, in this context, refers to mental growth. Though physical growth generally levels off before age twenty, mental growth may continue throughout the life span of the individual. Factors associated with the continuing growth or obsolescence of managers are detailed on pages 213 to 216. One of the most effective antidotes to mental stagnation and vocational obsolescence is a challenging job, as described on pages 95 to 105.
- Achievement refers to the need for achievement (n Ach) that McClelland has shown to be a key motive when it can find expression. Individuals

[14]J. K. Galbraith, *The Affluent Society*, Houghton Mifflin, Boston, 1958.

differ from each other in terms of their need for achievement, and a given individual's level of achievement motivation will vary with his opportunity to find expression for it. When jobs offer little opportunity for satisfying achievement needs, high achievers seek outlets for their talents within or outside the organization. Jobs rich in opportunity for growth and achievement attract and retain high achievers. Low n Ach people in such an environment may develop n Ach through the multiple influences of a challenging role, peer pressure, and image emulation. By the same token, jobs lacking in challenge tend to attract and retain low achievers whose needs are satisfied largely through the maintenance factors such as security, benefits, affiliation, and comfortable surroundings.

- The term *responsibility* refers to a sense of commitment to a worthwhile job. It has long been recognized that a sense of responsibility is a function of level in the organization—people high in management generally having a proportionally higher sense of responsibility than people at lower levels. A study of factors relating to motivation of managers at Texas Instruments[15] demonstrated this relationship, but it also revealed that level of motivation was more strongly related to style of supervision than it was to level in the organization. Figure 1-3 shows the relationship of level of motivation to level of management and boss's style of supervision. Level of motivation was based on the extent to which 1344 managers rated their jobs in terms of factors such as challenge, interest, utilization of talent, freedom to act, sense of achievement, and personal growth. Upper management consisted of the president and two levels below him, lower management of first- and second-level supervision, and middle management the levels in between. The boss's style was measured in terms of descriptions provided by subordinates—"developmental" and "reductive" being synonymous with McGregor's theory Y and theory X, respectively, and "traditional" representing a middle ground. Hence, a person's sense of commitment or responsibility is often a function of his boss's style of supervision.

- *Recognition,* as a motivation need, refers to earned recognition stemming from meritorious performance. Unearned recognition or friendliness, defined as a condition of security in the outer circle, is needed for keeping communication channels open so that when vital issues arise, they may be surfaced and dealt with. But, within the inner circle, recognition as positive feedback for a job well done is a reinforcement of motivated behavior. Recognition at its best does not depend on the value judgments of an authority figure to translate achievements into praise,

[15]M. Scott Myers, "Conditions for Manager Motivation," *Harvard Business Review*, Jan.–Feb. 1966.

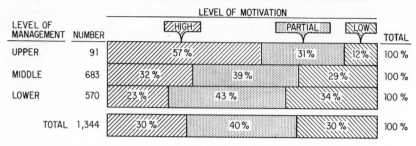

RELATIONSHIP OF MOTIVATION TO LEVEL OF MANAGEMENT
LEVEL OF MOTIVATION

LEVEL OF MANAGEMENT	NUMBER	HIGH	PARTIAL	LOW	TOTAL
UPPER	91	57%	31%	12%	100%
MIDDLE	683	32%	39%	29%	100%
LOWER	570	23%	43%	34%	100%
TOTAL	1,344	30%	40%	30%	100%

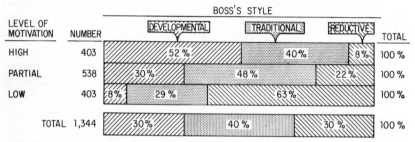

RELATIONSHIP OF MOTIVATION TO BOSS'S STYLE
BOSS'S STYLE

LEVEL OF MOTIVATION	NUMBER	DEVELOPMENTAL	TRADITIONAL	REDUCTIVE	TOTAL
HIGH	403	52%	40%	8%	100%
PARTIAL	538	30%	48%	22%	100%
LOW	403	8% 29%	63%		100%
TOTAL	1,344	30%	40%	30%	100%

FIG. 1-3 Motivation related to organizational level and style of supervision.

advancements, respect, awards, pay increases, and other rewards. Recognition in the form of "attaboys" dispensed by value judgment places unjustified faith in the objectivity, reliability, sensitivity, attentiveness, and competence of the judge, and tends to foster dependency relationships.

Ideally, recognition should not depend on an intermediary, but should be a natural expression of feedback from achievement itself. When the astronauts landed on the moon, or when Jonas Salk discovered polio vaccine, or when Babe Ruth batted a home run (or when Casey struck out!), they didn't need a supervisor to give them recognition. They received feedback naturally and spontaneously, and the quality of this feedback was not distorted by the interpretation of an intermediary. Hence, recognition at its best is primarily an expression of direct feedback.

Though achievement and responsibility may be their own rewards, they too are reinforced when someone upon whom the individual depends for continuing opportunity recognizes him for his achievements. As long as the supervisor's authority is the basis for continuing opportunity and his judgment assures an equitable relationship between accomplishments and rewards, his expressed feelings are a constructive part of the feedback.

The diagram in Figure 1-2 suggests that only work itself offers motivational opportunity. While the job for which the person was hired usually has the greatest potential for satisfying motivation needs, certain media in the outer circle, such as company newspapers, attitude surveys, and recreational activities also provide outlets for the constructive expression of talent in the work place. In the Eaton Corporation, many media peripheral to the work itself have been found to add motivational dimensions to monotonous jobs. The enriched work places of Eaton, as described on pages 115 to 119, represent a de facto broadening of the responsibilities of workers whose jobs were previously rather narrowly circumscribed. Moreover, worker involvement in a variety of administrative matters narrows the perceptual gap which characteristically polarizes management against labor.

The Need for Equilibrium   The relative importance of the four motivation needs and the six maintenance needs is situational, as can readily be seen in an everyday situation. For example, a given maintenance need, such as "physical," may loom as the most important if it is the main source of current dissatisfaction. But once the air-conditioning or noise-level problem, or whatever is the focus of concern, is solved, other factors may assume greater importance. If product obsolescence and organizational stagnation stymie growth opportunity, growth needs assume greater importance. However, thwarted growth needs are often unwittingly sublimated and expressed as amplified concern for maintenance factors. Increasingly, the real problems of the people at work are lack of inner-circle opportunities, though outer-circle factors linger as the issue of conflict, as noted earlier. Both maintenance and motivational needs must be satisfied, not so that one can replace the other but rather to provide better balance between the two.

People in upper levels of management have relatively more opportunity to satisfy inner-circle needs, but they devote much of their effort in coping with "labor" problems stemming from the inability of people at lower levels to get into the inner circle. Management's mission, then, must be to get people into the inner circle, not as altruistic missionaries for participation, but rather as practical business managers providing outlets for human talent in the pursuit of organizational goals.

The Texas Instruments Motivation Seminar

The preceding intellectual message was the foundation for the Texas Instruments motivation seminar. Though the scope, content, and duration of the seminar vary with the trainer and operation, the basic outline includes six 2-hour sessions:

1.   Statement of objectives. The role of theory; review of research.

2.   Development of a theory; relationship to other theories.

3.   Self-examination. Application of theory to filmed problem.

4.   Texas Instruments management philosophy as foundation for motivation. Home assignment.

5.   Application of theory to actual problems.

6.   Application of theory to actual problems. Self-evaluation.

The seminar is conducted with peer groups of eight to twelve supervisors, usually from a common operation. It is desirable to mix the mainstream and staff support personnel in the seminar to reinforce the total team concept and to overcome the functional isolation sometimes encountered. Participation in the seminar is largely voluntary, but is encouraged by the fact that the president and vice presidents initiate the program by their participation and support.

In the first session the objectives of the seminar are defined:

1.   To develop an understanding of a useful theory of management.

2.   To stimulate participants to examine their supervisory jobs in terms of opportunities to apply principles and techniques of motivation theory.

3.   To develop attitudes and skills necessary for day-to-day application of motivation theory.

Also during the first session each participant is asked to discuss theories or concepts he found useful in supervision. The universal application of theory, consciously or subconsciously, is established. Texas Instruments motivation research is described and illustrative data are gathered from participants and interpreted in terms of motivation-maintenance theory.

Session 2 includes lecture and discussion to give participants an understanding of the intellectual message presented on pages 10 to 15. Discussion of the relationship between motivation-maintenance theory and other theories such as those presented in Figure 1-1 was optionally included.

Session 3 begins with a question-and-answer period followed by a multiple-choice test of knowledge of motivation-maintenance theory. Papers are self-scored from answers furnished orally by the conference leader, and incorrect responses are discussed and clarified. A 10-minute filmed problem in delegation is presented and analyzed by the participants.

Session 4 begins with a lecture-discussion on Texas Instruments' management philosophy, an analysis of organizational climate factors, and examples of the intended use and the undesired abuse of management systems. Participants are given a home assignment to prepare a list of previous, current, or anticipated problems in motivation and to classify them according to motivation-maintenance criteria.

Session 5 starts with a blackboard listing of motivation problems compiled by the participants. Each participant elaborates on one of his problems and presents his motivation-maintenance diagnosis of it. Participants as a total group or in subgroups analyzed problems or groups of problems.

Session 6 is usually a continuation of problem analysis and is concluded with a self-evaluation in terms of McGregor's theory X and theory Y assumptions, as illustrated in Figure 1-4. Session 6 is sometimes extended into additional application sessions at the option of the participants.

Further Examples of Theory Translation

The translation of theory ideally has the potential for influencing the person to be changed in four ways: first, to discover and accept the fact that he has a problem; second, to provide insights and procedures for diagnosing the problem; third, to provide a frame of reference and a systematic approach for implementing remedial actions; and finally, to enable him to measure his progress. Innovative approaches for translating theory are unlimited, and the Texas Instruments motivation seminar and the four examples below serve simply to illustrate five separate and potentially successful translation processes.

Analysis of Assumptions and Styles of Management   Many training programs have based management development efforts on the concepts of McGregor's theory X and theory Y, summarized on pages 43 to 44. Figures 1-4 and 1-5 are work sheets to enable individuals to define their own assumptions about people and to describe their supervisors' styles of managing. In completing the statements about his assumptions, the supervisor is able to determine where he falls on the theory X–theory Y continuum. The system is limited, of course, by its brevity and by the deliberate or subconscious desire of the individual to provide the "correct" answers rather than the ones that describe his actual assumptions. The supervisory style work sheet, particularly if completed by his subordinates, represents a validity check on his own self-defined assumptions. Use of these two work sheets helps illustrate the distinction between, as well as the interdependence of, values and behavior. When they are used in conjunction with problem analysis, such as sessions 5 and 6 in the Texas Instruments motivation seminar, managers develop an understanding of their need not only to change their supervisory practices, but more important, to embark on the long-range process of acquiring additional insights and changed values and habits.

Profile of Organizational Characteristics   Rensis Likert's four systems are translated into meaningful exercises by a profiling process illustrated in abbreviated form in Figure 1-6. Individuals or groups may collaborate in completing this questionnaire by consensus or averages, diagnosing the organization in terms of leadership, motivation, communi-

Statements below, arranged in pairs, represent assumptions about people. Assign a weight from 0 to 10 to each statement to show the relative strength of your belief in the statements in each pair. The points assigned for each pair must in each case total 10.

1 –   It's only human nature for people to do as little work as they can get away with.
  –   When people avoid work, it's usually because their work has been deprived of its meaning.   _____
                                                                                                    10

2 –   If employees have access to any information they want, they tend to have better attitudes and behave more responsibly.
  –   If employees have access to more information than they need to do their immediate tasks, they will usually misuse it.   _____
                                                                                                    10

3 –   One problem in asking for the ideas of employees is that their perspective is too limited for their suggestions to be of much practical value.
  –   Asking employees for their ideas broadens their perspective and results in the development of useful suggestions.   _____
                                                                                                    10

4 –   If people don't use much imagination and ingenuity on the job, it's probably because relatively few people have much of either.
  –   Most people are imaginative and creative but may not show it because of limitations imposed by supervision and the job.   _____
                                                                                                    10

5 –   People tend to raise their standards if they are accountable for their own behavior and for correcting their own mistakes.
  –   People tend to lower their standards if they are not punished for their misbehavior and mistakes.   _____
                                                                                                    10

6 –   It's better to give people both good and bad news because most employees want the whole story, no matter how painful it is.
  –   It's better to withhold unfavorable news about business because most employees really want to hear only the good news.   _____
                                                                                                    10

7 –   Because a supervisor is entitled to more respect than those below him in the organization, it weakens his prestige to admit that a subordinate was right and he was wrong.
  –   Because people at all levels are entitled to equal respect, a supervisor's prestige is increased when he supports this principle by admitting that a subordinate was right and he was wrong.   _____
                                                                                                    10

8 –   If you give people enough money, they are less likely to be concerned with such intangibles as responsibility and recognition.
  –   If you give people interesting and challenging work, they are less likely to complain about such things as pay and supplemental benefits.   _____
                                                                                                    10

9 –   If people are allowed to set their own goals and standards of performance, they tend to set them higher than the boss would.
  –   If people are allowed to set their own goals and standards of performance, they tend to set them lower than the boss would.   _____
                                                                                                    10

10 – The more knowledge and freedom a person has regarding his job, the more controls are needed to keep him in line.
  –   The more knowledge and freedom a person has regarding his job, the fewer controls are needed to insure satisfactory job performance.   _____
                                                                                                    10

FIG. 1-4 My assumptions.

cation, decisions, goals, and control processes. Typically a group will profile both the actual and the ideal pattern for their organization. The difference between the actual and the ideal represents the challenge or goal to be undertaken within the organization through the appropriate mix of individuals, levels, and functions. Participation in the problem-solving task forces can result in the development of remedial strategies and commitment to their implementation. The comparison of current conditions

Statements below, arranged in pairs, represent supervisory style. Assign a weight from 0 to 10 to each statement to show the relative accuracy of the statements in each pair for describing your supervisor's style. The points assigned for each pair must in each case total 10.

1 – Easy to talk to, even when under pressure.
  – You have to pick carefully the time when you talk to him.
  <u>   </u> <u>   </u>
  10

2 – May ask for ideas, but usually his mind is already made up.
  – Tries to see the merit in your ideas even if they conflict with his.
  <u>   </u> <u>   </u>
  10

3 – Tries to help his people understand company objectives.
  – Lets his people figure out for themselves how company objectives apply to them.
  <u>   </u> <u>   </u>
  10

4 – Tries to give his people access to all the information they want.
  – Gives his people the information he thinks they need.
  <u>   </u> <u>   </u>
  10

5 – Tends to set his people's job goals and tell them how to achieve them.
  – Involves his people in solving problems and setting job goals.
  <u>   </u> <u>   </u>
  10

6 – Tends to discourage his people from trying new approaches.
  – Tries to encourage people to reach out in new directions.
  <u>   </u> <u>   </u>
  10

7 – Takes your mistakes in stride, so long as you learn from them.
  – Allows little room for mistakes, especially those that might embarrass him.
  <u>   </u> <u>   </u>
  10

8 – Tries mainly to correct mistakes and figure out how they can be prevented in the future.
  – When something goes wrong, tries primarily to find out who caused it.
  <u>   </u> <u>   </u>
  10

9 – His expectations of subordinates tend to fluctuate.
  – Consistent, high expectations of subordinates.
  <u>   </u> <u>   </u>
  10

10 – Expects superior performance and gives credit when you do it.
  – Expects you to do an adequate job, doesn't say much unless something goes wrong.
  <u>   </u> <u>   </u>
  10

FIG. 1-5   My supervisor's style.

against previous profiles provides the system user with feedback on the success of his remedial actions.

Blake's Managerial Grid   Blake and Mouton's two-factor grid, illustrated in Figure 1-7, allows individuals and groups to diagnose their own managerial styles and the styles of others in terms of concern for production and people. By completing questionnaires in which they describe actual behavior and define ideal styles, they become focused on the mission of developing 9,9 managerial style and strategies for the organization. The marketing of the managerial grid illustrates the potential that can be exploited for any sound theory when the application of a theory is backed by strong entrepreneurial interests. Blake and his associates have written five textbooks providing theoretical and testimonial evidence of the usefulness of the grid and, at the writing of this book, the grid marketing bro-

Organizational variables	SYSTEM 1	SYSTEM 2	SYSTEM 3	SYSTEM 4	Item no.
LEADERSHIP					
How much confidence is shown in subordinates?	None	Condescending	Substantial	Complete	1
How free do they feel to talk to superiors about job?	Not at all	Not very	Rather free	Fully free	2
Are subordinates' ideas sought and used, if worthy?	Seldom	Sometimes	Usually	Always	3
MOTIVATION					
Is predominant use made of (1) fear, (2) threats, (3) punishment, (4) rewards, (5) involvement?	1, 2, 3, occasionally 4	4, some 3	4, some 3 and 5	5, 4, based on group	4
Where is responsibility felt for achieving organization's goals?	Mostly at top	Top and middle	Fairly general	At all levels	5
How much cooperative teamwork exists?	None	Little	Some	Great deal	6
COMMUNICATION					
What is the direction of information flow?	Downward	Mostly downward	Down and up	Down, up and sideways	7
How is downward communication accepted?	With suspicion	Possibly with suspicion	With caution	With a receptive mind	8
How accurate is upward communication?	Often wrong	Censored for the boss	Limited accuracy	Accurate	9
How well do superiors know problems faced by subordinates?	Know little	Some knowledge	Quite well	Very well	10
DECISIONS					
At what level are decisions made?	Mostly at top	Policy at top, some delegation	Broad policy at top, more delegation	Throughout but well integrated	11
Are subordinates involved in decisions related to their work?	Not at all	Occasionally consulted	Generally consulted	Fully involved	12
What does decision-making process contribute to motivation?	Nothing, often weakens it	Relatively little	Some contribution	Substantial contribution	13
GOALS					
How are organizational goals established?	Orders issued	Orders, some comments invited	After discussion, by orders	By group action (except in crisis)	14
How much covert resistance to goals is present?	Strong resistance	Moderate resistance	Some resistance at times	Little or none	15
CONTROL					
How concentrated are review and control functions?	Highly at top	Relatively highly at top	Moderate delegation to lower levels	Quite widely shared	16
Is there an informal organization resisting the formal one?	Yes	Usually	Sometimes	No---same goals as formal	17
What are cost, productivity, and other control data used for?	Policing, punishment	Reward and punishment	Reward, some self-guidance	Self-guidance, problem-solving	18

FIG. 1-6 Profile of organizational characteristics.

chures for a 1-year period included schedules for public seminars at sixty-three locations—twenty-seven within the United States and thirty-six elsewhere throughout the world.

Power Structure Seminar   John Paré developed a profiling system to enable individuals and groups to diagnose the power structure within retail store operations in terms of the four sources of power reflected in Figure 1-8. After diagnosing the actual structure and concurring on optimal structure, the group then becomes involved in formulating strategies for overcoming the gap between actual and optimal. The power

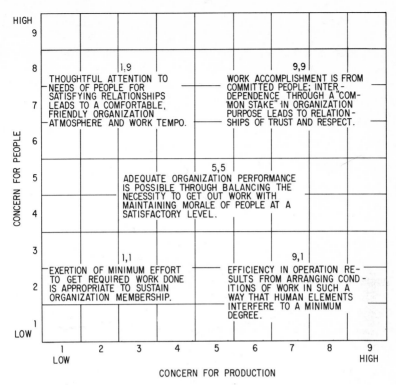

FIG. 1-7 The managerial grid. (R. R. Blake and J. S. Mouton, *The Managerial Grid*, Gulf Publishing Company, Houston, 1964, p. 10.)

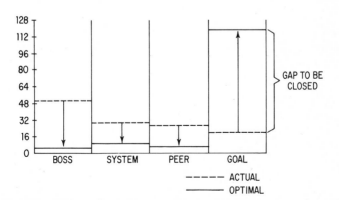

FIG. 1-8 Power structure profile sheet.

21

structure seminar has been highly successful in increasing organizational effectiveness in department stores, and its application illustrates a phenomenon noted in the discussion of management systems on pages 69 to 79. People's attitudes and perceptions are a primary cause of a system's successes and failures, and the success of the power structure seminar in replacing other frameworks is probably as much a function of the attitudes of the users as it is of the intrinsic characteristics of the system itself.

Changing Values in the Work Place

The foregoing discussion on relationships, goals, and systems does not recognize the rich variations in value systems that exist in the work place. Indeed most discussions of people at work confer upon them a rather monolithic syndrome of personality characteristics which set them apart from accountants or engineers, for example, each of whom tend to be described in terms of unique personality traits. In reality, there are more similarities than differences among the various vocational groupings, and a wide variety of differences within any given group.

Each person in the work place has a built-in set of values which he or she uses subconsciously as a yardstick for judging himself and other members of the organization. Informal relationships within peer groups are influenced by these differences. These real or imagined differences have even greater impact on relationships between vocational groups. Thus adversary relationships between management and labor may stem from social distance which inhibits communication between the two classes. Hence workers may label managers as arbitrary, insensitive, and authoritarian, while managers see workers as lazy, irresponsible, and incompetent. Managers commonly assume, for example, that one of the big differences between management and labor is that managers like their work and workers do not like theirs.

Managers sometimes marvel at the metamorphic change in values that takes place when a worker is promoted into supervision. The promoted worker, in turn, is surprised to discover at his new level some of the same personality differences and similarities observed in his previous peer groups. Hence interpersonal conflict is a function of both value differences and class distinctions.

Progressive managers are learning to reduce the social distance created by traditional status symbols and protocol. However, they have been less sensitive or responsive to the role of individual differences as the basis for conflict. Indeed, they are often intolerant of, and unable to understand, people whose values differ from their own. Supervisory problems are often symptoms of clashing value systems. A manufacturing manager expressed it this way:

People here aren't like they were when I was working my way up in the organization. We were here on time, put in a good day's work, and were pleased when the boss singled us out for a tough job. We seized every opportunity to work overtime and did everything we could to get ahead.

We have very few of that type today. Their minds seem to be elsewhere and they're not ambitious as we were. Some refuse transfers, even if they lead to promotions. The other day I had to discipline one of these long-hair types for violating a safety rule. I laid him off three days without pay. You know what he said to me? He said, "May I have the other two days off, too?"

Most of them aren't troublemakers, exactly—they just don't seem to give a hoot for the company, their jobs or their careers. Some of them *are* troublemakers. They are often tardy or absent and will lie, cheat and steal. They know that because they're from the ghetto, and EEO is breathing down our necks, we'll probably go easy on them.

This manager's lament is widely shared by peers who learned supervisory techniques through experience and training programs strongly influenced by tradition. The problem is not restricted to business organizations, but is encountered in all walks of life by parents and teachers, clergymen, government officials, union leaders, athletic coaches, and others. While some managers see these problems as symptoms of illness in society, what they actually represent is a freer expression of disparate values by its members.

John Gardner,[16] in recognizing the zeal with which traditional managers attempt to remold the values and life styles of nonconformists, writes:

A free society will not specify too closely the kinds of meaning different individuals will find or the things about which they should generate conviction. People differ in their goals and convictions and in the whole style of commitment. We must ask that their goals fall within the moral framework to which we all pay allegiance, but we cannot prescribe the things that will unlock their deepest motivations. Those earnest spirits who believe that a man cannot be counted worthy unless he burns with zeal for civic affairs could not be more misguided. And we are wrong when we follow the current fashion of identifying moral strength too exclusively with fighting for a cause. Nothing could be more admirable nor more appealing to a performance-minded people such as ourselves. But, such an emphasis hardly does justice to the rich variety of moral excellences that man has sought and occasionally achieved in the course of history.

A good many of the most valuable people in any society will never

---

[16]John Gardner, "Individuality, Commitment, and Meaning," in *Current Perspectives in Social Psychology*, Edward P. Hollander and Raymond G. Hunt (eds.), Oxford University Press, 1967.

burn with zeal for anything except the integrity and health and well-being of their own families—and if they achieve those goals, we need ask little more of them. There are other valuable members of a society who will never generate conviction about anything beyond the productive output of their hands or minds—and a sensible society will be grateful for their contributions.

Clare Graves[17] offers a framework for understanding the increasingly disparate value systems in today's society. Based on his observation and research begun in the early 1950s as a professor of psychology at Union College, Dr. Graves found that people seem to evolve through stages of "psychological existence" descriptive of personal values and lifestyles. Relatively independent of age and intelligence, a person's mode of psychological existence can become arrested at a given level, or it can move to another stage or return to a previous level, depending on that person's cultural conditioning and his or her perception of the opportunities and constraints in the environment. Graves refers to this framework as an open system to underscore the point that the number of stages is not limited. Tentative research findings have permitted definition of seven such levels or stages of psychological existence. These are described below and summarized in Figure 1-9.

Stage 1.   The *reactive* stage of existence is most commonly observed in newborn babies or in people psychologically arrested in, or regressed to, infancy. They are unaware of themselves or others as human beings, and simply react to hunger, thirst, need to urinate or defecate, fear of falling, sex, and other basic physiological needs. Few people remain at this stage as they move toward adulthood, and those few are not generally found on payrolls of organizations.

Stage 2.   Most people, as a matter of course, move out of the reactive existence to a *tribalistic* stage. Tribalism is characterized by concern with feelings of pain, temperature control, and safety, and by tacit submission to an authority figure, whether he be a supervisor, policeman, government official, teacher, priest, parent, big brother, or gang leader. Tribalism, in its purest form, is commonly observed in primitive cultures, where the tribal chieftain is boss; and magic, witchcraft, ritual, superstition, and tradition play important roles in his lifestyle.

Stage 3.   *Egocentrism* is an overly assertive form of rugged individualism. This person's behavior reflects a philosophy which seems to say, "To hell with the rest of the world, I'm for myself." He, or she, is characteristically unscrupulous, selfish, aggressive, restless, impulsive and,

[17]Clare Graves, "Levels of Existence: An Open System Theory of Values," *Journal of Humanistic Psychology*, Fall 1970, vol. 10, no. 2. See also M. Scott Myers and Susan S. Myers, "Adapting to the New Work Ethic," *Business Quarterly*, Winter 1973.

Stage 7 EXISTENTIAL. This employee likes a job where the goals and problems are more important than the money, prestige, or symbols of status. He prefers work of his own choosing that offers continuing challenge and requires imagination and initiative. To him, a good boss is one who gives him access to the information he needs and lets him do the job in his own way.

Stage 6 SOCIOCENTRIC. A job that allows the development of friendly relationships with people in his work group appeals to this employee. Working with people toward a common goal is more important than getting caught up in a materialistic rat race. He likes a boss who fosters close harmony by being more a friendly person than a boss.

Stage 5 ENTREPRENEURIAL. The preferred job for this employee is varied, allows free wheeling and dealing, and offers pay and bonus on the basis of results. He feels responsible for his own success and is constantly on the lookout for new opportunities. A good boss for this employee understands the politics of getting the job done, knows how to bargain, and is willing to bend the rules.

Stage 4 CONFORMIST. This employee likes job security, well-defined rules, and equal treatment. He feels entitled to some good breaks in exchange for his loyalty. His mode of dress and subservience to protocol cause him to blend with the masses and reflect strongly lack of individuality. He reacts strongly against value encroachments.

Stage 3 EGOCENTRIC. The two major requirements of a job for this employee are that it pays well and keeps people off his back. He shuns work that ties him down, but will do it if he must to get the money he wants. He responds well to a tough boss, but also responds to participative methods under peer pressure and respected leadership.

Stage 2 TRIBALISTIC. This employee is best suited to routine work, friendly people, fair play, and, above all, a good boss. He likes a boss who tells him exactly what to do and how to do it, and who encourages him by doing it with him. An employee at this level may realize his job lacks status, but he finds it acceptable under conditions of peer solidarity and supervisory respect.

Stage 1 REACTIVE. This level of psychological development is restricted primarily to infants, people with serious brain deterioration, and certain psychopathic conditions. For practical purposes, employees are not ordinarily found at Stage 1.

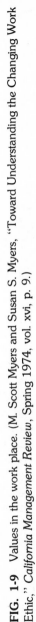

FIG. 1-9 Values in the work place. (M. Scott Myers and Susan S. Myers, "Toward Understanding the Changing Work Ethic," *California Management Review*, Spring 1974, vol. xvi, p. 9.)

in general, not psychologically inclined to live within the constraints imposed by society's accepted moral framework. To this person, might is right, and authoritarian management seems necessary to keep him in line. Though typical group techniques may not at first seem successful for this type of person, structured participative management of the type described in Chapter 4 promises to be an effective strategy for getting him out of this egocentric mode.

Stage 4.   Persons at the *conformity* stage of existence have low tolerance for ambiguity, difficulty in accepting people whose values differ from their own, and a need to get others to accept their values. They usually subordinate themselves to a philosophy, cause, or religion, and tend to be attracted to roles circumscribed by dogma or clearly defined rules. Though often perceived as docile, the conformist will assert or sacrifice himself in violence if his values are threatened. Conformists prefer authoritarianism to autonomy, but will respond to participation if it is prescribed by an acceptable authority, and if it does not violate deep-seated values. They like specific job descriptions and procedures, and have little tolerance for supervisory indecision or weakness. From the beginning of the Industrial Revolution until recently, people at this stage have been the mainstay of the hourly work force. This value system is also frequently found in management ranks in bureaucratic organizations where people are often rewarded for not "rocking the boat" and for perpetuating the *status quo*.

Stage 5.   The fifth stage of psychological existence is characterized by *entrepreneurial*, manipulative, or materialistic behavior. Persons at this stage are typically products of the Horatio Alger, rags-to-riches philosophy—striving to achieve their goals through the manipulation of people and systems. They thrive on gamesmanship, politics, competition, and entrepreneurial effort; measure their success in terms of materialistic gain and power; and are inclined to prize self-earned (as against inherited) status symbols. In the wage rolls, they may not blend well with peer groups, as they are characterized by ambition and initiative which tend to undermine solidarity. In many organizations, they are found in management levels, having been promoted because of their demonstrated competence in manipulating resources.

Stage 6.   People at the sixth, or *sociocentric*, stage of existence have high affiliation needs. Getting along or being a "good person" is often more important than getting ahead, and the approval of their peers is valued over individual fame. At this level there may be a return of religiousness, not for its ritual or dogma, but rather for its spiritual attitude and concern with social issues. Many members of the so-called "hippie" cult were sociocentric—their shabby appearance being a symbolic rejection of the organization-man image expected by the establishment. A person at this level responds well to participative methods, but might revolt if products or services served what he perceived to be destructive causes. He tends to articulate his protests openly, but characteristically dislikes violence and would counter authoritarianism with passive resistance. Sociocentrics are frequently perceived as "cop-outs" by people at stages 4 and 5, and their nonconformist behavior is not generally rewarded, or even tolerated, in business organizations. As a result, persons at this level who do not ultimately capitulate by adopting organizationally accepted modes of manipulation and conformity, or adapt by evolving to the seventh stage of psychological existence, may become organizational problems because of alcoholism, drug abuse, or other self-punitive behavior.

Stage 7.   People at the seventh, or *existential*, mode have high tolerance for ambiguity and nonconformity. They prefer to do jobs in their own way without constraints of authority or bureaucracy, showing little tolerance for detailed job descriptions, written procedures, and the arbitrary use of authority. Level 7's include people like Ralph Nader and Aileen Hernandez, who tend to be goal-oriented, but toward broader arenas and longer time perspectives than those in stage 5. As managers, they, too, are concerned with the organizational profits, the quarterly review, and the annual plan, but they are also concerned with the 10-year or 50-year plan and the impact of the organization on its members, society, and the environment. Like people in stage 6, they are concerned with the dignity of their fellow man and are repelled by the use of violence. Their independent behavior, disinterest in rank-oriented status symbols, and outspoken intolerance of constraints imposed by bureaucratic ritual are threatening to many managers of types 4 and 5, and they may be expelled from the organization for reasons of nonconformity or insubordination.

Guidelines for Compatibility

Managers are, with increasing frequency, finding themselves out of step with the people they supervise or the people they report to. Conformity behavior, once taken for granted, is no longer the norm. Not only are the managers out of step, but so are many of the systems which they use to achieve organizational goals. Since systems reflect the values of their designers and administrators, it is only natural to find people responding to systems as they do to the managers who created and administer them. Figure 1-10 is a chart of capsule descriptors of supervisory values, systems characteristics, and subordinate or systems user values. These capsule descriptors are derived from items in a questionnaire designed around Graves' framework.[18]

The three left columns of Figure 1-10 show characteristic supervisory

[18]M. Scott Myers and Susan S. Myers, *Values for Working*, Form A, Copyright 1972, Dallas, Tex.

SUPERVISION | SYSTEMS

		PERFORMANCE REVIEW	COMMUNICATION	CAREER PLANNING	COMPENSATION	ATTITUDE SURVEY	JOB POSTING
7	S	We work together in setting goals and reviewing progress.	We discuss things informally, and I give them access to any information they want.	Self-development is the key; people should have the opportunity to plan their own careers.	A smorgasbord approach which rewards merit and adapts to individual needs.	A democratic process involving all people in analyzing problems and suggesting improvements.	A system for maximizing organizational effectiveness by encouraging the natural flow of talent.
7	E	I like to have a major role in defining my goals and methods for achieving them.	I like to feel free to talk to anyone, and to get the information I want.	I am responsible for my own career, and require the opportunity to develop my capabilities.	A good system rewards merit and doesn't tie you to the organization.	Greater commitment and solidarity are achieved when people have a hand in solving problems.	Now that I know what the openings and requirements are, I can run my own maze.
6	S	I try to review their performance without hurting their feelings.	I want to be on good terms with them so they will feel they can discuss anything with me.	Every career should include the ingredients of social and civic responsibility.	Pay and benefits tailored to the needs of the people and their circumstances.	A vehicle for diagnosing and solving human problems.	A system providing opportunity for employees to find compatible work groups and supervisors.
6	E	He should use this occasion to get better acquainted with us.	He's easy to talk to and is interested in us personally.	Our careers should be oriented toward bettering relationships among all people.	Money should serve all people, and be more equitably distributed.	Working with others in analyzing survey results is a good way to improve human relations.	I like being able to find a job where the people and work don't clash with my values.
5	S	I find that the carrot and stick works best.	I give them the information I think they need to get the job done.	I keep track of their progress and specify developmental programs and assignments.	Distribution of money according to amount of responsibility and level of performance.	A management tool for taking the pulse of an organization.	A controlled, competitive system to upgrade the best employees into company job openings.
5	E	I like to set my own goals and get recognition for achieving them.	If I'm to do a good job, I need to know everything my boss knows.	My career depends on my taking the initiative in finding opportunity for advancement.	Money is a measure of my success.	If what we learn from an attitude survey can make our employees more productive, I'm all for it.	It's one way to find advancement opportunities, but it helps to know the right people.

4	**S**	I define the goals and standards I expect them to follow.	I give them the information they should have, and keep our relations businesslike.	I define their career paths and promotional opportunities and give them continuous guidance.	Compensation programs based on community and industry surveys and standard practice.	The systematic measurement of attitudes toward company goals, policies and practices.	The orderly, systematic and fair implementation of a promotion-from-within policy.
	E	We need to know the company goals and how we can support them.	He should tell us what we're supposed to know to do our job properly.	I will be promoted when I earn it through productiveness and loyalty.	Money is a reward for loyalty and hard work, and should not be subject to favoritism.	Management is asking for our help, and it is our duty to answer all questions as honestly as possible.	I will be given the job I bid on if I deserve it.
3	**S**	I make clear what he has to do if he wants to keep his job.	I tell them whatever I feel like telling them.	It's every man for himself — don't look to me for your breaks.	Manipulative, arbitrary and secretive use of money.	Rigged questions and whitewashed reports.	Posting of jobs that can't be filled more economically from the outside.
	E	I don't like anyone finding fault with me and telling me how to act.	The less I hear from my boss, the better.	I don't want anyone planning my life — I'll look after No. 1 myself.	I'll work for the highest bidder.	I don't want any part of a stool pigeon system that can be used against me.	It's no use trying — the cards are stacked against you.
2	**S**	I tell them how I think they did and how they can improve.	I explain company rules to them and talk with them about their problems.	They expect me to tell them what to do and to take care of them.	A fair and uniform system administered by the boss.	A way of letting employees know the company is interested in their ideas.	A way of increasing job security by filling job openings from within.
	E	I want him to tell me if I've done what he wanted me to do, and if I've let him down.	He tells us what to do in a friendly way and lets us know he'll help us.	What's most important is that I'll always have a steady job and a good boss.	I need steady pay to make ends meet.	My boss should know how we feel so he can help us.	I'll bid on a job if my supervisor tells me to.

FIG. 1-10 Values reflected by people and their systems. S = supervisor system; E = employee. (*California Management Review*, University of California, Berkeley, Spring 1974, p. 16.)

(S) attitudes toward subordinates at each of the seven stages as they relate to the supervisory functions of performance review, communication and career planning. Immediately beneath each supervisory value statement at each level is shown a characteristic value statement for the supervised employee (E) at that stage.

The right side of Figure 1-10 contains descriptors and values relating to three personnel management systems—compensation, attitude survey, and job posting. At each stage is a capsule descriptor of the system as it might characteristically be conceived by a system designer (S) at that stage of psychological existence. Immediately beneath each system designer viewpoint is summarized an attitude toward the system as it might characteristically be expressed by an employee (E) at that stage of existence.

This chart identifies conditions of compatibility and conflict within the organization. For example, in considering the "communication" relationships, the level 7 supervisor's view ("We discuss things informally, and I give them access to any information they want") is compatible with the needs of the people he supervises who are in levels 7, 6, and 5:

7:   "I like to feel free to talk to anyone, to get the information I want."

6:   "He's easy to talk to, and is interested in us personally."

5:   "If I'm to do a good job, I need to know everything my boss knows."

However, in reading further down the column, it becomes apparent that the needs of people at levels 4, 3, and 2 are less compatible:

4:   "He should tell us what we're supposed to know to do our job properly."

3:   "The less I hear from my boss, the better."

2:   "He tells us what to do in a friendly way and lets us know he'll help us."

Those at levels 4 and 2 want more structure, and those at level 3 need more structure, than a supervisor at level 7 might naturally provide.

However, the actual situation in organizations is more serious than the partial incompatibility reflected in the above example. Managers are typically oriented more toward level 5 or 4 than 7 and, consequently, encounter more conflict. For example, the level 5 supervisor's communication philosophy ("I give them the information I think they need to get the job done"), is not easily compatible with any level except 4 ("He should tell us what we're supposed to know to do our job properly"). This means that level 5, a common type of leadership style, has little opportunity to succeed unless he surrounds himself with conformists. This is ultimately self-defeating, of course, as the organization would, in the long run, be immobilized by excessive conformity.

The same phenomenon exists regarding the compatibility of people and management systems. Compensation, attitude surveys, and job-posting systems designed in terms of stage 7 concepts are usually compatible with 7, 6, and 5 values, but less so with 4, 3, and 2 values. Since systems are customarily designed in terms of stage 4 and 5 concepts, they tend to meet stages 2, 3, and 4 requirements and to frustrate people at stages 5, 6, and 7. In other words, systems in traditional organizations are more acceptable to people at the conformist, egocentric, and tribalistic stages than they are for the entrepreneurial self-starters in stages 5, 6, and 7. Paradoxically, systems are usually designed by level 4 conformists to curb the creative nonconformist behavior of people at levels 5, 6, and 7. This stems in part from the fact that the job of systems and procedures writer is more likely to attract level 4 conformists than any other type (except perhaps level 2 tribalists). Hence, as a counterbalancing influence, a stage 7 editor is needed to remove the unnecessary and inflexible constraints typically reflected in policy and procedure statements.

These realms of natural incompatibility can be overcome through understanding and deliberate adaptation. It was pointed out earlier in the chapter that psychological level is not correlated strongly with intelligence but, rather, determines the way in which intelligence is used. Hence, training programs can help supervisors and nonsupervisors at any level to understand the problem of potential incompatibility and to learn how to adapt to each other. The objective of such training programs should not be for supervisors to learn to diagnose other individuals but, rather, for them to learn to anticipate, recognize, and understand the different value systems they will encounter.

The new work ethic is not a new set of values; rather, it is a heterogeneity of values and a shift in the source of influence. The seven stages of psychological existence described above have long existed, but for several centuries business organizations and most realms of society have been dominated by entrepreneurs and conformists, whose influence has been unchallenged until recently. Now, leaders are also emerging from other value systems. Heterogeneous values are permeating our culture at an accelerating rate through various media.

Figure 1-11 portrays the modern supervisor's challenge. Traditional supervisory training programs reflected assumptions that supervisors were level 5 people charged with the responsibility of motivating level 4 or level 2 followers. Traditional supervisory duties were:

1. To set goals for subordinates and to define work methods
2. To train subordinates in job skills
3. To establish standards of performance
4. To evaluate and critique subordinates' performance

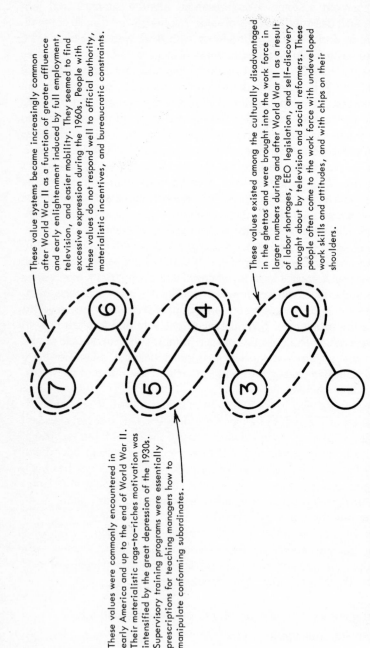

These value systems became increasingly common after World War II as a function of greater affluence and early enlightenment induced by full employment, television, and easier mobility. They seemed to find excessive expression during the 1960s. People with these values do not respond well to official authority, materialistic incentives, and bureaucratic constraints.

These values existed among the culturally disadvantaged in the ghettos and were brought into the work force in larger numbers during and after World War II as a result of labor shortages, EEO legislation, and self-discovery brought about by television and social reformers. These people often come to the work force with undeveloped work skills and attitudes, and with chips on their shoulders.

These values were commonly encountered in early America and up to the end of World War II. Their materialistic rags-to-riches motivation was intensified by the great depression of the 1930s. Supervisory training programs were essentially prescriptions for teaching managers how to manipulate conforming subordinates.

FIG. 1-11   The supervisor's challenge. The supervisor, who is frequently appointed to his leadership role because of his loyal conformity and manipulative capability, now finds himself in the uncomfortable role of leading people of all value systems, many of whom he neither understands nor accepts. (M. Scott Myers, *Managing Without Unions*, Addison-Wesley Publishing Company, Reading, Mass., 1976, p. 21.)

5. To discipline incorrect behavior and to set examples
6. To motivate through strong leadership and persuasion
7. To develop and install new methods
8. To give career guidance to subordinates
9. To praise achievements and punish failures

Though people at stages 2 and 4 tend to acquiesce to this traditional leadership style, people at stages 3, 5, 6, and 7 rebel—openly or covertly. Moreover, since stage 2 people are often identified with stage 3 egocentrics through ethnic and socioeconomic ties, they often emulate stage 3 behavior. Hence, the supervisor's leadership repertoire must be broadened to enable him to deal with the whole spectrum of value systems.

Value conflicts are not resolved, of course, by simply adopting the mod clothing and language of a cultural fad. Such conflicts can be ameliorated only by learning to operate from a new source of influence. Two primary sources of influence exist in every organization: official authority and the natural expression of "people power" by members of the organization. Traditional level 4 or 5 managers have tended to operate from influence derived from official authority. To succeed with the new work ethic, managers must learn to apply systems and supervisory techniques which are compatible with all value systems. This means learning how to let the influence of talent find free and constructive expression.

Can Every Employee Be a Manager?

The question is sometimes raised, "Is it possible for a tribalistic or egocentric person to assume a managerial responsibility for his or her job?" The answer is a qualified "yes," provided the definition of "manager" refers to the process of managing a job within the limitations established by the individual's capabilities and aspirations.

In a real sense, each person manages his or her own life away from the job. The opportunity for self-management on the job is but an extension of this responsibility in the work place. And just as the individual in the home and community learns to manage within the legal, moral, financial, and social constraints imposed by society, he or she is potentially capable of performing within the constraints of the work place.

Some individuals do not manage their own lives successfully in the home and community, and seem to require occasional rescue by friends, family, welfare agencies, and counselors. However, the "help" they receive from these protectors is often dispensed in a Parent-Child style (see pages 39 to 43) that fosters and perpetuates dependency relationships and incompetence. By the same token, these same individuals in their work place cannot be expected to be made responsible through the

Parent-Child use of permissiveness, coercion, paternalism, threats, persuasion, and manipulation. If ever they are to become responsibly self-reliant, it will be through the influence of Adult-Adult leadership. Indeed, learning to be responsible in the work place could influence their lifestyles away from the job.

But just as some persons choose complex or simple lifestyles away from the job, so do individuals differ in their preferred vocational roles on the job. At one extreme, some desire complex and continuously challenging jobs; at the other extreme, others prefer simple routine jobs. However complex or simple the job, the incumbents have one desire in common: the freedom to choose the kind of work they prefer and to relate to it in a way that is compatible with their own personal values. Hence, the concept "every employee a manager" can have meaning for persons at all levels of talent, though their preferred job-management roles may differ substantially in terms of scope and variety.

Differences among individuals regarding their preferred job roles become understandable when examined in terms of levels of psychological existence, described earlier. Such a framework helps explain why and how people differ in their choice of vocational roles, as well as their lifestyles away from the job.

As humans grow out of the reactive stage of infancy, they develop peer relationships which tend to be characterized by ritual, common attitudes, solidarity, conformity in dress code, and subservience to "tribal chieftains." During childhood, older siblings, dominant associates, parents, television personalities, clergymen, teachers, and policemen are their usual tribal chieftains. If this *tribalistic* value orientation carries over into their adult life in the work place, their supervisor or union leader might become the authority figure they look up to for direction, protection, discipline and affirmation. Being a manager of a job at this psychological level means pleasing the supervisor by carrying out duties which he has prescribed, or obeying a union leader. Delegation of planning and controlling functions to this person is a valued vote of confidence from the tribal chieftain. Having a whole job is intrinsically satisfying but, more importantly, doing it well earns praise from the boss.

The *egocentric* person is often expelled from the work force as a "troublemaker," and sometimes "the baby is thrown out with the bath water" when the creative talent of such a person is not constructively harnessed. To the traditional supervisor the concept "every employee a manager" seems unattainable for persons at this stage of development. However, self-management is an appealing concept to egocentrics, and their defiant behavior is but an irresponsible expression of their desire to escape regimentation and to be self-reliant. An appropriate combination of Adult-Adult supervision, peer pressure, and a joint stake in the success of the organization has the potential for giving constructive expression to egocentric talent.

The *conformist* stage of psychological existence is often characterized as a "procedure manual mentality"—one not associated with the initiative and self-reliance of a manager. However, extremes in conformity behavior are usually a function of extremes in suppressed talent. Paradoxically, the official prescription of a more creative role, along with mechanisms for managing innovation (such as Work Simplification, described in Chapter 4) may begin unfreezing the conformist behavior. If such a person believes it to be his duty and right to be a manager of his job, as officially prescribed by an accepted authority figure, he will tackle it with the zeal of a crusader, even to the extent of bending the rules a bit. Further, managing a meaningful job may ultimately dissipate the bonds of conformity, in which case the individual may evolve to other stages of psychological existence.

The *entrepreneurial* personality responds naturally and enthusiastically to the opportunity to be manager of his or her responsibility. Being a manager of his own job is this person's natural desire and expectation, and he resents supervisory intervention and is intolerant of constraints imposed by policies and procedures. Perhaps the primary shortcoming of the entrepreneurial type is a tendency to be excessively competitive and to be insensitive to other persons' needs to be responsible.

The *sociocentric* personality can also relate enthusiastically to the "every employee a manager" concept. However, involvement in the counterculture revolution makes it essential that sociocentrics fully understand organizational goals and constraints. Though their informality and their sometimes unkempt appearance may be disconcerting to traditional managers, they are capable of productive effort in a climate of approval, provided they are not involved with what they see as harmful products such as napalm, bombs, tobacco, or pesticides. Managing their own jobs is an appealing concept to sociocentrics, particularly when they can relate to supervisors on a first-name basis and are free to experience solidarity with other members of the work force.

The *existential* personality type is by definition already in charge of his life, and the opportunity to manage a job is a natural extension of his lifestyle. He is a goal-oriented person whose behavior seems to say, "OK, I understand the job to be done; now leave me alone and let me do it in my way." Being his own manager is the only acceptable condition of employment for the existentialist, and, if deprived of this opportunity, he is likely to leave the organization or to become preoccupied with personal goals on company time.

In summary, "every employee a manager" is a universally applicable concept, but one which depends on appropriate job conditions for its fullest implementation. Every person has the potential for managing some jobs, but not all jobs. However, every person has the potential for managing certain components of any job, or combinations of several jobs. The realization of this potential depends on matching the person's talents and aspirations with the appropriate job, particularly if the employee has an influential role in the matching process. The "job" in this case refers not only to the work itself but also to style of supervision, procedural constraints, peer relationships, and other climate factors in the work place.

2

Conditions for Human Effectiveness

This chapter attempts to integrate three strategies commonly used as the focus for organizational development: human relations, management by objectives, and the systems approach. Human relations gained emphasis when experiments in the 1920s showed that the depersonalizing processes of the Industrial Revolution needed an antidote, and it was realized that the technology of managing humans differed from the process of managing equipment. The Industrial Revolution, with its emphasis on the scientific method, and, more recently, management systems specialists have attempted to organize materiel and humans, but usually without adequate sensitivity to the needs of the people who must make the systems work. Proponents of management by objectives, while recognizing the need for aligning people's goals and their systems with organizational goals, have not placed sufficient emphasis on this strategy at the lower levels of the organization.

Human relations, management by objectives, and systems technology collectively have the potential for overcoming the shortcomings of any one of these strategies. Labeled herein as interpersonal competence, meaningful goals, and helpful systems, these three conditions are shown in Figure 2-1 to be interdependent and essential for human effectiveness at all levels. The satisfaction of these three conditions leads to achievement and self-actualization in terms of criteria meaningful to both the organization and its members. Thus, this diagram constitutes a framework for defining the requirements for organizational effectiveness, and as such, it can also serve as a checklist to aid the manager in diagnosing administrative problems.

INTERPERSONAL COMPETENCE

Organizational relationships are usually defined formally through organization charts and job descriptions. Though formal relationships are the basis for many informal relationships, many social and technical (sociotechnical)

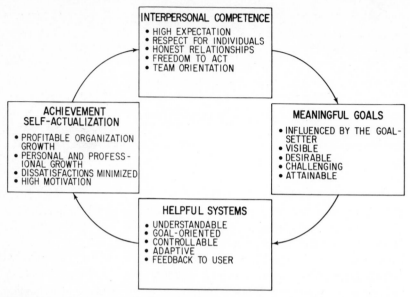

FIG. 2-1   A framework for human effectiveness.

relationships form quite independently of the formal organization. People may form social or "primary"[1] groups because they do the same kind of work, are of similar ethnic or regional origin, have similar interests, are the same age or sex, or have similar seniority in the firm. However, more often people come together simply because they are near each other in the work area. The structure of a primary group is not stable but changes in a fluid process as membership, job relationships, and work assignments change and as events alter the roles of individuals within the group. Primary groups based on work-station relationships may be preempted by other primary-group memberships in other role relationships such as in ride pools, coffee bars or lunch rooms, and bowling teams. However, these other groups do not detract from the work-group membership and, in fact, may even be a source of enrichment to it.

Large organizations are composed of small informal groups held together by the process of face-to-face communications. A primary group will sometimes develop its own jargon, which tends to create group solidarity and serves as a means of identifying group membership. These small primary groups vary in size, but average six to ten people. Because problems of communication increase with the size of the group, a group tends to break up or subdivide after it has reached a certain critical size.

[1]J. A. C. Brown, *The Social Psychology of Industry*, Penguin, Baltimore, 1965, pp. 124–256.

When a person enters a job with the intention of permanent employment, he will naturally strive to succeed and develop primary-group relationships. Interpersonal competence through primary groups is most likely to exist in skilled trades where turnover is low, where the plant is located in a relatively small and stable community, and where the work force is stable and not subject to fluctuations of seasonal employment, temporary help, layoffs, or high turnover for whatever reason.

The primary group is the medium through which individuals acquire their attitudes, values, and goals. It is also a fundamental source of discipline and social control. In most organizations, members of primary or natural work groups expect a fair share of the group's work from each other, and will rally against the member who benefits at the expense of another. Because the informal working group is the main source of social control, attempts to change human behavior should be made through the medium of the group rather than through the individual. The supervisor should try to exercise legitimate influence through such groups and should avoid breaking them up.

Interpersonal Transactions

People relate to one another in the work place through the languages of words, behavior, and systems. The language of words is the spoken or written words that people hear or read. The language of behavior is nonverbal communications such as facial expressions, gestures, supervisory styles, social interactions, recreational groupings, task-force endeavors, and freedom of action. The language of systems is procedural media such as attitude surveys, job posting, grievance procedures, public address systems, performance reviews, work standards, and other processes utilizing standardized forms and equipment.

These three types of communication media obviously are not mutually exclusive. For instance, performance reviews usually involve all three—words, behavior, and systems. Information is conveyed via written and spoken words to the person being evaluated. Vivid messages are also conveyed by the supervisor's mannerisms, facial expressions, and tone of voice. The standard forms and procedures represent a system which circumscribes the communication process.

Behavior and systems may be thought of as the language of action and are generally found to be more influential than the language of words. It is sometimes said that when the language of action differs from the language of words, the language of action is the only one "heard." For example, with the language of words a management spokesperson may say, "People are our most important assets," but with the language of behavior may convey a contradictory message. And with the language of systems, management may reinforce this contradiction through the inappropriate use of time clocks, signal bells, work standards, and status symbols.

Some standard practices in communication have become less appropriate as people have become more enlightened. Enlightened people do not like to be talked down to, as some parents talk down to children, and as some managers talk to subordinates. Most people respond better if they are addressed as adults. However, unenlightened people who are more accustomed to dependency relationships may expect to hear the voice of authority, accept it as normal, and even welcome it as an expression of protective parental concern.

The late Eric Berne[2] pointed out that each personality has three components, which for the purpose of explanation to nonpsychologists, he labeled Parent, Adult, and Child. Each person has these three dimensions within his or her personality, ready to respond to appropriate cues. The Parent is talking when a supervisor says, "I warn you not to be late again"; the Adult says, "We needed you at eight o'clock this morning"; and the Child says, "Please don't come in late; you'll get us both in trouble."

When the Parent part of the personality is being asserted, it may be expressed in one of two ways—critical or protective. The Critical Parent may be judgmental, fault-finding, self-righteous, hostile, tough, or dogmatic. The Protective Parent may be sympathetic, kind, helpful, nurturing, indulgent, and lenient.

The Adult component of the personality is rational, logical, factual, and unemotional. It is the data processor within us, and sometimes it is referred to as our computer. It is also the component of our personality that enables us to understand the influence of the Parent and the Child.

The Child component of the personality may be expressed in one of two ways—as a Natural Child or as an Adapted Child. The Natural Child may be creative, intuitive, fun-loving, charming, and optimistic or self-indulgent, selfish, domineering, and manipulative. The Adapted Child tends to be compliant, courteous, depressed, whining, withdrawing, and tribalistic.

It should be noted that the concepts of Parent, Adult, and Child are not related to chronological age or to roles in a family. People of all ages have these three components in their personalities. Very young, as well as older, people may have strong Parent tapes; that is, their minds may have recordings of them, like cassette tapes, imprinted by their parents or other authority figures. Typical Parent tapes are:

If at first you don't succeed, try, try again.

Eat all the food on your plate.

[2]Eric Berne, *Transactional Analysis in Psychotherapy*, Grove Press, New York, 1961.

Boys don't cry.

Girls don't get dirty.

Never tell a lie.

By the same token, older people may have strong Child components, and hence we see sixty-five-year-olds enjoying a party, going to a picnic, watching television, eating ice cream, pouting about a disappointment, or withdrawing within themselves.

People of all ages, then, have active Parent, Child, and Adult personality components. The Adult component enables us to take an objective look at ourselves, to understand how our Parent and Child are influencing our behavior, and to help us decide whether or not to permit this to happen. For example, the obese person who spots coconut cream pie when he goes through the cafeteria line hears three voices:

Child: "Wow! Coconut cream pie! That's what I want!"

Parent: "You shouldn't eat it, fatty!"

Adult: "I'd enjoy it for five minutes and carry it around for five weeks."

The Child may dominate and the Parent may arouse guilt feelings, but the Adult may analyze what is happening and, if the desire for pie is strong enough, work out a calorie budget to compensate during the next meal.

In the work place, a person's perceptions and expectations are influenced by the component that may be dominant. Consider, for example, the immediate reaction of the individual who is told, "Hey, Joe, the boss wants to see you in his office—right now!" Depending on which component of his personality is activated at that time, Joe may experience any of the following feelings:

Critical Parent: "Why can't he leave me alone when I'm busy?"

Protective Parent: "Don't worry, Joe; everything will be OK."

Adult: "I wonder what he wants to see me about."

Natural Child: "Wow, maybe I'm getting a promotion!"

Adapted Child: "Oh, no—I hope I didn't do anything wrong."

In his supervisor's office, Joe may receive either positive or negative strokes. Speaking from his Adult, the supervisor may give him a positive stroke: "Thanks for coming in, Joe, I would like your advice. The superintendent wants to know when we could get the new compressor installed. What shall I tell him?" Or speaking from his Parent, the supervisor could give Joe negative strokes on the same subject: "Where in the devil were you, Joe? I promised the super we'd have the new compressor installed by tomorrow noon. Drop whatever you're doing and get on it, or it's your neck and mine. Now don't tell me your problems; I don't want to hear from you till the job is done."

The use of positive strokes is more likely to evoke an Adult-Adult discussion between Joe and his supervisor, resulting in mutual respect and self-confidence. The negative strokes clearly represent a Parent-Child encounter, which evokes a "Yes, sir" from Joe's Adapted Child, resulting in lingering resentment and conformity or rebellion.

A positive stroke in its simplest form may be a smile or a friendly gesture—a warm sign of acceptance. A negative stroke may be a frown, a sneer, or a criticism—a putdown. In the work environment, asking for suggestions and listening to them are positive strokes. Not listening to ideas or giving "idiot-proof" job instructions are negative strokes. Not all positive strokes have to be good news. In a performance review discussion, for example, adverse information handled as feedback rather than criticism represents a display of confidence and respect which makes it a positive stroke.

As a consequence of continuous use of positive or negative strokes, people tend to develop a rather permanent set of attitudes toward themselves, others, and life in general. This attitudinal life position is sometimes referred to as degree of "OKness." A person who is consistently treated as an adult and given many positive strokes tends to develop feelings of OKness about self and others. This person's basic position is "I'm OK, you're OK"; the world is a pretty good place, and it's fun to be alive. But the person who is given many positive strokes from permissively protective authority figures may develop a spoiled-brat syndrome: "I'm OK, you're not OK." Individuals who have received a lifetime of negative strokes may develop the position "I'm not OK, you're OK" or "I'm not OK, you're not OK." This is particularly true of persons whose initiative has been continuously quashed or who have been unfairly and inescapably disadvantaged in competitive pursuits.

Many individuals appear to carry through life a characteristic position of OKness which predictably manifests itself in most circumstances. For most people, however, feelings of OKness are situational. For example, an employee may feel in the work place "I'm OK, you're not OK," may feel in church "I'm not OK, you're OK," but may feel at home "I'm OK, you're OK."

People are sometimes polarized into positions through their group identity. In a company of stressful labor relations, management people seem to assume a uniform position toward workers of "We're OK, they're not OK." Workers, in turn, assume the same position "We're OK, but management is not OK." As long as these basic group postures exist, it is not realistic to expect collaboration between the two parties.

Strokes and life positions are interdependent. When our Critical Parent or defiant Natural Child causes us to dispense negative strokes, we may evoke an "I'm not OK" or "You're not OK" attitude from the recipients. When our Adult or Natural Child applies positive strokes, we usually evoke "You're OK" responses. However, people in the "We're OK, you're not OK" position find it unnatural and difficult to dispense positive strokes to an adversary, and so the mutually self-defeating win-lose cycle is perpetuated. The interruption of this win-lose cycle can be constructively activated by intervention processes described in Chapter 7.

The Role of Assumptions

McGregor's famous book, *The Human Side of Enterprise*,[3] illustrates the theme that people's behavior reflects their values or attitudes. One type of attitude, which he called "theory X," embodies a set of assumptions which, when translated into behavior, tends to bring out the worst in people. A contrasting set of assumptions, which he labeled "theory Y," provides more options for bringing out the best in people. Though the terminology of transactional analysis was not widely known when McGregor wrote his book, theory X values are usually expressed as a Critical or Protective Parent in a Parent-Child relationship, from the position, "I'm OK, you're not OK." Theory Y would generally find expression in Adult-Adult relationships, though at times, when appropriate, might also be expressed as Parent-Child, Adult-Child, and Child-Child transactions. Theory Y is usually a manifestation of the position, "I'm OK, you're OK."

The goal-oriented, developmental (theory Y) supervisor embraces a set of values which reflects confidence in and respect for his fellow man. Though he recognizes that not all persons have earned respect and confidence, he assumes that they are capable of doing so and that an individual is competent and has integrity until he learns otherwise.

He recognizes that many people find work unpleasant, but tends to see this as more of an indictment of job design or style of supervision than of the inherent characteristics of the job incumbent. He believes that people are not naturally lazy, but seem so when work has been deprived of its meaning. He assumes that most people are imaginative and creative and that if they fail to display these traits, it is largely a result of constraints imposed by supervision or apathy stemming from the absence of challenge. He believes that freedom and responsibility go hand in hand and that the more information he shares with people, the more they will tend to think and behave responsibly. He has consistently high expectations of others and assumes that, with access to information and freedom to pursue goals, they will set and achieve high goals without continuing intervention.[4]

---

[3] Douglas McGregor, *The Human Side of Enterprise*, McGraw-Hill, New York, 1960.

[4] For further elaboration on the role of a manager's expectations, see J. Sterling Livingston, "Pygmalion in Management," *Harvard Business Review*, July–Aug. 1969, pp. 81–89.

In his view, it is better to give people both good and bad news, believing most people capable of accepting the whole story, no matter how painful it is. He assumes that mistakes are inevitable and should provide a basis for learning, as punishment tends primarily to evoke defensiveness. Though he recognizes the importance of money and believes that it should be distributed according to merit, he assumes that most people are more strongly motivated by interesting and challenging work.

The authority-oriented, reductive (theory X) supervisor, in contrast, tends to quash initiative or evoke defensiveness through behavior reflecting lack of confidence in and respect for others. Though his assumptions cannot be neatly catalogued as a pure syndrome, the following characteristics usually cluster together. He assumes that people naturally tend to do as little work as possible, and believes close supervision and a little fear are needed to prevent them from lowering their standards or to push them toward higher goals. In his opinion, few people have much imagination and ingenuity, and the perspective of most is too limited to expect them to provide realistic suggestions. Moreover, he interprets his role as "superior" literally, assuming that it entitles him to respect and believing his prestige would be weakened if he asked for suggestions or admitted to the superiority of a subordinate's ideas. He assumes that people are not usually responsible, are not to be trusted with information, and are not capable of accepting unpleasant news. The more knowledge and freedom people have regarding their job, the more controls are assumed to be needed to keep them in line because, "If you give them an inch, they'll take a mile." Though he readily admits that people like responsibility, recognition, and other forms of "mollycoddling," he feels that they are bound to gripe about something and that the only real way to motivate them and keep them happy is to give them enough money. He is usually unable to differentiate between happiness and motivation.

Supervisory Style

The supervisory style of the goal-oriented manager is characterized by balanced concern for the needs of the organization and its members. His behavior reflects confidence in, and respect for, others. He makes time, even during busy schedules, to listen, and will attempt to see the merit of ideas which conflict with his own. He solves problems by sharing company information with people under his supervision and by involving them in problem solving and goal setting. He encourages people to reach out in new directions, taking mistakes in stride, and tries mainly to discover how mistakes can be avoided in the future. He expects and acknowledges superior performance.

Authoritarian assumptions more often find expression in a style of management which reflects high concern for the organization or self, but little concern or respect for its members. He sets job goals for his subordinates (or abandons them without the information that would enable subordinates to set their own goals), doles out information, discourages them from deviating from specified procedures, expects adequate performance, and says little unless something goes wrong. In paying lip service to new theory, he may ask for ideas, but his mind is usually already made up, and when confronted with conflict, he may try to suppress it or may capitulate by attempting to appease the troublemakers. There is little room for mistakes in his organization, especially mistakes that might embarrass him. When something goes wrong, he tries primarily to find out who caused it, and see to it that the culprit is punished.

Trends in organization development favor goal orientation over authority orientation as a foundation for human effectiveness. Few thoughtful managers today would deliberately defend the traditional application of authority. Many managers have assisted in the preparation of formal statements of philosophy to idealize their organization as democratically goal-oriented, and they may have conscientiously committed themselves to this principle through both written and spoken words. However, in many ways, both subtle and flagrant, as a result of habit, tradition, policy, systems, insensitivity, and introspective myopia, some managers continue to use authority as their primary source of power.

The Reductive Use of Authority

The most overt forms of authority orientation are reflected in "superior-subordinate" relationships which imply "ownership" of subordinates by the supervisor. The supervisor demands rather than requests actions from his subordinates, and will, for example, without apparent consideration for their convenience, summon them to his office or otherwise interrupt their activity. He phones orders to underlings without inquiring about their availability, or simply barks to the subordinate's secretary, for example, "Tell Bill to come to my office." Though he may drive his points home in meetings by shouting and pounding the conference table, he makes it generally understood that subordinates will not respond with shouting and table pounding. He preempts conference rooms reserved by subordinates, calls subordinates out of training programs, bypasses a subordinate's secretary, interrupts subordinates' staff meetings, disregards social relationships and commitments, conscripts a subordinate's secretary for personal use or to lend to some higher-up, or criticizes a subordinate's mode of dress or hair style, for example, reminding him with an authority-laden smile, "There are no sideburns at the top, Dave."

Tradition has bestowed rank with privileges so commonplace that they find unquestioned acceptance, usually without conscious awareness of their original and lingering significance. Class distinctions are created or

C. /

reinforced through authority-based privileges and symbols such as exclusive dining and parking facilities, office size and furnishings, distinctive identification badges, and mode of attire. Special coffee service, exemption from parking rules, disregard of time signal bells, nonobservance of lunch and coffee schedules, and circumvention of job-posting procedures are examples of common privileges of rank, unthinkingly or flagrantly perpetuated by managers long after they have declared themselves officially against authority orientation. Symbols associated with these privileges tend to increase social distance and inhibit communication, thus creating and exaggerating cleavages between groups at various levels of the organization.

The authority-oriented supervisor rarely stands on convictions born of professional competence but, rather, devotes much of his energy to aligning himself with the power structure of the organization. If a project managed by a subordinate is viewed favorably by upper management, he becomes identified with it and gradually and subtly reverses the delegation process until he is pulled into the limelight and becomes the official spokesman for the project. The subordinate, characteristically led on with expectations of presenting a proposal personally, completes the necessary research and development work, only to have the boss whisk it away to an unknown fate. If the project loses favor in the eyes of upper management, the boss quickly divests himself of it by redelegating it.

The "chain of command" is the authoritarian's primary basis for both official and unofficial relationships. He expects all information to flow upward or downward through him or other "official channels." A subordinate who wishes to contact a member at his boss's level or above, for example, to be guest speaker at a graduation banquet, soon learns that the transaction must be performed by the boss. However, the subordinate is free to contact those at his own level or below. The authority-oriented person tends to choose persons at his own level or above for luncheon dates or social activities, though he would find it acceptable to accompany a *group* of his subordinates to lunch. For him, social stratification within, and even outside, the organization is determined largely by position in the official hierarchy.

If one of the authoritarian's subordinates loses favor with a higher-up, for whatever reason, his own perception of the subordinate is altered, and he readily turns and "takes the second bite" at the heels of the subordinate. He may salve his conscience by uttering feeble demurrals, damning the subordinate with faint praise, but will ultimately acquiesce and obediently perform the painful ceremony of admonishment, transfer, demotion, or termination with the courage displayed by all official axmen.

Occasionally, goal-oriented work groups form within the authoritarian's organization, made up of individuals whose professional competence immunizes them against his arbitrary use of power. He holds them in awe because he respects power of any kind, and as long as they incur top management favor and support, he does not stand in their way. However, his relationship to them is not usually one of goal-oriented reciprocity. For the authoritarian, solidarity or equality is an uncomfortable experience. Hence, he tends to abandon them or disengage himself from involvement in their efforts. If the group finally disbands and leaves his organization in reaction to his style of leadership, and he is faced with the mission of restaffing the vacated positions, he vows he will never again let another "power-base" develop within his organization.

Slightly more subtle are the cat-and-mouse tactics employed by the boss to remind underlings that their security and freedom exist only through his magnanimity. Further examples of subtle misuse of authority include the arbitrary withholding and dispensing of information according to whim, the last-moment scheduling or canceling of meetings, the delaying and extending of staff meetings, the extraction of "reasons" for personal leave, the selective distribution of homemade Christmas cakes to his favorites, and the dog-in-the-manger authorization to use company-financed club facilities.

When the authoritarian supervisor chairs a staff meeting, for example, to solve a problem or to evaluate a proposal, his subordinates develop an infallible method for taking the "right" position on any issue: They learn to read his facial expression. They sit in watchful silence until the chief speaks and then converge on an elaboration of his viewpoint. So firmly established become these cue-reading patterns that subordinates, as well as the boss, are often deceived into interpreting conformity as consensus.

The boss's authority is often adopted by his secretary through a process of authority by association. His secretary's "requests" for information frequently come through as orders to subordinates and their secretaries. Exempted from timekeeping regulations, rotational relief assignments, and many standard ground rules, the secretary gradually activates a conditioning process which increases subordinate acquiescence and alienation, and also increases his or her secretarial imperiousness. Attempts to give feedback to the boss regarding his secretary's "little-dictator" syndrome characteristically evoke a defensiveness that effectively shuts off future feedback attempts.

Perhaps the most discouraging aspect of the misuse of authority is the supervisor's insensitivity to this syndrome. It should be noted that authority orientation is not usually an expression of intentional or deliberate malice. It is more often a form of pathology, perhaps a result of years of adapting to authoritarianism in the home, schools, the church, the armed forces, and previous jobs. The intelligent authoritarian typically experiences occasional flashes of insight and brief periods of remorse. In fact, a true authoritarian is also a masochist who pathologically enjoys punishment or criticism—as long as it comes from a respected authority and represents an opportunity for atonement from which he can recover. When he becomes aware of alienation in his group, he may attempt to win goodwill through the paternalistic generosity of an office party, a home barbecue, a Christmas turkey, or other irrelevant tactics. Paternalism, of course, only increases social distance. His attempts to change are sincere, but most such attempts are superficial veneers which fail to conceal the real personality that he exposes through his day-by-day language of action.

Finally, it must be noted that the authority-oriented supervisor should not bear the full brunt of his ineptness. The managers above him, who appointed him and reinforced his behavior through rewards, authoritarian systems, and their own leadership styles, are the primary problem. If he *can* change, he certainly will not do it until he gets different cues from above, as his behavior largely reflects his attempts, usually subconscious, to build himself in their image.

Figure 2-2 shows how 1344 managers were described by highly motivated and poorly motivated subordinates.[5] Highly motivated managers use descriptors characterizing goal-oriented supervisors, defined on page 43. Poorly motivated managers were almost evenly balanced in describing their boss as authority-oriented or goal-oriented, with more emphasis on reductive descriptors. These results suggest that interpersonal competence, as defined in these terms, is a requisite for high motivation, but that interpersonal competence alone does not ensure it. Other requirements for high motivation are meaningful goals and helpful systems, as portrayed in Figure 2-1.

Effective Teams

McGregor's discussion of the implications of theory X and theory Y noted that managerial behavior, practices, and systems rather commonly reflected theory X assumptions. However, in research conducted at the MIT Sloan School of Management during the 1950s, McGregor found that the more successful organizations followed practices which were apparently based on theory Y assumptions. For instance, with regard to the use of task-oriented groups or teams engaged in problem-solving–goal-setting missions, it was observed that the successful group with a genuine unity of purpose tended to display certain characteristics.

Characteristics of Effective Groups

1. *Climate.* The "atmosphere," which can be sensed in a few minutes of observation, tends to be informal, comfortable, and relaxed. There are no

[5]M. Scott Myers, "Conditions for Manager Motivation," *Harvard Business Review*, Jan.–Feb. 1966, p. 63.

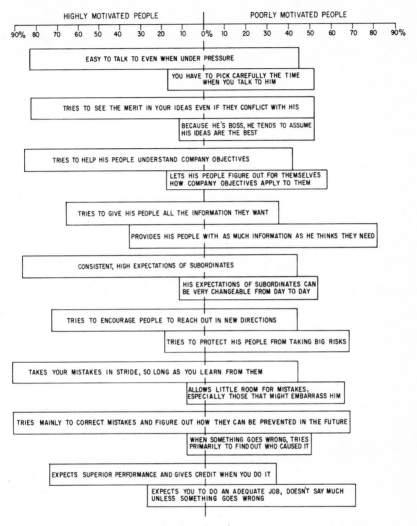

FIG. 2-2   How people describe their bosses.

obvious tensions. It is a working atmosphere in which people are involved and interested. There are no signs of boredom.

2.   *Discussion.* There is a lot of discussion in which virtually everyone participates, but it remains pertinent to the task of the group. If the discussion gets off the subject, someone brings it back in short order.

3.   *Goals.* The task or the objective of the group is well understood and accepted by the members. There will have been free discussion of the objective at some point until it was formulated in such a way that the members of the group could commit themselves to it.

4. *Listening.* The members listen to one another. The discussion does not have the quality of jumping from one idea to another unrelated one. Every idea is given a hearing. People do not seem to be afraid of appearing foolish by putting forth a creative thought, even if it seems fairly extreme.

5. *Disagreement.* There is disagreement. The group is comfortable with this and shows no signs of having to avoid conflict or to keep everything on a plane of sweetness and light. Disagreements are not suppressed or over-ridden by premature group action. The reasons are carefully examined, and the group seeks to resolve them rather than to dominate the dissenter.

On the other hand, there is no "tyranny of the minority." Individuals who disagree do not appear to be trying to dominate the group or to express hostility. Their disagreement is an expression of a genuine differ-ence of opinion, and they expect a hearing in order that a solution may be found. Sometimes there are basic disagreements which cannot be re-solved. The group finds it possible to live with them, accepting them but not permitting them to block its efforts. Under some conditions, action will be deferred to permit further study of an issue among the members. On other occasions, where the disagreement cannot be resolved and action is necessary, it will be taken, but with open caution and recognition that the action may be subject to later reconsideration.

6. *Consensus.* Most decisions are reached by a kind of consensus in which it is clear that everybody is in general agreement and willing to go along. However, there is little tendency for individuals who oppose the action to keep their opposition private and thus let an apparent consensus mask real disagreement. Formal voting is at a minimum; the group does not accept a simple majority as a proper basis for action.

7. *Criticism.* Criticism is frequent, frank, and relatively comfortable. There is little evidence of personal attack, either openly or in a hidden fashion. The criticism has a constructive flavor in that it is oriented toward removing obstacles that face the group and preventing them from getting the job done.

8. *Candor.* People are free in expressing their feelings as well as their ideas, both on the problem and on the group's operation. There is little pussyfooting; there are few "hidden agendas." Everybody appears to know quite well how everybody else feels about any matter under discus-sion.

9. *Action plan.* When action is taken, clear assignments are made and accepted.

10. *Chairmanship.* The person chairing the group does not dominate it nor, on the contrary, does the group defer unduly to the leader. In fact as one observes the activity, it is clear that the leadership shifts from time to time, depending on the circumstances. Different members, because of their knowledge or experience, are in a position at various times to act as "resources" for the group. The members utilize them in this fashion, and they occupy leadership roles while they are thus being used. There is little evidence of a struggle for power as the group operates. The issue is not who controls but how to get the job done.

11. *Feedback.* The group is self-conscious about its own operations. Frequently, it will pause during the meeting to examine how well it is doing or what may be interfering with its operations. The problem may be a matter of procedure, or it may be an individual whose behavior is interfering with the accomplishment of the group's objectives. Whatever it is, it gets open discussion until a solution is found.

Characteristics of Ineffective Groups

In studying the characteristics of groups that are relatively ineffective in accomplishing their purposes, McGregor reported the following characteristics.

1. *Climate.* The "atmosphere" is likely to reflect either indifference and boredom (people whispering to each other or carrying on side conversations, individuals who are obviously not involved) or tension (undercurrents of hostility and antagonism, stiffness and undue formality). The group is clearly not challenged by its task or genuinely involved in it.

2. *Discussion.* A few people tend to dominate the discussion. Often their contributions are way off the point. Little is done by anyone to keep the group clearly on the track.

3. *Goals.* From the things said, it is difficult to understand what the group task is or what its objectives are. These may have been stated by the chairman initially, but there is no evidence that the group either understands or accepts a common objective. On the contrary, it is usually evident that different people have different, private, and personal objectives which they are attempting to achieve in the group, and these are often in conflict with one another and with the group's task.

4. *Listening.* People do not really listen to one another. Ideas are ignored and overridden. The discussion jumps around with little coherence and no sense of movement along a track. One gets the impression that there is much talking for effect: People make speeches which are obviously intended to impress someone else rather than being relevant to the task at hand. Conversation with members after the meeting will reveal that they have failed to express ideas or feelings which they may have had for fear they would be criticized or regarded as silly. Some members feel that the leader or the other members are constantly making judgments of them in terms of evaluations of the contributions they make, and so they are extremely careful about what they say.

5. *Disagreement.* Disagreements are generally not dealt with effectively by the group. They may be completely suppressed by a leader who fears conflict. On the other hand, they may result in open warfare, the consequence of which is domination by one subgroup over another. They may be "resolved" by a vote in which a very small majority wins the day and a large minority remains completely unconvinced.

There may be a "tyranny of the minority" in which an individual or a small subgroup is so aggressive that the majority accedes in order to preserve the peace or to get on with the task. In general, only the more aggressive members get their ideas considered, because the less aggressive people tend either to keep quiet altogether or to give up after short, ineffectual attempts to be heard.

6. *Consensus.* Actions are often taken prematurely before the real issues are either examined or resolved. There will be much grousing after the meeting by people who disliked the decision but failed to speak up about it in the meeting itself. A simple majority is considered sufficient for action, and the minority is expected to go along. Most of the time, however, the minority remains resentful and uncommitted to the decision.

7. *Criticism.* Criticism may be present, but it is embarrassing and tension-producing. It may be in the form of a personal attack on another person, and the members are uncomfortable with this and unable to cope with it. Criticism of ideas tends to be destructive, putting certain members on the defensive. Sometimes *every* idea proposed will be "clobbered" by someone else. In such situations, no one will be willing to take the risk of offering an idea.

8. *Candor.* Personal feelings are hidden rather than brought out in the open. The general attitude of the group is that feelings are inappropriate for discussion and would be too explosive if brought out on the table.

9. *Action plan.* Action decisions tend to be unclear; no one really knows who is going to do what. Even when assignments of responsibility are made, there is often considerable doubt as to whether they will be carried out.

10. *Chairmanship.* The leadership remains clearly with the committee chairman. This person may be weak or strong, but she or he always sits "at the head of the table."

11. *Feedback.* The group tends to avoid any objective discussion of how it is functioning as a group. There is often more discussion after the meeting of what went wrong and why, but these matters are seldom brought up and considered during the meeting itself, where they might be resolved.

How a Group Measures Its Effectiveness

The principles elaborated above regarding the functioning of effective and ineffective groups can serve as guidelines for helping a group give itself feedback on how well it is doing as a group. Figure 2-3 summarizes these criteria in a group feedback form. The recommended use is to have a supply of these forms on hand and when a meeting seems not to be functioning as desired, to stop and have each member complete a form. The group average or median for each item is the score for that item. Similarly, a highly successful meeting might be followed by self-assessment

1. Climate	0	1	2	3	4	5	6	7	8	9	
	indifference, boredom						involvement, interest				
2. Discussion	0	1	2	3	4	5	6	7	8	9	
	unbalanced, irrelevant						widespread, relevant				
3. Goals	0	1	2	3	4	5	6	7	8	9	
	unclear, conflicting						understood, accepted				
4. Listening	0	1	2	3	4	5	6	7	8	9	
	ideas ignored, overridden						attentive, respectful				
5. Disagreement	0	1	2	3	4	5	6	7	8	9	
	conflict suppressed, open warfare, or tyranny of the minority						thoughtful acceptance of conflict, rational expression of difference				
6. Consensus	0	1	2	3	4	5	6	7	8	9	
	premature action, resentful minority(ies)						working through to agreement				
7. Criticism	0	1	2	3	4	5	6	7	8	9	
	tension-producing, personal attacks						obstacle-directed discussion				
8. Candor	0	1	2	3	4	5	6	7	8	9	
	hidden feelings						free expression of feelings				
9. Action plan	0	1	2	3	4	5	6	7	8	9	
	unclear assignments, uncommitted acceptance						clear, accepted assignments				
10. Chairmanship	0	1	2	3	4	5	6	7	8	9	
	domineering, arbitrary, Parent-Child						democratic, thoughtful, Adult-Adult				
11. Feedback	0	1	2	3	4	5	6	7	8	9	
	fault finding after meeting						self-examination during meeting				

FIG. 2-3 Group feedback form. (M. Scott Myers, *Managing With Unions*, Addison-Wesley Publishing Company, Reading, Mass., 1978, p. 69.)

in the same manner. The potentially perfect score for the whole form is 99, and the absolute low is 0. In practice, groups don't hit these extremes, but a well-functioning group scores above 75 and a poorly functioning group below 50.

MEANINGFUL GOALS

Everyone has goals. Some goals are set by the individuals pursuing them, some are set with the participation of others, some are set exclusively by others. Generally speaking, individuals most actively pursue the goals they set themselves. When too many of a person's goals are set by others, he reacts individually or collectively by setting goals to circumvent, violate, or change these goals. These goals of avoidance and rebellion then become personal goals. Therein lies the crux of the problem of goal setting in industry.

The higher a person's position in the organization, the more degrees of freedom he has to set goals. If the person at the top defines his goals with the genuine involvement of the people below him, his goals are also their goals.

But if goal setting is a "top management" function to be "sold" downward through the use of persuasion, authority, bribery, and manipulation, people respond with words and actions that say, "Those are not my goals, they are management's goals." If "management" is seen as an enemy, the individual fights back in subtle or overt ways, often ingeniously, sometimes subconsciously, to thwart management goals; if management is perceived as benevolent and friendly, he may curb his inner frustrations, turn out a fair day's work, and appreciate the well-intended praise and rewards of management. But most of the time he thinks and talks about his own goals—which he finds off the job.

Some Dynamics of Goal Setting

Goals are related to satisfaction according to this equation:

$$\text{Satisfaction} = \frac{\text{achievements}}{\text{goals}}$$

Goals nearly always exceed achievements, and hence, satisfaction increases as achievements approach goals. But in reality, this satisfaction is illusory and fleeting because, as an individual's achievements approach a particular goal, he begins raising his goals or directing them elsewhere. For example, a person's goal to jog a mile per day, when achieved, may be adjusted to a goal to run three miles per day. When he is hungry, his immediate goal is to eat. Having satisfied that goal, he redirects his aspiration, say to reading a book or completing some office homework.

The equation also has long-range application. For example, a high school graduate's goal may be a bachelor's degree in electrical engineering. When he gains the satisfaction of attaining this goal (usually before graduation day), he sets a new goal—perhaps to get a job as an engineer in a certain company, or to pursue an advanced degree. While working toward these long-range goals, he has, of course, set and achieved (or set, failed to achieve, and readjusted) many short-range goals such as pledging a particular fraternity, earning an A in calculus, getting a passing D in history, taking a particular girl to the spring dance, winning a tennis match, and learning to parallel on snow skis.

Victor Vroom[6] defines the attractiveness of a particular goal as a function of the net desirability of any number of consequences of its attainment. Further, the level of motivation with which an individual pursues a goal is a function of the net value of the anticipated consequences of having achieved the goal. Thus, a high school graduate may volunteer for an undesirable military assignment to earn educational assistance to get a college education which he values more than he dislikes the military assignment. While performing his uninspiring military duties, he may unexpectedly discover an opportunity to apply for a military-sponsored educational assignment which is relevant to his professional interests and which will also grant him college credits. He pursues the assignment with newly kindled enthusiasm, for now the presumed negative value of the military assignment itself has the potential of leading to a positive outcome to be coupled with the positive value of his long-range college plan.

Goal-setting problems often arise from supervisory assumptions that people have little interest in organizational goals. This view stems largely from the fact that many supervisors, not understanding the characteristics of meaningful goals, assign only tasks or duties to people. Tasks and duties must be performed, of course, to achieve the supervisor's goals, but the supervisor often has little success in getting others to perform tasks and duties with the enthusiasm he feels toward his goals. The corrective mission, in this case, becomes one of helping the supervisor understand the need for a framework or hierarchy of goals within the organization that is meaningful at any level. Tasks and duties take on meaning when those who perform them can relate them to a meaningful chunk of a hierarchy of goals and see the relationship between their efforts and the attainment of these goals. Job efforts have maximum meaning when they include the planning and measurement of achievements in accordance with the plan-do-control concept described on pages 101 to 104.

[6]V. H. Vroom, *Work and Motivation*, John Wiley, New York, 1964.

Finding a Goal-Setting Arena

Most people ultimately find the arena in life in which they can achieve goals, usually by trial-and-error processes. The new college graduate entering industry usually finds ever-blossoming opportunities for setting and achieving increasingly higher goals. Since his college degree opens many doors, his success in the company is largely a function of his ambition and talent. His economic maintenance needs are routinely met through his expanding compensation package and are not his primary concern as long as his broadening professional role in the organization provides growth, responsibility, and recognition for the achievement of challenging goals. Indeed, he may become so engrossed in self-actualizing experiences on the job that he gradually, voluntarily, and sometimes unconsciously, disengages himself from outside interests to devote ever-increasing amounts of time and energy to the job, which is *his* arena for goal setting and achievement.

But his former high school classmate who entered industry without a college degree usually finds the industrial work place only temporarily rewarding. Having escaped parental control and satisfied his immediate maintenance needs, he casts about impatiently for new opportunities, only to find them reserved for the newcomer with a degree, who is often younger and less experienced than he. His alternatives are few, difficult, and not often satisfying. He can do double duty and acquire the requisite academic credentials by attending classes after working hours, he can earn advancement through sheer talent, initiative, and perseverance, or he can abandon the organization—physically or mentally.

Most who enter industry without benefit of a college degree stay in the work force physically, job-hopping occasionally, preoccupied during duty hours with wages, hours, and working conditions, finding and gradually accepting their identity through their work roles and memberships in peer groups. But their compliant performance of simplified tasks is undemanding of their talents, and their interests and energies are channeled outward to their arena for self-actualization—off the job.

Off the job, the individual may satisfy growth needs through travel, reading, Toastmasters, stamp collecting, bird watching, ham radio, technical group memberships, and miscellaneous challenging pursuits. Achievement opportunities abound in a variety of activities, such as bowling, fishing, hunting, skiing, flying, sailing, painting, stock speculation, photography, mountain climbing, linguistics, ceramics, and home workshop projects. Vicarious achievement is experienced through spectator sports, movies, television, and reading. He may experience a sense of responsibility as a scoutmaster or Sunday school teacher, and through school board membership, public office, PTA leadership, and participation in social action groups. Recognition needs may be satisfied through many of the foregoing, plus activities such as little theater, ballroom dancing, public speaking, competitive sports, and social group membership. While his contemporary with a degree is gradually channeling more of his energy into the pursuit of organizational goals, the employee without a degree is more often disengaging himself from organizational commitment and finding expression for his talents in the pursuit of meaningful goals off the job.

Hence, the manager and the worker go separate ways in pursuit of goals. The problem is circular and self-perpetuating. The manager finds he must do extra duty to make up for the lack of commitment to goals at the lower levels. But people at the lower level pursue goals outside the organization because managers have reserved the more interesting aspects of their jobs for themselves.

The Consequences of Overcommitment

It is not uncommon to encounter overcommitment to the job at the higher management levels—overcommitment in the sense that the individual is deprived of a well-rounded life of responsible citizenship. The avid corporate goal setter rarely has enough energy and time left over from his company duties to attend to his personal and professional growth, his physical well-being, his family and community responsibilities. The more engaged he becomes in the pursuit of meaningful goals on the job, the more tunnel-visioned he becomes and the more disengaged he becomes from involvement with the members of his family, and hence, the less opportunity he has to experience goal setting within family and community units. Moreover, his family's familiarity with his vocational role is usually so fragmentary that it offers little opportunity for them to experience his achievements vicariously.

Members of the corporate goal setter's family often have life roles similar in many respects to the work roles of lower-level workers in his organization. Like the traditional hourly paid worker, they do not share his higher-order corporate goals as a foundation for their goal setting. It would be unrealistic, of course, for them to expect to share his job goals unless they were also members of his organization. Of course, however, each family, like each organization, does have unique goals which need the involvement, support, and commitment of all members of the family unit, including the person who earns the income to pay the bills. But checkbook benevolence is not an adequate substitute for personal participation. Many business organizations, however, seem to thrive, at least temporarily, at the expense of a community whose wives and children display symptoms of ennui and neuroses as a result of absentee spouses and parents, over-committed to corporate goals.

The Consequences of Undercommitment

The other population, composed primarily of hourly, nonexempt workers, may have just as much imbalance in their lives. Their goal-setting efforts within the organization, because of their alienation, are often unofficial and counterproductive, aimed at counteracting limitations imposed by corporate goal setters. Because they have little opportunity to apply their talents in influencing company goals or in managing challenging jobs which support them, their talents find expression at work in pursuit of goals associated with wages, hours, and working conditions, which tradition and labor legislation have placed within their realm of jurisdiction. Higher wages, paid leave, broadened insurance, liberal retirement benefits, and shorter hours are only intermediate goals, of course, as they provide the means to achieve the goals which are attractive to the workers off the job. In addition, of course, the fun of engaging management in the adversary bargaining process breaks the monotony of an otherwise humdrum existence.

In the absence of challenging jobs, workers' goals become associated with a wide spectrum of maintenance factors extrinsic to work itself. The workers seem to have capricious and vacillating interests in issues peripheral to the job, such as improving the grievance procedure, revising work rules, changing the content of the company newspaper, using the bulletin boards, getting better-sounding job titles, changing the cafeteria menu, getting the new typewriter or the chair at the end of the assembly line, avoiding the noisy work area, being located near the lunch facilities and rest rooms, and having convenient parking facilities. Goals often relate to social needs such as gaining acceptance and status within work groups, meeting friends at the coffee bar, joining a particular group at lunch time, organizing office parties, finding a congenial ride pool, planning recreational outings, and participating in special-interest-group activities.

Most nonproductive or unofficial work-place preoccupations serve primarily to make time at work more bearable or to reinforce off-the-job pursuits. As noted earlier, workers' after-hours goals involve them in sports and outings, professional societies, community projects, civic undertakings, social affairs, and family activities. Efforts directed toward these off-the-job activities sometimes seem wasteful to the corporate goal setter, but off-the-job activities have greater potential than company activities for involving the family and, hence, for contributing to family cohesiveness and community stability. Thus, wage earners, because of their freedom from the organization, as well as their greater numbers, have a disproportionately greater influence on the values and behavior patterns of a culture.

Unfortunately, ability to meet responsible citizenship roles may be inversely related to the time available to do so. When the growth and responsibility needs of people are thwarted on the job, as is often the case

with wage earners, they become culturally co
maintenance-seeking habits and attitudes which
tive leadership roles in their families and commun
porate goal setter, whose leadership talents are ofter
developed through his involvement in responsible ro
least time to utilize this competence in the family and
then, a balance should be sought in which more of
setter's leadership can be devoted to the community and
of the wage earner's leadership talents can be developed
sible goal-oriented job activities.

Requirements for Meaningful Goals

Attractive goals can give meaning to almost any type of activity, on or off
the job. Ideally, of course, work itself is intrinsically interesting. However,
even distasteful, enervating, and humdrum activities are usually tolerated
as long as they lead to meaningful goals. Otherwise, diapers would not be
changed, dishes would not be washed, and lawns would not be mowed.
Factors which give meaning to goals and, thus, inspire people to achieve
them, may be defined in terms of the characteristics of goals themselves,
and the impact that the pursuit or attainment of goals has on the goal
setter.

Goals which have maximum motivation value are

1. Influenced by the goal setter
2. Visible
3. Desirable
4. Challenging
5. Attainable

and they lead to the satisfaction of needs for

6. Growth
7. Achievement
8. Responsibility
9. Recognition
10. Affiliation
11. Security

"Company success" can be a motivational goal in satisfying the above
conditions, but only in terms of criteria meaningful to each job holder. To
the president, it might be return on investment, share of the available
market, or profitability. To a brand manager, company success may be

a greater share of the market from competitive brands. An en-
s goal might be a technological breakthrough needed to solve a
oduct performance problem. Members of an assembly line contribute to
company success when they are producing units to meet quantity and
quality goals which they, themselves, have set. To the extent that each of
these goal setters identifies his goal with company success, and his goal
meets the criteria enumerated above, it can be said that "company success" is a meaningful goal.

Consider, for contrast, goal setting through the participative task-force
approach, as described in Chapter 3, versus traditional supervisory goal
setting. In the participative process, the supervisor convenes the operators
in a conference room, shares cost information with them, explains the
company commitment to a goal established by the competitive bidding
process, and asks for their ideas. Suggestions obtained from the operators
through this conference approach leads to process improvements, greater
cooperation and commitment, and the attainment of goals which, in the
case cited, surpassed the competitive bid constraints.

Prior to the group problem-solving–goal-setting process, the operators
had been assigned to work stations on a line balanced by engineers, and
had been given job instruction by supervisory and engineering personnel.
Attempts to improve the line through "better engineering" and to "motivate" the assemblers by persuasion and enforcement of standards did not
evoke the desired performance ultimately achieved through the group
process. Analysis of these two processes in terms of eleven criteria of
meaningful goals, presented in Table 2-1, shows the task force to be
preferable to the traditional approach on every point.

The eleven criteria of meaningful goals are not presented as an
exhaustive list of factors which can give meaning to goals, but, rather, as
ideal characteristics and consequences of work itself. The relative importance of factors varies among individuals and may fluctuate for any given
individual. Moreover, even meaningless work satisfies needs for money
and other goals which may be extrinsic to the job, as noted on pages 100
to 101. Most of the characteristics in Table 2-1 can be, and often are,
satisfied by off-the-job goals. In addition, it must be recognized that some
goals are desirable simply because they represent steppingstones to other
goals.

Goal-Setting Opportunities in Industry

Two kinds of goal-setting opportunities exist within the organization. One
of these is within the context of the work itself for which the individual was
employed, and the other is in managing systems peripheral to the work
itself which are normally administered by staff people.

TABLE 2-1   A Comparison of Goal-Setting Techniques on the Assembly Line

Characteristics of meaningful goals	Participative goal setting	Supervisory goal setting
1. Influenced by goal setter	Operators participate with supervisor and others to help set goals based on analysis of problems.	Operators receive goals from supervisor, usually in terms of engineered standards.
2. Visible	Operators see goals as customer goals in terms of quantity, quality and delivery dates.	Operators see performance goals in terms of standards established by "management."
3. Desirable	Achievement of goals desirable for meeting personal commitments and to earn merit pay.	Achievement of goals desirable to earn merit pay and to avoid punishment.
4. Challenging	Both mental and physical challenges to raise and achieve self-established goals.	Physical challenge to meet quantity and quality goals, and sometimes mental challenge to "beat the system."
5. Attainable	Attainability determined by group problem solving, consensus, and cooperation.	Goals usually established at levels where a majority can meet standard.
6. Growth	Operators broaden perspective, develop problem-solving skills and mature attitudes.	Little on-the-job learning opportunity beyond immediate job skills.
7. Achievement	Achievement motive recurrently stimulated and satisfied by goal setting.	Achievement motive satisfied by attaining and exceeding standards, or by thwarting system.
8. Responsibility	Responsibility for the project results naturally from voluntary commitment to goals.	Responsible for following instructions and being loyal to the supervisor and the company.
9. Recognition	Recognition from within and outside the group for attainment of goals, and from prestige of group membership.	Praise from supervision for high performance, and acceptance from peers for supporting unofficial goals.
10. Affiliation	Joint stake effort increases interpersonal and group cohesiveness.	Social needs satisfied through informal cliques.
11. Security	Feelings of self-confidence fostered by knowledge, competence and freedom.	Feelings of insecurity fostered by unpredictability of the job situation and dependency relationship.

Goal setting related to work itself finds natural expression in vertically enriched jobs, defined on page 97 and illustrated throughout this book. For example, problem solving–goal setting, defined on pages 138 to 143, enables members of work groups, individually and collectively, to set goals within the charter of higher-echelon goals established by market surveys, competitive bidding, and strategic planning. The goal-setting performance review process defined on pages 234 to 244 offers opportunity for individuals to assist in establishing their short- and long-range goals, and in evaluating their own achievements. Work Simplification, defined on pages 130 to 138, permits goal setting as an individual or group process and, properly administered, affords many goal-setting opportunities which foster facilitative interaction with supervision. In addition to these formalized processes, of course, effective supervisors routinely foster goal-setting behavior through an informal day-to-day practice of sharing job information and problems with the people who are responsible for implementing the solutions.

Supplemental benefits and personnel services are administered through management systems serving employees who are in a real sense the customers or users of the systems. The goals of these systems, such as group insurance, retirement, profit sharing, job posting, company newspapers, grievance procedures, and eating facilities, are usually established by top management. All these systems offer opportunity for the involvement of the users at the lower levels of the organization, as illustrated in the administration of the group insurance program on pages 195 to 198, the attitude measurement program on pages 143 to 149, and the job-posting system on pages 227 to 231.

Involvement of individuals and groups in the goal-setting process of company systems results in the application of more talent, in the development of better systems, and in better understanding and acceptance by the users. Though the involvement of employees in planning and control functions results in what might be perceived by traditionalists as "nonproductive" time away from their jobs, it is found in practice that systems introduced top-down by upper levels often create more misunderstanding and hence more resentment and nonproductive efforts than systems designed through the involvement of the users.

Many peripheral systems have been overlooked as media for goal setting for job incumbents at lower levels. Chapter 3 lists examples from Eaton Corporation that provide opportunities for employees to participate in such activities. Figure 5-1 shows the potential for diverse opportunities for employee involvement under conditions of organizational democracy.

Entrepreneurial behavior by managers is often deplored on the assumption that it results in the quashing of spirit at the lower levels of the organization. The indictment should not be made against entrepreneurial behavior, per se, but rather against reserving it only for top management. As Charles Hughes[7] points out, ideally every employee should be able to think of himself as an entrepreneur, not working for a company, but working for himself within a company, providing his services and talents in exchange for compensation and other benefits, much in the same way that a service station owner provides products and services in exchange for compensation. The difference in commitment between a service station owner-operator and a hired service station operator need not reflect the extreme contrast often in evidence. Given an opportunity to utilize his talents, a stake in the success of the enterprise, and accountability for his behavior, the hired operator could think and act like an entrepreneur.

HELPFUL SYSTEMS

When the tiny Lilliputians discovered the giant Gulliver[8] asleep on their shores, they staked him to the ground, as shown in Figure 2-4, so that when he awakened he could not move. They were acting on the assumption that anyone so large and powerful was probably dangerous. His roar of protest evoked a panicky retreat and a retaliation with tiny arrows and spears. His initial entreaties for release and offers of friendly assistance were rebuffed with suspicion, and he was transported at great expense and trouble to the Emperor. As the Lilliputians gradually became accustomed to his presence, and as he learned their language and won their trust through dialogue and helpful acts, they cautiously began freeing him. He earned their confidence, respect, and goodwill by adhering to their laws, by assisting them in their agricultural and construction activities, and by defending their shores against invaders. He was granted freedom within their specified guidelines, fed at a cost 2000 times a Lilliputian's requirements, and given access to the Emperor.

Centuries later, Gulliver is reappearing in the form of giant and mysterious machines. Gulliver still talks to, and takes orders from, the Emperor of Lilliput, better known today as the "plant manager." He still has a voracious appetite, and the Lilliputians sometimes feel dwarfed and frightened by him—particularly when they first see him. He is often seen as a source of oppression that takes the fun out of life at work. Many would prefer to see him staked down, and though they are assured by the Emperor that he is friendly and helpful, they must learn this from firsthand experience.

Business systems become increasingly complex by a spiraling process.

[7]Charles L. Hughes, *Goal Setting: Key to Individual and Organizational Effectiveness*, American Management Association, New York, 1965.

[8]Jonathan Swift, *Gulliver's Travels*, Macmillan, New York, 1894, p. 5.

FIG. 2-4   The Lilliputians meet Gulliver. (Copyright 1894 by Macmillan & Co.)

Computer technology, expanding exponentially, provides ability to store, retrieve, manipulate, transmit, and display data at increasingly faster rates and lower costs. This capability, serving the mainstream and support functions of an organization, accelerates the organization's growth and complexity, at the same time increasing its dependency on massive and complicated networks of systems and their meticulously detailed and coordinated subsystems. System-imposed conformity, in combination with bigness-induced depersonalization, fosters alienation and apathy or hostility. Thus, systems themselves, depending upon how they were developed, have a primary role in generating the attitudes and perceptions that cause them to succeed or fail.

Many systems encountered by people at work do little to bring out the best in the workers; instead, the systems evoke anxiety, resentment, and "system-fighting" behavior. When systems are more restrictive than helpful, they inspire ingenuity, and sometimes dishonesty, to circumvent them. But pressures from supervision tend to quash spontaneity and encourage people to conform to established practices. Jobs are usually designed to fit the lowest level of talent. The design of a keypunch operator's job, for example, is commonly guided by the directive "Assume that they can't think." Thus, creativity among keypunch operators is seldom expected or rewarded and may actually provoke admonishments, System-controlled processes, such as the paced assembly line, though intended to increase efficiency, may do just the opposite. Man as an appendage to a machine must share its inefficiencies. The ore refinery, for example, geared to process 1000 tons per day, enables the refinery operators to "stay busy" when the intake of raw material drops to 500 tons. Also, some systems compete, to their mutual detriment. In the chemical industry, for example, engineering and operations may be inadvertently placed in conflict by inappropriate criteria of performance. Engineering may be rewarded for constructing processing plants at lower "per-square-foot" cost, even though a greater expenditure might result in greater efficiency by operations and, hence, greater return on investment to the company,. Systems may also interfere simply because they are required by tradition, protocol, or authority. Rules sometimes remain in the rulebooks long after people have devised informal and efficient shortcuts which disregard the official rules. Such a situation has double-edged potential for punishment, as people may be admonished for either "violating rules" or "slavish conformity." Finally, some systems perpetuate social stratification by prescribing rules according to status, such as time-keeping procedures, parking privileges, dining facilities, dress code, paid leave, and certain supplemental benefits.

Why Play Is Fun

People's firsthand experience with recreational activities off the job provides examples of systems which could serve as models for improving systems on the job. The bowler in Figure 2-5 could be attracted to the sport for a variety of reasons:

1. He has a visible goal.
2. He has a challenging but attainable goal.
3. He is performing according to his own personally accepted standards.
4. He is competing with himself and others.
5. He has an opportunity to improve his skills.
6. He is there of his own free will.
7. He receives immediate feedback.
8. He has opportunity to satisfy social needs.
9. He can dissipate hostility.
10. He is engaged in a healthful physical exercise.
11. He receives recognition.

However, meaning could be taken away from the bowler's activity by doing to the bowling game what seems to have been done to many jobs in

FIG. 2-5   Why play is fun.

industry. Consider, for example, the consequences of the following modifications of the bowling game:

1.   Eliminating the bowling pins so the bowler is merely rolling a ball down an empty alley.

2.   Hiding the pins from the bowler by hanging a drape halfway down the alley to prevent feedback.

3.   Under either of the foregoing conditions, having a "supervisor" give the bowler an opinion of how well he is doing—along with some "constructive criticism."

4.   Changing the rules of the game and standards of performance without involving the bowler in the change process, or even telling him why the changes were made.

5.   Making attendance at the bowling alley mandatory under threat of penalty.

6.   Preventing social interaction among bowlers or discouraging team effort.

7.   Giving most of the credit and recognition to the supervisor for performance of the bowlers under his supervision.

8.   Mechanizing the bowling process so the bowler need merely press a button to activate the bowling ball.

9.   Keeping bowlers on the job by threat of job security or by paying them enough money to make the "time" in the bowling alley worth their while.

Bowling, under these conditions would, of course, lose it and bowlers would look for activities away from the bowling alle, the needs which were satisfied by the original bowling game.

When Work Is Fun

The characteristics of effective management systems, defined later, are examples of systems designed to satisfy the motivation and maintenance needs of people at work. These examples include the job-posting system described on pages 227 to 231, the performance review system on pages 234 to 244, the attitude survey on pages 143 to 149, work simplification on pages 130 to 138, and problem solving–goal setting on pages 138 to 143.

The problem-solving–goal-setting approach satisfies many characteristics of a helpful system in that it not only leads to job enrichment but also is, in itself, a form of job enrichment. For example, assemblers confronted with the company's problem of losing money on the production of radar units were given the opportunity to apply their talents in solving the problem. Their supervisor shared information with them regarding the duration of the contract, its dollar magnitude, delivery schedules, and the manufacturing costs stemming from overhead, materials, and labor. He asked them for their suggestions in reducing costs, particularly in regard to lowering the man-hours below the 100-hour breakeven point. After a two-hour meeting to compile, discuss, discard, and select ideas, the group set a goal of 86 hours. As shown by the chart in Figure 2-6, they surpassed their goal and achieved a 75-man-hour level. In subsequent meetings in which the group was expanded to include engineers, inspectors, and assemblers from other lines, they continued the goal-setting session until they reached a 41-hour level by year-end.

The problem-solving–goal-setting system has many of the characteristics of the natural bowling game, such as visible, challenging, and attainable goals; feedback; competition; social interaction and team involvement; and earned recognition.

In another application, when janitors and their supervisors became involved in a problem-solving–goal-setting process in an attempt to "work smarter, not harder," they first established the criteria of building maintenance and then took part in planning their own work. The results reflected in Figure 2-7 show improvements in terms of labor costs, quality of performance, and turnover. The work force was reduced from 121 to 70, the reductions being accommodated through job transfers and normal turnover. Quality of performance increased from 65 to 83 percent cleanliness level, and turnover dropped from 100 percent to 20 percent per quarter. Reduction in turnover illustrates the potential of even unprestigious work

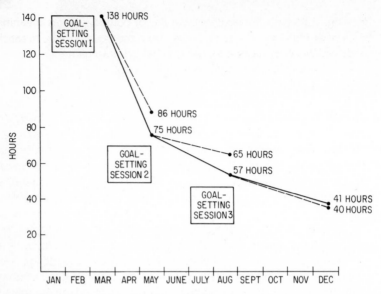

FIG. 2-6 Goal setting in radar assembly.

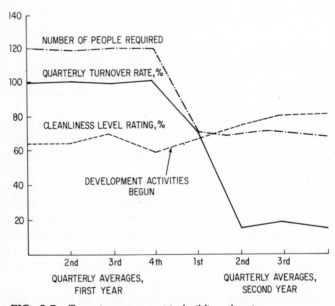

FIG. 2-7 Team improvement in building cleaning.

for developing group cohesiveness and pride through worthwhile and recognized achievements.

These examples of helpful systems, drawn from the lower level of the organization, show that processes traditionally applied at higher levels are also applicable at lower levels. Moreover, these examples of helpful systems at lower levels can serve as models for applying similar processes at upper levels.

The Design of Effective Systems[9]

A "management system" is a process of people interacting to apply resources to achieve goals. System designers tend to place major emphasis on hardware and software (technology), but system effectiveness is primarily dependent on the human factor. Computers, machines, buildings, materials, and money lie idle and lifeless in the absence of human effort; hence, all management is the management of human effort. The materiel with which people interact may be organized to facilitate their efforts and to inspire their commitment, or it may be organized in a way that impedes their efforts and evokes their opposition.

When people encounter difficulty in the pursuit of goals, there is a tendency to blame "the system." For example, problems encountered in terminating a book-club membership, in changing a mailing address, in getting a charge account error corrected, in clearing an expense account, or in getting an accounts receivable balanced are usually attributed to "the system." Physical aspects of systems are convenient scapegoats at the customer-complaint desk, and systems' administrators (users) often attribute their own limitations to the allegation that their data were "lost in the computer." Attempts to remedy a system usually lead back to the system designer.

Role of the System Designer

Systems designers often defend their design of software and use of hardware, asserting that a system failed only because people misused it. Within that point of view lies the crux of most management system problems.

The systems designer is correct in diagnosing systems failures as human failures. But he usually fails to recognize that his responsibility embraces the human factor—that the system designer's role is one of facilitating human processes, and that helpful systems function as exten-

[9]Much of this section is abstracted from documents coauthored in 1968 with Charles L. Kettler, coordinator of Texas Instruments' management systems development committee, and A. Graham Sterling, manager of control and administration in Texas Instruments' materials group.

sions of man, not man as an appendage of systems. Furthermore, the system designer often overlooks his responsibility for seeing to it that the system user is adequately trained to administer the system. Systems failures sometimes result from designer permissiveness in allowing the user to divest himself of the responsibility for helping design the system. Because of sheer job pressure, the user may welcome the staff man's takeover.

Sometimes system users try to participate in the design of their system, and the system designers may even urge them to do so. But the system user frequently encounters the same problem in talking to the system designer that the production foreman sometimes encounters in trying to talk to the personnel psychologist: In neither case is the staff man's jargon fully understood. The system user may be as confused by the designer's use of such terms as "SYSGEN," "time sharing," "syntax-directed," "bombout," and "real-time" as the foreman was by the psychologist's use of "emotional stability," "exophoria," "IQ," "manic-depressive," and "ego drive." In both cases, the staff man has failed to adapt his terminology to the boundaries of his customer's language.

A system user can no more divest himself of responsibility for system design than the foreman can delegate the handling of grievances and job instruction to the personnel department. When system designers and personnel managers permit this type of disengagement, the results almost always are ineffective systems and inept foremen.

Informal Systems

Systems may be official or unofficial, formal or informal, simple or complex, but all come into existence because of needs of individuals or groups at any level of the organization. For example, the office check pool (based on the highest poker hand to be found in paycheck serial nuimbers) is an informal and unofficial system that forms almost spontaneously, and is perpetuated by a combination of social, financial, diversion, and risk-taking needs of the members. Failing to understand the check pool as a symptom of boredom, management may attack the check pool as a violation of company rules on gambling, and may try to develop a system for stopping it. Attempts to quash the check pool may be implemented through a system of posted notices, newspaper inserts, public pronouncements, and supervisory instruction, all reinforced by specific or implicit threats of punishment. But if the need to perpetuate the check pool is strong enough, or if the joy of circumventing authority is great enough, the pool system goes underground, thereby satisfying rebellion needs provoked by management edict, and perhaps increasing the system's value in satisfying social (group cohesiveness), diversion, and risk-taking needs.

All systems are circular and give feedback to the user. Check pool members contribute their dollars and obtain feedback in terms of observed payoff to the highest "poker hand." Attempts by management to intervene merely activate a countersystem for evading detection, which gives the members additional feedback in terms of not getting caught or, if their system fails, in getting caught. Similarly, management's control system for preventing participation in the check pool gives feedback to management in terms of official reports of conformity or violation. Feedback may or may not be valid.

Formal Systems Development

Formal and complex management systems are developed and refined through a continuous circular process that may be defined in terms of seven phases. Though any phase, and particularly phase 5, may lead directly back to any preceding phase, the development of a system generally follows a circular evolutionary process, diagrammed in Figure 2-8.

Phase 1.   *Goal setting* is initiated in response to a need to create a new system or modify an old one. Goals are expressed quantitatively and qualitatively in terms of end results desired and resources available.

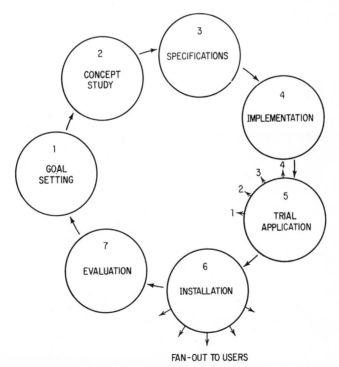

FAN-OUT TO USERS

FIG. 2-8   Seven phases of system development.

Phase 2.   The *concept study* is a systematic consideration of how to achieve the stated goals, and the long- and short-range impact of the system on the user, on other systems, or uninvolved bystanders, and on the community, in terms of social, economic, and legal considerations. The concept study ends with the selection of one of several alternative approaches for achieving the established goals.

Phase 3.   *Specifications* define the details of how the system will implement the concepts to achieve the goals. They are established in terms of costs, time limits, personnel, machines, equipment, materials, facilities, responsibility, and evaluation criteria.

Phase 4.   The system is *implemented* by committing hardware, software, manpower, services, space, and budget; by designing trial applications; and by defining error signals.

Phase 5.   *Trial applications* are made with real or simulated data in representative situations; errors are corrected; the system is refined; and management and user commitment is confirmed. Phase 5 may lead directly back to any previous phase.

Phase 6.   The system is *installed* by instructing users, transferring system management to users, informing affected publics, establishing review schedules, and monitoring initial applications. Systems with potential for broad organizational application should be "fanned out" immediately to other operations to maximize system payout.

Phase 7.   The system is *evaluated* by measuring performance against goals, impact on other systems, deviations from design, and identifying goal adjustments required.

A Specimen Management System

The job-posting system, described on pages 227 to 231, as an internal staffing system, illustrates the cyclical and evolutionary process for developing a management system.[10] Job posting existed as a simple and informal process at Texas Instruments for several years. In its earliest form it consisted of dittoed lists of job openings which rarely crossed organizational and geographical boundaries. Feedback to management through the grapevine and the annual attitude survey reflected inadequacies in the job-posting system in terms of ambiguous ground rules and arbitrary supervisory practice.

System shortcomings included allegations that favoritism was a basis for many promotions, seniority was disregarded, education was em-

---

[10]Described by Mark Shepherd, chairman of the board of Texas Instruments, in his EIA presidential address at the Industrial Relations Conference in San Diego, Calif., Apr. 22, 1969.

phasized to the exclusion of experience, qualifications for job openings were not specified, and advancement opportunities were restricted to the departments in which the opportunities occurred.

Supervisory practice complaints alleged that supervisors withheld job opportunity information, sometimes resented transfer requests, refused or delayed transfers, and too often gave priority to outside applicants.

In terms of the system development cycle illustrated in Figure 2-8, these reactions to the job-posting system represented an informal phase 7 evaluation of an ongoing system. This feedback precipitated the formation of an official task force to improve the system.

Preliminary work by the phase 1, goal-setting task force confirmed the phase 7 evaluation described above and further noted the following shortcomings in the existing system:

1. Job openings were published too infrequently.
2. Many job openings were not posted.
3. Posted openings were primarily for lower job grades.
4. Dates for posting and closing job openings were not specified.
5. Job postings were not easily accessible to all.
6. Job specifications were too sketchy.

The systematic evaluation of the existing system was a major basis for defining the goals for its improvement. However, since most of the feedback was from the employees as the primary users of the system, it was necessary to broaden the scope of the goal-setting process to include balanced consideration of the goals of the organization and the impact of job-posting on other systems. The system development task force was comprised of a heterogeneous membership of line and staff persons, chaired by a seasoned industrial relations generalist.[11] Though the permanent membership of the central task force numbered about eight persons, *ad hoc* involvement of people from all levels and major functions of the company through five satellite task forces totaled approximately 900. The involvement process employed here in many respects paralleled the group insurance task-force strategy outlined on pages 195 to 198.

The task-force strategy led routinely and naturally into the phase 2 concept study. Though it was recognized that job posting could lead to increased internal mobility, the advantages of the system appeared to outweigh its disadvantages greatly:

1. Its role in facilitating promotions, transfers, and reassignments would support the company's promotion-from-within policy, and thereby lead to

[11]A. E. Prescott, manager of internal staffing for Texas Instruments in 1967, chaired the central job-posting system task force whose achievements are outlined in this section.

better utilization of manpower and the retention of talent within the organization.

2. It would reduce the loss of people from the work force due to faulty placement or work-force reduction and, hence, would lead to increased organizational and community stability.

3. It would facilitate the placement of people returning from leave of absence, as well as the upgrading of persons who improved their qualifications through skills training and educational programs.

4. It would lower interdepartmental mobility barriers and, thus, lead to broader unification of the total work force and implementation of equal-opportunity policy.

5. It would provide information, a procedure, and an incentive for individuals to take charge of their own career development, and would correspondingly reduce their dependence on supervision.

Phase 3 specifications were established in terms of overhead, hardware, software, and manpower costs. Evaluation criteria were established to include employee (user) reaction as measured through attitude surveys, frequency of usage, and grapevine testimonials; and impact on the organization in terms of reduced turnover and staffing costs, disruption of work standards and schedules, and general acceptance by supervision.

Phases 4 and 5 of the system were implemented through the joint efforts of a skeletal staff of corporate and division personnel applying the system in Texas operations. Space, personnel, and budget had been allocated by Corporate Personnel, with concomitant pledges of support from the divisions. Immediate and favorable reaction to initial applications resulted in early commitment of support from top management to expand the program to all domestic operations and appropriate opportunities in international operations that might be staffed from domestic operations. Much of phase 5 had been accomplished earlier through the application of the informal and local job-posting systems that had preceded the development of the more formalized and comprehensive system. To the users, the most apparent changes were the more comprehensive coverage of the job opportunity bulletin, illustrated in Figure 7-6, and a simple procedure for actuating the system.

Phase 6 was formally and officially completed when capital, overhead, and expense budgets were approved, administrative staff and support personnel were selected and trained, and the system was described in the company newspaper. Approximately 10 percent of the domestic work force utilized the system for promotion and transfers during the first year. More than 20 percent of the positions filled were for salaried-exempt classifications. Administration of the program followed the procedure illustrated in Figure 7-7.

General reaction to the system, particularly from the users' viewpoint, was favorable. However, a gradual groundswell of dissatisfaction, largely from operating managers, brought phases 7 and 1 into formal and rigorous application. The central task force was reactivated with nineteen members to determine whether or not to continue the system and, if it was to be continued, to identify and correct problems leading to dissatisfaction with the system. Nine geographically deployed division task forces, involving 125 system users from all levels and functions, compiled a list of problems and possible solutions, and forwarded them to the central task force. The central task force consolidated the division recommendations and returned them to the divisions for review, revision, and ratification. Finally, the central task force consolidated the division revisions for corporate review.

The company president and operating vice-presidents held a day-long meeting to review the system with its problems and possible solutions, and to decide whether or not to continue it. The review, aided by testimonials from line and staff managers, revealed the following problems associated with the job opportunity system and allowed planning of the modifications listed below.

Problems identified by the phase 7 analysis:

1.   Large numbers of bids by a few individuals delayed the candidate evaluation process and feedback to bidders.

2.   Bids were submitted on jobs in the outdated monthly bulletins by persons who were not aware of updated interim weekly bulletins posted on bulletin boards.

3.   Lateral transfers filled many positions representing promotional opportunities from lower job grades.

4.   Profitability of some operating departments was reduced by work interruptions caused by frequent transfers.

5.   People were transferring before achieving their competence levels, depriving managers of a fair return on training or security clearance investments.

6.   Some supervisors were engaging in "gamesmanship" by delaying transfers or negotiating under-the-table transfers under the pretense of following official job-posting procedures.

Dissatisfactions arising from the job opportunity system illustrate a common phenomenon; namely, a system for removing dissatisfactions has the potential itself for being the focus of new or even worse dissatisfactions than the ones it was intended to remove. This principle is also illustrated in connection with the discussion of paid suggestions systems on pages 184 to 185.

Modifications incorporated into the system by the new phase 1 activity:

1.   Limit concurrent job bids per person to two, except for individuals made available for reassignment.

2.   Simplify coding of new job postings.

3.   Permit lateral transfers only when
  • progression on the present job is blocked
  • the job family or salary schedule is being changed
  • the change is part of a planned career development program
  • the change is necessary to assign displaced personnel.

4.   Effect a temporary "transfer-out moratorium" if necessary, to protect vital understaffed work groups.

5.   Require 6 months on the job for nonexempt personnel and 12 months for exempt, before bidding on new job.

6.   Provide continuing education and information to users regarding the system and its revisions.

These changes were communicated back to the work force via informal one-to-one and group discussions, the employee newspaper, and revisions of procedure handbooks. In the decade following the phase 7 evaluation described above, three similar evaluations were made, with necessary adjustments introduced into the system.

Characteristics of Effective and Ineffective Systems

This evolutionary process, perpetuated by feedback from the users, represents an ideal model of an effective self-correcting management system. Tracing the evolution of the job-posting system through its seven developmental phases reveals characteristics common to most effective systems. Because of their involvement in the evolutionary process, users understand and agree with its purpose. It is a system *they* can actuate simply by submitting a completed job bid to their personnel department, without fear of supervisory reprisal. Actually, many people actuate the system with one or more covert inquiries. It is primarily their initiative that enables them to discover opportunities; and because the system minimizes dependency on, or unwanted intervention by, supervision, the user is in control all the way. Finally, the system gives the user direct feedback in terms of a disqualification or acceptance notification. In summary, a management system is considered effective when the people whose job performance is influenced by the system:

1. Understand its purpose
2. Agree with its purpose
3. Know how to use it
4. Are in control of it
5. Can influence its revision
6. Receive timely feedback from it

Stated negatively, as a basis for understanding system failure, it may be generalized that a management system is not effective when the people whose job performance is influenced by the system:

1. Do not understand its purpose
2. Disagree with its purpose
3. Do not know how to use it
4. Feel they are unnecessarily restricted by it
5. Feel it is hopeless to try to change it
6. Receive inadequate feedback from it

The Key Role of the User

It is noteworthy that the conditions for effective and ineffective systems noted above are almost exclusively functions of systems users' attitudes and perceptions. When people feel they belong to an organization, they tend to support its systems. This feeling of belonging in turn is fostered by the opportunity to participate in the development of systems. This observation is illustrated by comparing the behavior of two groups of machine operators toward their respective assembly lines.

One group, in a paper carton factory, was idled for a few hours (with pay) while industrial engineers introduced improvements into their line. The operators clustered near the coke machine, laughing, drinking cokes, and smoking. When the engineers completed the installation, they briefed the operators on the changes, and asked for questions. Receiving no questions, they assumed the installation would be an improvement. but the system actually reduced the line yield, and hence, the line was less effective than before. The engineered changes had altered role relationships on the line, and even before giving it a fair trial, the operators had conspired, perhaps unconsciously, to make the system fail.

In contrast, a superintendent and a foreman in an electronics assembly department involved the operators in planning and balancing their own assembly line and setting their first week's production goals. They achieved their Friday evening goal on Wednesday and went on almost to double their first week's goal. From an engineering point of view, the electronic assembly line was not as well designed as the paper carton line, but it worked because the operators made it work.

In general, it may be said that people's attitudes and perceptions are the primary causes of all systems successes and failures,

- Enabling poorly designed systems to succeed
- Causing well-designed systems to fail

Qualifications of Systems Designers

It was noted earlier that system designers, recognizing the importance of the users' attitudes to the system's success, have taken the initiative in familiarizing themselves with their users' operations, or have attempted to involve users in the development of their systems. It was also noted that these cooperative efforts were often discouraged by the job demands of the user or the system designer's jargon. Moreover, it was illustrated in the job-posting system that sensitivity to the human factor—the causes of commitment and alienation—is an essential ingredient for developing and managing effective systems. Thus it is apparent that system designers must apply three types of competence in developing workable systems:

1.   Knowledge of data-processing technology

2.   Knowledge of the functions or operations to be served by the system, and the proposed system's relation to, and potential impact on, other systems

3.   Sensitivity to the factors evoking human commitment and alienation in the development and application of management systems

Management's Role

The hardware and software available for facilitating modern management systems have almost unlimited potential, to be exploited or limited by the people who interact with them. People who man the work force also have untapped potential, to be utilized or limited by the systems they interact with. If the synergistic relationships are to exist between people and their systems, human development and system development must be guided by persons who understand both people and systems.

Thus, formalized and effective management systems cannot be established as the warp and the woof of the organization if system development is relegated to staff functions. Many organizations try it, just as they try to delegate the planning function to staff personnel. Neither will succeed, of course, as planning and control functions are mainstream processes which must be managed by the persons who are to implement them.

Simply stated, a manager is responsible for managing materiel, manpower, and technology to achieve organizational goals. The manager's responsibility in managing management systems is to see to it that system development is not an isolated, uncoordinated, or unilateral process but, rather, a joint or task force effort, appropriately balanced with systems technology, mainstream user participation, and human effectiveness expertise.

3

Quality of Work Life

During the 1960s, personnel journals and textbooks reflected much emphasis on the concept of job enrichment or job enlargement.[1] This interest extended into the 1970s, but was gradually supplanted by a broader concept of "life enrichment" or "quality of working life."[2] This broadened emphasis was born of the realization that work itself, important as it is, is not the only medium through which meaning is given to life in the work place. In fact, several organizations, most notably the Eaton Corporation cited on page 115, were effecting improved industrial relations and productivity by modifying systems peripheral to the work itself.

However, proponents of strategies for motivating employees through improved peripheral systems or organizational climate factors soon realized that they did not have the exclusive antidote for employee alienation—that both work itself and peripheral systems are influential in shaping attitudes and improving job performance.

Moreover, it became increasingly apparent to practitioners that life-enrichment efforts would gain little momentum if viewed by their intended beneficiaries as a paternalistic or manipulative ploy to take advantage of them. Traditional union leaders tended to view job-enrichment programs as veiled attempts to thwart union organizers or to effect speedups and reduce work forces. Management-directed strategies to create conditions for motivation seemed oblivious to Allan Mogensen's principle (see pages 130 to 138) that people are more likely to accept change when they can

[1]For example, Frederick Herzberg, *The Motivation to Work*, John Wiley, New York, 1959; "One More Time: How Do You Motivate Employees?" *Harvard Business Review*, Jan.–Feb. 1968; Robert N. Ford, "Job Enrichment Lessons from AT&T," *Harvard Business Review*, Jan.–Feb. 1973; *Motivation through the Work Itself*, American Management Association, New York, 1969; M. Scott Myers, "Every Employee a Manager," *California Management Review*, Spring 1968; John R. Maher, *New Perspective in Job Enrichment*, Van Nostrand Reinhold, New York, 1971.

[2]This broader view is reflected in *Quality of Working Life: The Canadian Scene*, a quarterly report initiated in 1979 by the Government of Canada through its Department of Labor in Ottawa. Also see publications cited later in this chapter by Work in America Institute and the National Center for Productivity and Quality of Working Life.

influence the change process. This principle is also illustrated on pages 143 to 149 in connection with the administration of attitude surveys. The job incumbent's role in developing a system may evoke more enthusiasm and commitment than the application of the system itself. This principle supports the conclusion that any effort to bring about change in the work place is more likely to succeed if it is planned and implemented by the people who are to be influenced by it.

Job-enrichment efforts directed to the hourly paid workers were not always supported by supervisors, particularly when they were bypassed in the planning process. Some supervisors felt that the new participative approach would further erode their already diminished and ambiguous responsibilities. Certainly the autocratic supervisor who called all the shots and ran a tight ship felt threatened by an edict which required him to be "soft" with employees. It was particularly frustrating to receive edicts from managers who did not practice what they preached. Union shop stewards also felt threatened if required to implement a program ratified by higher-level union officials. Employees, in turn, who sensed foot-dragging on the part of their union leaders and supervisors could not be expected to support such an effort without feeling uncooperative or insubordinate.

A program pitfall is the failure to recognize the dual purpose of the quality-of-work-life effort. Improving the quality of workers' lives at the expense of the organization would not of course receive sustained support from executives who are measured in terms of financial criteria of organizational success. Conversely, if quality-of-work-life efforts are undertaken to improve productivity to the detriment of employee attitudes, even though pay and job security are enhanced, the program is doomed to failure. In short, the long-term success of an organization is born of a pursuit of organizational goals that are synergistically related to the needs of its members. This synergy is illustrated in the quality-of-work-life efforts implemented in the General Motors auto assembly plant in Tarrytown, New York.[3] In such an organization, people achieve their personal goals through the attainment of organizational goals. Thus, quality of working life as described herein presumes a balanced concern for organizational and individual goals.

The quality of work life in an organization is a function of the conditions described in Chapter 2 and portrayed in Figure 2-1. These three basic ingredients, interpersonal competence, meaningful goals, and helpful systems, are not independent variables, of course, as each influences the other two.

The systems of an organization are the vehicles through which em-

[3]Robert H. Guest, "Quality of Work Life—Learning from Tarrytown," *Harvard Business Review*, July–Aug. 1979.

ployee needs are satisfied or thwarted. In this chapter, quality of work life will be discussed within the framework of two kinds of systems: those related directly to work itself and those peripheral to the job or occupation the job incumbent was hired to perform. Work systems embrace the classical concepts of job enrichment or job enlargement, while peripheral systems include nonjob factors such as landscaping, eating arrangements, parking facilities, and dress code.

WORK SYSTEMS—HISTORICAL PERSPECTIVE[4]

Originally performed only as a means to survival, work has undergone several significant changes in history. According to Maslow's "hierarchy of needs" concept, when living is precarious, man devotes most of his attention to survival. Such was the case, of course, with the caveman, who was forced to devote most of his time to seeking food and shelter. For the caveman, work and living were one and the same, and work was indeed meaningful as it was essential to survival. His inability to predict or control his environment required him to react instead of to think. Hence, efforts to control or cope with his environment through the use of crude weapons and fire resulted more from serendipity than from knowledge and logic. The continued and refined usage of happenstance discoveries rewarded the more innovative individuals with survival. The banding together for protection resulted in the development of social and status relationships.

Gradually moving up his need hierarchy, man in the medieval period found himself more formally concerned with social and status matters. However, tradition and environment had by then chained him to the economic role and the social order to which he was born. Limited by inherited role and social position, men born to families of artisans became artisans, and men born to royal families became kings, with virtually no mobility in between. But within the limits of his inherited sphere, the individual had freedom to express himself in his work and social life. In this respect, man in the medieval years was able to create, make, and market his own products, as long as he stayed within a particular product line and marketplace. At the same time, he enjoyed a certain amount of security and cohesiveness as a result of his membership in a particular guild, the church, and a circumscribed social order. Within his own sphere of influence, then, and in spite of being a captive in the feudal system, man was free to set his own standards and goals and to experience the rewards of achievement.

[4]Adapted from an unpublished paper by Susan S. Myers, Southern Methodist University, Dallas, Tex., July, 1969.

Emerging Capitalism

Events during the Middle Ages charted another course for man on which he could, for the first time in history, alter his own destiny. Skilled and motivated artisans reaped the benefits of quality workmanship, and competition developed between them and between other small businessmen, providing an example of social Darwinism or the concept of survival of the fittest. More successful artisans were able to hire less successful artisans to work for them, thus elevating their own social positions as a result of their increased wealth and status. Concomitant with the possibility of social mobility was the opportunity for geographical mobility and the opening of trade routes within and between Europe and the Orient. The horizons of the *nouveau riche* of the Renaissance were bright, but the future of the exploited working masses was grim. As they lost their ability to maintain their traditional memberships and relationships in guilds, they lost proprietary interest in their work, and their social, economic, and political status deteriorated.

The combination of competition, capital, and economic opportunity enabled the "fittest" of the artisans to survive and prosper, but at the expense of the weaker ones. The fittest became masters with entrepreneurial freedom and power to act and realize their personal ambitions. Members of the working class, on the other hand, enjoyed only enough freedom to choose to become silversmiths, cobblers, or blacksmiths; after that, their futures were largely determined for them by their employers. Work was then, as it is now, meaningful for members of "management," who could shape their jobs as they pleased, but for the workers, work was performed as directed. The situation was summarized by Erich Fromm, who states, ". . . as the number of journeymen under one master increased, the more capital was needed to become a master and the more guilds assumed a monopolistic and exclusive character, the less were the opportunities of journeymen. The deterioration of their economic and social position was shown by their growing dissatisfaction, the formation of organizations of their own, by strikes and even violent insurrections."[5]

Although dissatisfied workers discovered their strength in numbers, it was not enough influence to stem the inexorable development of the labor-management dichotomy in the late fifteenth century. Social and economic injustices of the times gradually brought the uniform theology of the period into question. The church member was taught that he had equal status with his fellow man in the eyes and love of God and that, though he shared original sin with all, if he worked diligently to atone for his sins, he could be assured by his church of a place in heaven. The fact that the capitalists were reaping rewards at the expense of the working class sug-

[5]Erich Fromm, *Escape from Freedom*, Holt, Rinehart and Winston, New York, 1941, pp. 73–74.

gested that the church represented the rich man's religion, and the working man began developing an awareness of his own insignificance and powerlessness before the "official" church and the capitalists.

Birth of the Horatio Alger Philosophy

Thus the time was ripe for the Protestant theologies of Luther and Calvin. Both the working class and the middle class were ready to attack the authority and power of the wealthy and their church. Many of Luther's followers believed that the way to heaven was through good work and success on earth. Calvin taught that destiny for heaven or hell was predetermined but that success in life through moral and effortful living indicated predestined salvation. Luther and Calvin both emphasized the powerlessness and baseness of man and the need for faith in the submission to God. The theology of both resulted in stronger self-reliance and responsibility for salvation. Thus, both doctrines succeeded in placing the burden of salvation on the individual. Man became responsible for his own fate; no longer could the church lift the burden from his shoulders. Hence, the overdeveloped conscience and the latter-day Horatio Alger "rags to riches" theme were born. According to Fromm[6]:

> This new attitude towards effort and work as an aim in itself may be assumed to be the most important psychological change which has happened to man since the end of the Middle Ages. . . . What was new in modern society was that men came to be driven to work not so much by external pressure, but by an internal compulsion which made them work as only a very strict master could have made people do in other societies. The inner compulsion was more effective in harnessing all energies to work than any outer compulsion can ever be. Against external compulsion there is always a certain amount of rebelliousness which hampers the effectiveness of work or makes people unfit for any differentiated task requiring intelligence, initiative and responsibility. The compulsion to work by which man was turned into his own slave driver did not hamper these qualities. Undoubtedly, capitalism could not have been developed had not the greatest part of man's energy been channeled in the direction of work. There is no other period in history in which free men have given their energy so completely for the one purpose: work.

The Industrial Revolution

As a result of religious and political oppression in western Europe, the industrious rebels of the Reformation transferred their efforts to improve

[6]Ibid.

their lot to America. Firmly believing that God helps those who help themselves, members of the Protestant faith became associated with the rising commercial class. In a remarkably short time, they and their descendants had brought about the Industrial Revolution. Because of its impact on the economy and the people, perhaps the most far-reaching effect of the Industrial Revolution was the development of large industrial organizations.

Stimulated initially by the iron and steel mills, and nurtured by the railroads and entrepreneurs, big business was built across the country. Accompanying big business was the development of mass markets and mass-production techniques, including standardization of parts and processes, division of labor, and repetitive production of standard items, manufacture of interchangeable parts, and assembly of parts into finished products. And while big businesses mushroomed, many small businesses disappeared, their owner-managers being forced to sell their labor for nothing more than wages. Caught in a trap of specialization, division of labor, wage systems, and pyramidal authoritarian organizations, dissatisfied workers in the 1860s formally joined forces in the National Labor Union and Knights of Labor in an unsuccessful attempt to regain some of their former status as owners of enterprise. The wage system became permanent, however, in spite of their efforts to destroy it. Accepting this fact, then, a new labor organization, the American Federation of Labor (AFL) was formed in 1886 to help workers improve their position within the system. Organized on the basis of trades and inspired by Samuel Gompers, the AFL differed from previous unions in that it *rested upon the assumption of an inherent conflict of interest between labor and management and the permanent ban of most employees from the ranks of management.*

Early Attempts at Scientific Management

Threatened by the aggressive role of labor and the continuing need for new responses to industrialism, managers of business and industrial organizations sought better management techniques—not for altruistic reasons, but for increased efficiency and productivity. They were influenced first by Max Weber's concept of bureaucracy, introduced in 1900. Opposed to loosely structured organizations run by whim, Weber proposed highly structured organizations run by rules. Although bureaucracy was understandable as a reaction to arbitrariness, it proved to be inefficent and cumbersome in an environment of rapidly changing technologies.

More attractive to management at that time was Frederick W. Taylor's concept of scientific management, which placed more emphasis on efficiency and productivity. Believing that the nature of work had gradually evolved from an art to a science, Taylor recommended that each job should be fractionated, analyzed for efficiency techniques, and given to the highest-aptitude employees trained for one specific task. To maximize efficiency, Taylor further recommended that employees be motivated through piecework incentive systems of pay, by which the most productive would earn the highest wages. Taylor's research, coupled with that of his successor, Frank B. Gilbreth, is now often known as time and motion study.

Taylorism and expressions of its philosophy linger on in many of today's organizations in the forms of engineered labor standards, time and motion study, piecework incentive, paid suggestion plans, and a myriad of manipulative programs for "communication," "zero defects," "attitude measurement," "merit rating," "motivation," "recognition," and "morale." Though these programs may yield sporadic short-term gains, their ultimate impact, because of the way they are administered, is usually alienation and net loss.

The discovery that incentives other than wages, hours, and working conditions motivated employees came as a surprise to many managers when Elton Mayo uncovered the importance of the attitude of the worker toward his job at Western Electric's Hawthorne Plant in 1927. Moreover, he called attention to the effects of groups on productivity, noting that cohesive groups had the power to raise or lower production according to their attitudes toward their jobs and the company.

The shift in emphasis away from improving individual efficiency to human relations and improved group processes was a natural consequence of trends toward mass production and automation. While machines and processes have been made increasingly complex, the workers who monitor the machines are experiencing diminishing demands on their intellect, initiative, and creativity. Recognizing that automation is making man an appendage of machines, Charles Walker[7] calls attention to the need to return the machine to its proper role as an appendage of man. Attempts to remedy the stultifying relationship between man and machines initiated the concepts of human engineering and job enrichment, whereby machines are designed to meet the abilities and limitations of man, and humans are taught to amplify the efficiency of machines.

Emergence of Formalized Job Enrichment

Realizing that the dimensions of a job exceed the conventional formula of wages, hours, and working conditions, Walker cites several other work

---

[7]Charles R. Walker (former director, Yale Technology Project), "Changing Character of Human Work under the Impact of Technological Change" (multilith), Wellfleet, Mass., 1965.

dimensions useful as analytic tools in determining both productivity and satisfaction on the job:

1. Knowledge and skill requirement
2. Pacing or rate of performance
3. Degree of repetitiveness or variety
4. Relation to the total product or process
5. Relationships with people as individuals or as groups
6. Style of supervision and of managerial controls
7. Degree of worker's autonomy in determining work methods
8. Relation of work to personal development

To the extent that these dimensions are known about a job, and improved in accordance with technological and psychological changes, there is potential for putting meaning back into work. As employers recognize the need to design machines to fit man, they also see the importance of designing jobs to meet man's needs. In answer to the question of how the design of a job affects the meaningfulness of a job, Peter Vaill[8] concluded, on the basis of research on the working lives of factory workers, that jobs are more meaningful when (1) they offer the worker continuous opportunity to learn on his job, (2) they encourage quality workmanship, (3) they allow the worker to set his own standards and goals, (4) they are experienced by the worker as psychologically whole, and (5) they show the relationship between the goals of a particular jobholder and company goals.

Regarding the relationship between the design of a job and the working environment, Vaill concluded that there is an inverse relationship between the degree of concern with wages, hours, and working conditions and job challenge and complexity. Vaill found the effect of improved job design resulted in greater willingness on the part of the workers to take an active, rather than a passive, role in the organization, thus leading to their increased commitment and self-confidence.

The evolutionary process of the nature of work and the worker, from the days of the caveman and the stone ax to the days of technicians and the computer, has offered man the opportunity to move upward through his hierarchy of need satisfactions. However, he is stopped short of self-actualization by a factor that has remained curiously constant throughout the ages: his dependency on powers beyond his influence. Mason Haire[9]

[8]Peter B. Vaill, "Industrial Engineering and Socio-Technical Systems," Paper presented before the AIIE, San Francisco, Calif., May 26, 1966, pp. 13–15.

[9]Lecture by Mason Haire to Fellows of Salzburg Seminar in American Management Dynamics, Salzburg, Austria, Mar. 21, 1969.

traces the source of power through several stages. Primeval man, of course, lived in a bewildering and overwhelming world in which his survival depended on his wariness in reacting to unpredictable and sometimes uninterpretable threats. *Fear of the unknown* was the major source of power to the caveman. In medieval times the *state,* often identical with the official religious organization, was the source of power. Conformity and servility were keys to acceptance. The late Middle Ages ushered in entrepreneur activity, with *ownership* or equity as the source of power. Loyalty and industriousness were keys to success. The Industrial Revolution placed a premium on production, and *production technology,* coupled with the Protestant's attitude toward industriousness, was the source of power. Midcentury emphasis on professional management and staff expertise has made the *professional manager and his systems* a velvet-gloved source of power. Success is usually measured in terms of professional competence and advancement in the organization. However, there is not room for all to succeed in these terms, and large numbers at the lower levels resort to emotional disengagement, if only to maintain their sanity. Tomorrow's manager will shun the use of authority and will organize physical resources and manpower to enable human talent at all levels to find expression in solving problems and achieving goals. The source of power, then, will be *human competence,* applied toward the synergistic achievement of the goals of the organization and its members. Only under conditions of responsible self-direction and self-control can self-actualization be realized.

STAGES OF LABOR RELATIONS[10]

Capitalism, as it is known in America, began in the Middle Ages, flourished during the Industrial Revolution, and hit a peak in the twentieth century. Late in the nineteenth century when Samuel Gompers, William Haywood, and other union leaders sought to defend workers against exploitive entrepreneurs, they made explicit an adversary relationship that had been implicitly evolving since the Middle Ages. Viewed in historical perspective since the days of Samuel Gompers, three stages or models of labor relations may be defined: stage 1, win-lose adversary; stage 2, collaborative adversary; and stage 3, organizational democracy. These three stages are portrayed on a continuum in Figure 3-1.

Stage 1:   Win-Lose Adversary

Win-lose adversary relationships characterize a majority of unionized organizations but are also found in some nonunion situations. Unionism was

[10]Excerpted from M. Scott Myers, *Managing with Unions,* Addison-Wesley Publishing, Reading, Mass., 1978, pp. 119–124.

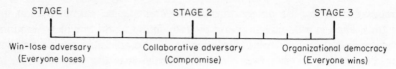

FIG. 3-1   Three stages of labor relations.

born under this model by leaders who articulated the cleavage between management and labor rather explicitly. Samuel Gompers, who founded the AFL union, wrote, "We recognize the solidarity of the whole working class to work harmoniously against their common enemy—the capitalists. . . . United we are a power to be respected; divided we are the slaves of capitalists."[11] William Haywood wrote "The working class and the employing class have nothing in common. . . . Between these two classes a struggle must go on until the workers of the world organize as a class, take possession of the earth and the machinery of production, and abolish the wage system. . . . It is the historic mission of the working class to do away with capitalism."[12]

Early union leaders encountered bitter opposition to the union movement from employers, government officials, and other conservative defenders of the free-enterprise system. Early unions were attacked as socialistic and anti-American by ruthless capitalists who used the power of laws, economics, politics, and violence to crush the unions. Unions countered, of course, with similar tactics; and with the help of counterbalancing legislation, after a bitter struggle spanning several decades, unions established a power base for perpetuating a hostile adversary relationship in circumstances which in many cases no longer justify them. Union leaders under this model feel compelled from time to time to foment a crisis or issue which enables them to exercise their clout and thereby demonstrate their value to their constituency.

The strike by the UAW of General Motors in 1970 was not wanted by most of the 180,000 strikers from the ninety-six plants affected, nor could many of them explain the reasons for it. However, the international union leadership appeared to have a need to demonstrate that it had the power to bring the company to its knees. Actually, the whole demonstration was a wasteful sham in which the company ultimately collaborated by lending money to the union to help tide the workers over their period of unemployment. The total episode was a vivid illustration of the extent to which

[11]From Samuel Gompers, *Seventy Years of Life and Labor: An Autobiography*, copyright 1925 by E. P. Dutton & Co.; renewal, 1953, by Gertrude Gleaves Gompers. Reprinted by permission of the publishers, E. P. Dutton & Co., Inc.

[12]Statements from the constitution of the Industrial Workers of the World (IWW), founded in 1905 by William Haywood to unionize the vast majority of workers not eligible for membership in Gompers' trade unions.

top executives in the company and union shamelessly acquiesced to the tradition of win-lose gamesmanship, at the expense of the workers and the total society. The consequences of the 1970 strike were assessed tangibly by William Serrin[13] in terms of a variety of far-reaching impacts. General Motors lost more than $1 billion in profits and the production of 1.5 million cars and trucks. Dividends dropped from the usual $5.00 to $2.09 per share—a gap of $600 million. The union paid out $160 million in strike benefits, had to mortgage its Black Lake recreation and education center, and paid $2.5 million in interest on loans. More than 300,000 people, in addition to strikers and layoffs, were on reduced hours. The government lost $1 billion in taxes, the nation lost hundreds of millions of dollars in retail sales, and taxpayers paid $30 million in welfare payments.

Most courses in collective bargaining for company and union alike are based on the stage 1 win-lose adversary relationships. Bargainers are taught the fine points and loopholes of the law, briefed on trends and precedents established in other bargaining situations, refreshed on the motivation principles underlying their adversary's strategies, updated on the company's financial status and the results of compensation surveys, and encouraged to share and exchange their strategies for winning.

Under the philosophy engendered by stage 1, people who otherwise would harbor no malice toward one another are pressured by tradition to become identified as either management or labor, and are often required by the adversary system to role-play hostility or mistrust in their company-union relationships. Moreover, affiliational identity usually takes precedence over ethics when the two are in conflict.

Stage 2: Collaborative Adversary

Collaborative adversary relationships are typified by the case studies of company-union relationships completed in 1953 under the auspices of the National Planning Association.[14] This project focused on twelve major companies chosen because of their peaceful company-union relationships. Though collaborative relationships was the primary criterion for being selected for the study, in most cases the two parties operated from separate and admittedly conflicting charters: "The employer represents, and is concerned primarily with, a property interest which, in turn, is directly related to the financial interests of a limited number of stockholders or owners. The interest of the employees' organization or union is primarily that of people—a greater number in most cases—and is concerned with their material, as well as their spiritual and psychological, interest and

---

[13]William Serrin, *The Company and the Union*, Knopf, New York, 1973.

[14]Clinton S. Golden and Virginia D. Parker, *Causes of Industrial Peace under Collective Bargaining*, Harper, New York, 1955.

needs. . . . The two parties coexist, with each retaining its institutional sovereignty, working together in reasonable harmony in a climate of mutual respect and confidence."[15]

Though the companies and unions described in these case studies operated from different charters, their compatibility in sustaining industrial peace stemmed largely from their attitudes toward each other. Management accepted the collective-bargaining process, unionism as an institution, and considered a strong, democratic, and responsible union as an asset to the company. At the same time, the union respected the private ownership of industry and recognized the dependence of its members on the successful operation of business. These attitudes were conducive to prompt, mutually trustful conflict resolutions and widespread informal information sharing.

Two recent publications have provided new examples of union-company collaboration.[16] In most respects the cases described in these two booklets are contemporary examples of stage 2 collaborative adversary relationships. Most collaborative efforts between company and union represent a condition of détente, based on a compartmentalization of media into two categories—those which are "safe" for collaborative effort and those reserved for adversary collective bargaining. Irving Bluestone, vice president of the United Auto Workers, lists a number of topics for joint company-union effort, including alcoholism, drug addiction, emotional problems, preretirement programs, disciplinary counseling, health and safety programs, movement of work and workers, subcontracting of work, production scheduling, introduction of technological innovations, assignment of overtime, job design, and the decision-making process. However, he points out that while this collaboration is going on, "the parties remain adversaries with regard to subjects which lend themselves more naturally to the hard business of confrontation collective bargaining," such as "wages, fringe benefits, and job security."[17]

In no case are all issues of mutual concern to company and union open to democratic codetermination. Though the list of topics for collaborative effort has grown progressively, the union has clung tenaciously to wages, benefits, and job security to be negotiated through the traditional adversary process. This persevering concern for excluding a few issues

[15]Ibid., pp. 7, 8.

[16]*Recent Initiatives in Labor-Management Cooperation*, National Center for Productivity and Quality of Working Life, Washington, D.C., 1976; Joseph A. Loftus and Beatrice Walfish, *Breakthroughs in Union-Management Cooperation*, Work in America Institute, Scarsdale, N.Y., 1977.

[17]Irving Bluestone, "A Changing View of the Union-Management Relationship," *Breakthroughs in Union-Management Cooperation*, Work in America Institute, Scarsdale, N.Y., 1977, pp. 7–12.

from democratic resolution and administration suggests that not many union officials have become comfortable in a role of democratic facilitator. Some of them look on collaborative activities as a transitory fad and still regard the diminishing realm of confrontation as their real reason and means for being. When quality of working life becomes intermingled with bread-and-butter issues, as it did with the introduction of Scanlon plans in the Dana Corporation,[18] the internal union's initial assessment of the program was less than enthusiastic. Though the union's local constituency reacted positively to the opportunity to participate in improving productivity and the quality of work life, the international union's ostensible protest stemmed from the program's alleged excessive emphasis on productivity and plant performance. However, the workers themselves have not protested against this emphasis.

George Kuper, as executive director of the National Center for Production and Quality of Working Life, summarized four conditions necessary for workable company-union cooperation:

1. The opportunity must be present for participants to address both economic and noneconomic issues in the work place.

2. The people addressing these issues must be those who are directly affected by them. Labor-management committees, for instance, permit rank-and-file workers, participating on an equal basis with management, to become involved.

3. No matter what problem is under discussion, labor and management should perceive that they both stand to gain from its solution.

4. Last, and perhaps most important, control of the program must be jointly exercised rather than kept in the hands of either labor or management alone.[19]

James Scearce, former director of the Federal Mediation and Conciliation Service, summarizes the conditions for effective Stage 2 collaborative adversary relationships:

> Cooperation cannot be seen as a threat to the collective bargaining mechanism. It means working through the collective bargaining mechanism and within the union structure. If cooperative efforts are perceived as a threat to undermine the union's structure, or if they become a political threat to the established leadership, they won't get off the ground. Quite simply, you have to understand the real world of executive

[18]"The Scanlon Plan at the Dana Corporation," *Breakthroughs in Union-Management Cooperation*, Work in America Institute, Scarsdale, N.Y., 1977, pp. 17–29.

[19]George H. Kuper, "New Insights in Labor-Management Cooperation," *Breakthroughs in Union-Management Cooperation*, Work in America Institute, Scarsdale, N.Y., 1977, p. 6.

bargaining before you try to shape the ideal work place the way you think it should be.[20]

However, Scearce goes on to hint of the possibility of stage 3 industrial democracy evolving from patient acceptance of tradition as a non-threatening transitional process toward new patterns of management: "American industrial society has its own values and traditions. If we operate through existing institutions, however, with patience and solid programs, people will begin to open their minds to new approaches."[21] As these stage 2 relationships establish new norms and gradually alter the perceptions and values of the participants, potential is created for evolution toward stage 3 organizational democracy.

Stage 3:   Organizational Democracy

Organizational democracy is an ideal which, to many now embroiled in win-lose adversary relationships, would seem pure fantasy and completely contrary to what they believe they know about human nature. Organizational democracy is not based on the perpetuation of a two-class system, but rather on an organizational model not unlike the free society which exists outside the factory gates. Stage 3 is not a condition of détente with friendly and cooperative adversaries, but rather a matrix of conditions in the work place in which all members of the work force have an opportunity to participate in democratic processes for the purpose of creating wealth, establishing systems for equitable sharing, changing the climate of the organization, and enabling them to take charge of their own careers.

Nor is industrial democracy a form of socialism or communism; rather, it is a set of conditions inspiring expression of the entrepreneur spirit in which responsible, creative, and productive individuals and groups reap higher rewards than the less effective members of the organization. Moreover, these conditions result in competitive advantage in the business sector and cost effectiveness in the public sector.

The culture of a work place is strongly influenced by the interpersonal relationships within the organization, as discussed in Chapter 2. However, when people change their behavior from one style of leadership to another, the organization usually retains much of its previous flavor as a result of the inertia created by the systems installed under the preceding regime. Even when the systems are changed, changes in people's attitudes and perceptions take place slowly, as noted on pages 7 and 8.

In Figure 5-1, a variety of major and minor systems which affect the climate of an organization are presented. Each of these systems carries with

---

[20]James Scearce, "Labor-Management Cooperation: Myth or Reality?" *Breakthroughs in Union-Management Cooperation*, Work in America Institute, Scarsdale, N.Y., 1977, p. 47.
    [21]Ibid.

it a positive or negative valence. Few of these systems, functioning alone, would have a major impact on employee attitudes. However, if most of these subsystems each carry a small positive valence, the net impact in terms of employee attitudes is positive. But if most of these systems carry a small negative valence, the net effect is negative. Moreover, the interactive impact of these predominantly positive or predominantly negative factors tends to amplify their impact. A person seeking a single major cause of sour attitudes will invariably be thwarted. If the seemingly causal factor is isolated, attempts to introduce gimmicks to neutralize or reverse its negative valence are usually futile. For instance, job enrichment, when introduced by itself as a strategy for improving job attitudes, often fails because it represents only one of a vast collage of systems in the organization. Thus, attempts to restructure jobs to make every employee a manager will not be well received by hourly employees as long as they continue to be set apart from the management class by the color of hard hats, the use of time clocks, discriminatory parking privileges, signal bells, paycheck distribution schedules, and a myriad of other subtle symbols of the two-class system.

Sometimes a system is damaging to all members of the organization because of its intrinsic reductive design. This is true, for example, of the traditional authority-oriented performance-review system which causes a supervisor to talk down to his subordinates. However, the system may be redesigned to a goal-setting developmental process, but may still be damaging if it is not available to all members of the organization. Applying the goal-oriented performance review system only to supervisory personnel and excluding workers could accentuate the cleavage between management and labor to an even greater extent than applying the authority-oriented system uniformly to people at all levels. In the following discussion on meaningful work, greater emphasis is placed on the hourly worker's job, not only to make the job more interesting, but also to eliminate practices which symbolically put people into two classes.

MEANINGFUL WORK

Meaning is given or returned to work through processes which include job enrichment or job enlargement. Applications of job enrichment have shown tangible improvements in terms of diverse criteria such as reduced costs, higher yields, less scrap, accelerated learning time, fewer complaints and trips to the health center, reduced anxiety, improved attitudes and team efforts, and increased profits.

Most reports on job enrichment are situational descriptions which offer little guidance for applications in dissimilar circumstances. The slavish emulation of inappropriate examples usually leads to failure. Principles and techniques of job enrichment are useful only as guidelines, and each job must be studied in terms of the opportunities and constraints surrounding it. Jobs may be improved through horizontal or vertical job enlargement or through a combination of both, as illustrated in Figure 3-2. Horizontal job enlargement is characterized by increasing the variety of functions performed at a given level. As an intermediate step, it serves to reduce boredom and broaden the employee's perspective, thereby preparing him for vertical job enlargement. Vertically enlarged jobs enable employees to take part in the planning and control functions customarily restricted to persons in supervisory and staff functions.

The Management-Labor Dichotomy

The functions of management are commonly defined in business school terminology as planning, organizing, leading, and controlling, as illustrated in Figure 3-3. Management functions are descriptive of the job of a "manager," but not of the job of a "worker," For example, a manager in an automobile assembly plant might describe his own job in terms of planning, organizing, leading, and controlling, and would see his fifty foremen as concerned primarily with leading and controlling. Their main responsibility is supervising the 2000 workers on the assembly line who are doing the work, as reflected in Figure 3-4.

This typical management point of view excludes employees from the realm of management and creates, unwittingly if not deliberately, a dichotomy of people at work: workers as unintelligent, uninformed, uncreative, irresponsible, and immature persons dependent upon the direction and control of intelligent, informed, creative, responsible, and mature managers. Consequences of this viewpoint are widely evident in organizations and are reflected in Figure 3-5, which shows the cleavage between management and labor in terms of social distance and alienation.

Though the gap between the employer and the employed has a long heritage and, in some respects, seems inescapably inherent to the relationship, it has become more formalized and widened through the efforts of labor unions whose charters seem to depend on their success in convincing labor that management is their natural enemy. The union, while pressuring the company to share its wealth and the managers to relinquish their prerogatives, has at the same time clearly defined the laboring man's charter as being separate from, and indeed in conflict with, that of managers. Managers typically and naturally align themselves with the goals of the company, but workers divide their allegiance between the union and the company, sometimes with a closer identification with the union.

Though autocratic management, tradition, and labor union strategy all tend to perpetuate the two-class concept, two forces in America have the potential for narrowing or obliterating the gap between labor and management. One is the improving socioeconomic status and the consequent

Horizontal

1 – Assemblers on a transformer assembly line each performed a single operation as the assembly moved by on the conveyor belt. Jobs were enlarged horizontally by setting up work stations to permit each operator to assemble the entire unit. Operations now performed by each operator include cabling, upending, winding, soldering, laminating and symbolizing.

2 – A similar transformer assembly line provides horizontal job enlargement when assemblers are taught how to perform all operations and are rotated to different operations periodically, or as permitted by peer and supervisory consensus.

Vertical

3 – Assemblers on a radar assembly line are given information on customer contract commitments in terms of price, quality specifications, delivery schedules, and company data on materiel and personnel costs, breakeven performance, and potential profit margins. Assemblers and engineers work together in methods and design improvements. Assemblers inspect, adjust, and repair their own work, help test completed units, and receive copies of customer inspection reports.

4 – Female electronic assemblers involved in intricate assembling, bonding, soldering, and welding operations are given training in methods improvement and encouraged to make suggestions for improving manufacturing processes. Natural work groups of five to 20 assemblers each elect a "team captain" for a term of six months. In addition to performing her regular operations, the team captain collects work improvement ideas from members of her team, describes them on a standard form, credits the suggestors, presents the recommendations to their supervisor and superintendent at the end of the week, and gives the team feedback on idea utilization. Though most job operations remain the same, vertical job enlargement is achieved by providing increased opportunity for planning, reorganizing and controlling their work.

Horizontal Plus Vertical

5 – Jobs are enlarged horizontally in a clad metal rolling mill by qualifying operators to work interchangeably on breakdown rolling, finishing rolling, slitter, pickler, and abrader operations. After giving the operators training in methods improvement and basic metallurgy, jobs are enlarged vertically by involving them with engineering and supervisory personnel in problem-solving, goal-setting sessions for increasing production yields.

6 – Jobs in a large employee insurance section are enlarged horizontally by qualifying insurance clerks to work interchangeably in filing claims, mailing checks, enrolling and orienting new employees, checking premium and enrollment reports, adjusting payroll deductions, and interpreting policies to employees. Vertical enlargement involves clerks in insurance program planning meetings with personnel directors and carrier representatives, authorizes them to sign disbursement requests, attend a paperwork systems conference, recommend equipment replacements and to rearrange their work layout.

FIG. 3-2 Examples of horizontal and vertical job enlargement.

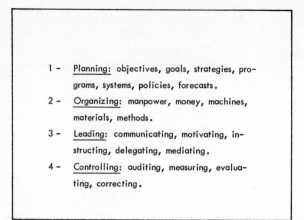

1 - <u>Planning</u>: objectives, goals, strategies, programs, systems, policies, forecasts.

2 - <u>Organizing</u>: manpower, money, machines,
materials, methods.

3 - <u>Leading</u>: communicating, motivating, instructing, delegating, mediating.

4 - <u>Controlling</u>: auditing, measuring, evaluating, correcting.

FIG. 3-3   The functions of management.

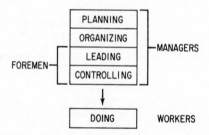

FIG. 3-4   The manager's traditional perception of the job.

FIG. 3-5   The management-labor dichotomy.

rising aspirations of the less privileged, accelerated by legislated equality in an increasingly enlightened and affluent society. The second force is a growing awareness by managers of the inevitability of democracy as the pattern for successful competition in an entrepreneurial society, and their acceptance of their role in initiating and supporting it. This chapter focuses on this second force: presenting a concept of meaningful work to guide tomorrow's managers in redefining working conditions and the roles of job incumbents.

The Changing Needs of Man

Maslow's[22] hierarchy-of-needs theory is useful in understanding the consequences of the increasing affluence of man. Primeval man's efforts were directed primarily toward survival needs—safety, food, and shelter—leaving little time or energy for preoccupation with his latent higher-order needs. As man's survival needs were satisfied, he became sensitized to social and status needs. Finally, in the affluence of recent decades, these lower-order or maintenance needs are being satisfied to the point that man is ready to realize his potential, to experience self-actualization in terms of growth, achievement, responsibility and recognition.

Management and the union both have contributed to the worker's readiness for self-actualization. Efficiency engineers of the Industrial Revolution, under the label of "scientific management," simplified tasks and created the mass-production technology. Jobs were fractionated for efficiency in training (and to escape management's dependency on prima donna journeymen) and to satisfy the implicit assumption that workers would be happy and efficient doing easy work for high pay. And though mass-production technology made man an appendage of machines and destroyed his journeyman's pride and autonomy, it helped to price automobiles, washing machines, refrigerators, and other consumer products within his reach. These and other effects of the mass-production economy accelerated the satisfaction of man's lower-order needs and readied him to become aware of his dormant and unfulfilled self-actualization needs.

The union's role was just as vital in readying the worker for self-actualization, for it forced managers to share company success with the wage earners, thereby narrowing the economic gap between the manager and the worker and further enabling him to buy the products of mass production. However, as noted on pages 89 to 91, the union, for reasons of self-preservation, sharpened the worker's identity as a member of labor rather than a member of management—preserving the social gap that might otherwise have been reduced through economic trends.

[22]Abraham H. Maslow, *Toward a Psychology of Being*, 2d ed., Van Nostrand, New York, 1968.

When Work Is Meaningless

In the eyes of many workers, work itself is a form of punishment. It is uninteresting, demeaning, oppressive, and generally unrelated to or in conflict with their personal goals. But it is an activity which they take in stride, or an unpleasantness they are willing to endure, to get the money needed to buy goods and services which are related to personal goals. The income itself, however, is not the sole motive for working.

Apart from the needs satisfied through income earned on the job, work itself, however dull and menial, can satisfy a wide variety of other motives:

- Work reduces role ambiguity. It establishes the worker's identity, and though the self-image may not be an attractive one, for most it is better than an undefined role. For some it is an "escape from freedom" which Eric Fromm[23] shows to be necessary for people who are culturally conditioned to associate security with roles prescribed by authority.

- Work offers socializing opportunity. Close and sustained association with others having similar goals, socioeconomic backgrounds, and interests are natural conditions for social interaction. However, social relationships, in the absence of a unifying achievement mission, can be disruptive to productivity. Broad-scale group cohesiveness and social interaction sometimes occur among the members of a work force who can find no better basis for uniting than to defy the management Goliath.

- Work increases solidarity. The performance of similar tasks, however routine, is a shared ritual which provides a basis for equality and role acceptance. "Misery loves company" only because of the solidarity created by shared misery. The individual who is promoted or transferred from the unifying circumscribed role becomes an outsider whose solidarity needs must be satisfied elsewhere. The saying, "God must have loved common man because he made so many of them" finds grateful acceptance by people who need solace for their inescapable commonness.

- Work bolsters security feelings. Apart from the security related to economics, for many persons, feelings of security require continuous affirmation from authority figures. Authority-oriented people, particularly when deprived of meaningful work roles, have unusually high requirements for feedback from the supervisor to satisfy their security and achievement needs. Dependency relationships to authority figures are also manifested, of course, by achievement-oriented people with thwarted achievement needs.

[23]Fromm, op. cit.

- Work is a substitute for unrealized potential. "Keeping busy" channels energy or thwarted intellectual capability and helps obscure the reality of unfulfilled potential. Though it is an escape mechanism, at least it is less destructive than alcoholism or other negative addictions, and it helps to buy freedom and the opportunity off the job which gives better expression to talent. Furthermore, evidence of fatigue from an "honest day's work" evokes social approval.

- Work is an escape from the home environment. Particularly for women whose homemaking roles are unfulfilling or completed, an outside job is a culturally accepted escape mechanism. Other reasons for wanting to get away from home include domestic conflict, neighborhood friction, unattractive home facilities, and loneliness.

- Work reduces feelings of guilt and worthlessness. In an achieving society where dignity and pride are earned through the traits of ambition, initiative, industriousness, and perseverance, idleness violates deep-seated values, and work for work's sake is virtuous. By Horatio Alger or Protestant ethic standards, idleness is the equivalent of stealing, and a strong conscience is a key motive for staying on the job.

The roles of meaningless work defined above relate to the personal needs of individuals which are not constructively aligned with company goals. Moreover, these roles may thwart long-range personal goals, as they usually increase dependency relationships and discourage the development of talent. However, when work itself is properly designed, it can satisfy other needs which are related to the achievement of long-range personal and organization goals.

For example, the manager's job is usually found to be challenging, related to company goals, and generally aligned with his long-range personal goals. The difference in job attitude between manager and worker is usually ascribed to immaturity of the worker, overlooking the fact that maturity is developed or impaired as a function of opportunity to be responsible.

Managers manage their jobs, while workers are managed by their jobs. Workers are frequently only appendages of machines or links between them—doing what is necessary to keep pace with uninspiring, inflexible, and demanding systems.

The Dimensions of Meaningful Work

Work itself, to be meaningful, must make tools the appendage of man and place man in a role not restricted to obedient *doing.* It must include *planning* and *controlling,* as well as *doing,* as illustrated in Figure 3-6.

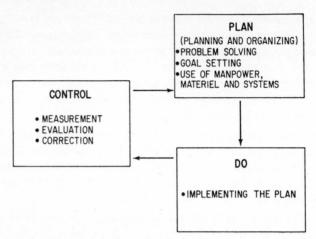

FIG. 3-6   Meaningful work model.

The *plan* phase includes the planning and organizing functions of work and consists of problem solving–goal setting and of planning the use of manpower, materiel, and systems. Planning is a dimension of work which makes it more meaningful by aligning it with goals. The *do* phase is the implementation of the plan, ideally involving the coordinated expenditure of physical and mental effort, utilizing aptitudes and special skills. *Control* includes measurement, evaluation, and correction—the feedback process for assessing achievements against goals. Feedback, even to a greater extent than planning, gives work its meaning, and its absence is a common cause of job dissatisfaction. The control phase is the basis for recycling planning, doing, and controlling. People who work for themselves generally have meaningful work in terms of a complete cycle of plan, do, and control.

The self-employed farmer, for example, plans and organizes in terms of market evaluation, crop rotation, seed selection, utilization of land, purchase of equipment, and the employment of manpower. He typically has a major role in implementing his plan—planting, cultivating, irrigating, harvesting, and marketing. Finally, he measures, evaluates, and corrects his program as necessary to provide for a better future cycle. An analogous pattern may be defined for others in the entrepreneurial situation of self-employment.

The Meaningful Work of Managers

Managers in industry, though seldom having as much autonomy as self-employed entrepreneurs, typically have jobs rich in plan, do, and control phases, particularly at the higher levels. Three typical management jobs

out of a seven-level hierarchy in a manufacturing organization a
fied below for analysis in terms of their customary plan, do, an
phases.

President

→ Operating vice president

Department manager

→ Manufacturing manager

Superintendent

→ Foreman

Operator

Figure 3-7 shows that the operating vice president, as division manager, plans in the realm of economic and technological trends, facilities
expansion, manpower and management systems, and policy formulation.
The doing aspect of his job involves him routinely with key customers, in
public relations roles, with visits to various operating sites, and in the
exchange of business information. His control functions include the measurement, evaluation, and correction of factors associated with customer
satisfaction, net sales, profits, cash flow, facilities utilization, return on investment, morale, and manpower development. Hence, the division di-

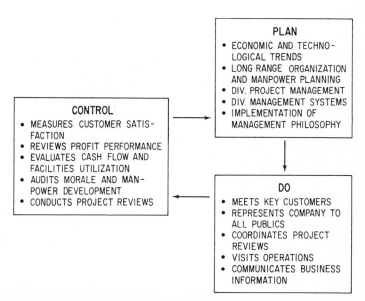

FIG. 3-7 Meaningful work—operating vice president.

rector's job is rich in plan, do, and control, much like that of the self-employed individual.

Similarly, Figure 3-8 shows the manufacturing manager's job to be relatively rich in the meaningful aspects of work. Though his job is narrower in scope and two levels below the division manager's position, it is nonetheless rich in plan, do, and control. A company is rarely plagued with the lack of commitment of a manufacturing manager or the people above him.

Where Meaningful Work Usually Stops

Even the foreman's job, two levels below the manufacturing manager, may be rich in terms of the ingredients of meaningful work. Figure 3-9 indicates that the foreman's job, though narrower in scope than the manufacturing manager's, offers him considerable latitude in managing his work. This example depicts a traditional authority-oriented supervisor, who will be contrasted later with a goal-oriented supervisor in Figure 7-2.

Though this foreman's job portrays a complete plan-do-control cycle, it is not fully satisfying to the incumbent because its authority orientation does not result in the delegation of a complete plan-do-control cycle of responsibility to the operator. Under this foreman, the operator lives in a world circumscribed by conformity pressures to follow instructions, work

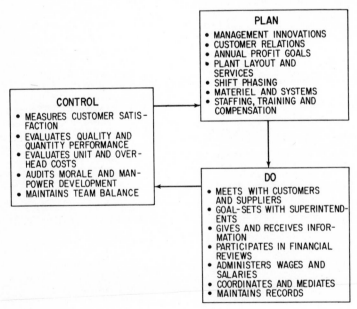

FIG. 3-8   Meaningful work—manufacturing manager.

harder, obey rules, get along with people, and be loyal to the supervisor and the company, quashing any pleasure that work itself might potentially offer. His role puts him in a category with materiel, to be manipulated by managers exercising their "management prerogatives" (as kings once exercised their "divine rights") in pursuit of "their" organizational goals. Conformity-oriented workers tend to behave like adolescent children responding to punishments and rewards of authoritarian parents, and their prerogatives, which are generally expressed in terms of rights wrested from management, are only incidentally aligned with company goals.

The Impact of Supervisory Style

Job enrichment sometimes results naturally from the intuitive practices of goal-oriented, emotionally mature managers who evoke commitment through a "language of action" which grants freedom and reflects respect, confidence, and high expectations. Unfortunately, many managers still see job enlargement as a form of benevolent autocracy. When job enrichment is attempted by reductive, authority-oriented managers, they usually fail to inspire the level of involvement and commitment achieved by goal-oriented managers. Their motives are suspect and their "language of action" comes through as manipulation and exploitation rather than as acts of trust, confidence, and respect.

Hence, job enrichment depends on style of supervision as well as job requirements and is not simply a matter of emulating patterns of work and relationships found to be successful elsewhere.

JOB ENRICHMENT PROCESSES

The foregoing examples show that meaningful work includes planning and controlling, as well as doing, and that conformity pressures by the authority-oriented supervisor defined in Figure 3-9 tend to prevent the break with tradition necessary for people under his supervision to experience the full plan-do-control cycle of work. Hence, the role of the supervisor is the key to job enrichment. The involvement of the supervisor in the enrichment process is necessary, if only because he is usually the person most familiar with all jobs in his work group. But, more importantly, his participation involves him in the redefinition of his own role and leads to self-initiated changes in his managerial style.

Job enrichment is a never-ending process and, particularly in a large organization, the logistics of improving all jobs simultaneously would be overwhelming. A realistic initial mission is to involve each supervisor at least once in a formal way, so that he can take the initiative in testing and

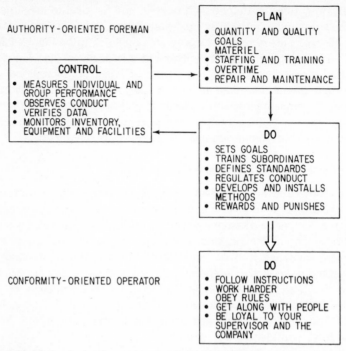

FIG. 3-9 Authority-oriented relationship between foreman and operator.

implementing enrichment techniques with other jobs under his supervision.

Job Incumbent Checklist

As part of the intellectual conditioning process described on pages 10 to 15, supervisors can analyze the meaningfulness of jobs under their supervision by answering questions related to each of the three phases of work, as illustrated in Figure 3-10. A supervisor's involvement in answering questions in this checklist may sensitize him to the gross disparity between the reality of his own work group and the theoretical model. The plan and control items in particular may at first appear unrealistic to him in terms of his perception of his people's competence, but he can be helped to a more realistic view by having him make a comparative analysis of a similar job managed by a person of similar talents in business for himself.

For example, analysis of a company oil driller's job in the field may show it to be largely devoid of planning and control phases when compared to the job of his free-lance counterpart who manages his own drilling

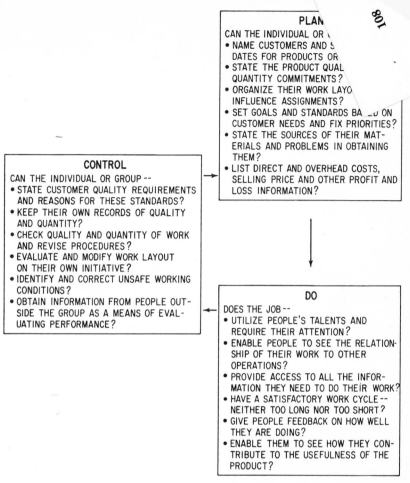

PLAN

CAN THE INDIVIDUAL OR
- NAME CUSTOMERS AND S
  DATES FOR PRODUCTS OR
- STATE THE PRODUCT QUAL
  QUANTITY COMMITMENTS?
- ORGANIZE THEIR WORK LAYO
  INFLUENCE ASSIGNMENTS?
- SET GOALS AND STANDARDS BA _D ON
  CUSTOMER NEEDS AND FIX PRIORITIES?
- STATE THE SOURCES OF THEIR MAT-
  ERIALS AND PROBLEMS IN OBTAINING
  THEM?
- LIST DIRECT AND OVERHEAD COSTS,
  SELLING PRICE AND OTHER PROFIT AND
  LOSS INFORMATION?

CONTROL

CAN THE INDIVIDUAL OR GROUP --
- STATE CUSTOMER QUALITY REQUIREMENTS
  AND REASONS FOR THESE STANDARDS?
- KEEP THEIR OWN RECORDS OF QUALITY
  AND QUANTITY?
- CHECK QUALITY AND QUANTITY OF WORK
  AND REVISE PROCEDURES?
- EVALUATE AND MODIFY WORK LAYOUT
  ON THEIR OWN INITIATIVE?
- IDENTIFY AND CORRECT UNSAFE WORKING
  CONDITIONS?
- OBTAIN INFORMATION FROM PEOPLE OUT-
  SIDE THE GROUP AS A MEANS OF EVAL-
  UATING PERFORMANCE?

DO

DOES THE JOB --
- UTILIZE PEOPLE'S TALENTS AND
  REQUIRE THEIR ATTENTION?
- ENABLE PEOPLE TO SEE THE RELATION-
  SHIP OF THEIR WORK TO OTHER
  OPERATIONS?
- PROVIDE ACCESS TO ALL THE INFOR-
  MATION THEY NEED TO DO THEIR WORK?
- HAVE A SATISFACTORY WORK CYCLE --
  NEITHER TOO LONG NOR TOO SHORT?
- GIVE PEOPLE FEEDBACK ON HOW WELL
  THEY ARE DOING?
- ENABLE THEM TO SEE HOW THEY CON-
  TRIBUTE TO THE USEFULNESS OF THE
  PRODUCT?

FIG. 3-10   Sample questions for analyzing meaningful work.

rig. The self-employed driller, who must manage the total plan-do-control cycle of his work to succeed in business, thus serves as a model for planning the enrichment of the company driller's job. Similar comparisons can be made for other occupations such as the salesclerk versus the self-employed haberdasher, the truck driver versus the self-employed trucker, or the toolroom supervisor versus the owner-operator of a machine shop.

This checklist approach is more appropriate as a sensitizing process for supervisors in training than it is for an actual enrichment process. Job-enrichment processes, to be fully effective, must also involve the job incumbents.

Management Task-force Approach[24]

Job enrichment may be approached through a task force composed of a vertical cross section of supervisors extending from the job incumbent's supervisor to the highest level possible. This slice is made up of people in line management of a given product or service, and may include horizontal cross sections at the lower levels. Ideally, the first job-enrichment workshop should be limited to fewer than ten people. Later on, larger task forces may be practical, with perhaps twenty members as an upper limit. The task-force approach of job enrichment is outlined in Figure 3-11.

These work groups should be isolated from their daily jobs, off the premises if feasible, away from interruptions. Supervisors sometimes resist the idea of spending time away from the job, particularly when they are deeply involved in day-to-day efforts for which they believe themselves indispensable. Of course, their "inescapable" problems are the ones most likely to be solved through job enrichment.

Supervisory training is a prerequisite to this process, and all participants in the task force should have completed at least 16 hours of orientation consisting of:

1. Motivation theory
2. Meaningful work
3. Work Simplification
4. Conference leadership

Motivation theory provides a foundation for understanding constructive and reactive behavior as a symptom of satisfied or thwarted needs. Meaningful work defines the proper or ideal balance of plan-do-control functions that give work its meaning. Work Simplification familiarizes the supervisor with techniques and principles which enable people to become their own industrial engineers in analyzing and improving their jobs. Conference leadership skills focus on communication processes which enable supervisors to avoid quashing individual initiative and creativity, and to obtain goal-oriented involvement of the group in solving problems and setting goals.

The mission of the supervisory group is to translate the abstractions of responsibility, achievement, recognition, and growth into tangible job factors. How can *responsibility* be added to this particular job? Who is responsible now for planning and assigning work and measuring results? Can any

---

[24]The management task-force approach is a combination of Texas Instruments' motivation seminar and plan-do-control concepts with Robert Ford's process, defined in his book *Motivation through the Work Itself*, American Management Association, New York, 1969, pp. 139–167.

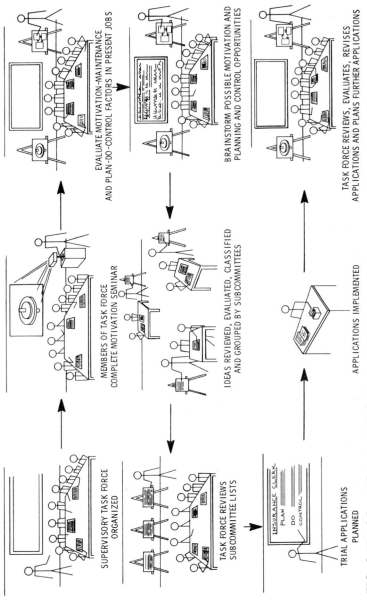

FIG. 3-11 Job enrichment—task-force approach.

SUPERVISORY TASK FORCE ORGANIZED

TASK FORCE REVIEWS SUBCOMMITTEE LISTS

TRIAL APPLICATIONS PLANNED

MEMBERS OF TASK FORCE COMPLETE MOTIVATION SEMINAR

IDEAS REVIEWED, EVALUATED, CLASSIFIED AND GROUPED BY SUBCOMMITTEES

APPLICATIONS IMPLEMENTED

EVALUATE MOTIVATION-MAINTENANCE AND PLAN-DO-CONTROL FACTORS IN PRESENT JOBS

BRAINSTORM POSSIBLE MOTIVATION AND PLANNING AND CONTROL OPPORTUNITIES

TASK FORCE REVIEWS, EVALUATES, REVISES APPLICATIONS AND PLANS FURTHER APPLICATIONS

109

of this responsibility be moved down to the job incumbent? How can the job be altered to provide a greater sense of *achievement?* Are accomplishments clearly definable or measurable? If not, what is obscuring goals or feedback? Bob Ford cited a case in AT&T where a supervisory task force found sixteen new ways of giving each service representative her own performance results. In another example, an operator was given copies of only her own defective toll tickets with the request to analyze and classify the defects.

Recognition and *growth* result from responsibility and achievement. Traditionally, the job incumbent is dependent on authority figures for recognition. But jobs can be designed so that participation in plan and control responsibilities gives the job incumbent natural opportunity for recognition, without reinforcing a dependency relationship to the supervisor. How can the worker get natural recognition from upper management, supervisors, peers, and others without relying unduly on the value judgments of supervisors?

Personal and professional growth is a natural consequence of progressive or varied challenges. People with greater ability thrive on a progression of increasingly difficult tasks or skills to master, and need opportunity for advancement to more challenging jobs. Some jobs, such as those in medicine, research, and top management, have a lifetime of challenge in them. The challenge of the supervisor is to vary job content flexibly to enable people of varying abilities to experience job satisfaction in accordance with their aspirations and capability.

A brainstorming session (with ground rules against criticism, ridicule, and inflexibility) for loading jobs with responsibility, achievement, recognition, and growth usually lasts a whole day, and may extend into the second day. Proceedings are summarized on large easel sheets and displayed around the conference room.

First-day guidelines include the instructions, "Think radically about the work flow and the purpose of the jobs involved in satisfying customer needs. What can be done to create more complete jobs for these employees?" Diagnose jobs in terms of the plan, do, and control phases—for both the job incumbent and his supervisor. Which *do* functions are perpetuated by tradition, and what would happen if they were eliminated? Which *plan* and *control* functions could be moved across or down to a job incumbent? Brainstorming sessions purposely preclude concern with the feasibility of implementing changes or the consequences of manpower surplus that might result from these changes.

Following the brainstorming session, an evaluation of the brainstorming list is begun. If the list is short (fewer than fifty items), the group usually works together to classify each suggestion into either motivation or maintenance categories, as defined in Figure 1-2. If the list is long (more than fifty items), and if conference time is limited, the task can be subdivided for subgroup assignment, each group reviewing all items for possible inclusion in one category. Motivational items are designed as horizontal or vertical job enlargement, as illustrated in Figure 3-2, and their impact is specified in terms of growth, achievement, responsibility, and recognition.

Maintenance items may be diagnosed in terms of economic, security, orientation, status, social, and physical factors, or, more simply, in terms of administrative roadblocks and other maintenance factors.

When all items have been classified by category, they are reviewed by the group in terms of feasibility. The least feasible are put aside (though not necessarily rejected), and the most feasible are listed by category on a clean easel sheet in rank order of feasibility.

The workshop then reconvenes as a total group, and each team reports on the merits and limitations of each item on its list and evokes and incorporates new ideas from the group. Also, at this point, for the first time, conferees are asked to designate the items in their list which they believe could and should be implemented. Job restructuring begins at this stage, especially if motivation factors are strongly represented in the items.

A list strong on roadblock items but weak in motivation categories may imply a basically or potentially rich job that has become hemmed in by rules and regulations. If so, motivation factors might be liberated by eliminating roadblocks.

Some maintenance items, because of their uniform application across the organization, cannot be altered for a job or a group. However, some changes can be spearheaded in small groups, and group efforts can sometimes lead to more broadly applied changes throughout the organization.

Near the end of the second day, the group decides whether a job-improvement trial is to be undertaken and which items are to be implemented. Supervisors, individually or in groups, are asked to pick a few items for trial application. They list obstacles and problems anticipated in implementing each item, with specific steps for overcoming them.

During trial applications—usually extending through a four- to six-week period—supervisors meet periodically to review progress, discuss problems, and continue brainstorming of additional jobs. Also during this period, implementation procedures and schedules are planned. Participation and support of top management are helpful ingredients in planning the strategy.

In beginning job enrichment, much can be done just by improving existing jobs. This is least threatening or disrupting to job incumbents and their supervisors. The next step might involve the collapsing or merging of several allied jobs. In both instances, it is helpful to itemize the planning and control functions of higher jobs which can be pulled down to make lower jobs more complete. When possible, routine functions are eliminated, perhaps through automation, or made more bearable by combining them with more interesting functions.

One key, but elusive, concept in making work more meaningful is the natural module of work—that is, all the work in connection with a particular assignment. For example, in one of the AT&T studies, a group of ten women was responsible for mailing out toll billings on staggered dates throughout the month. All bills for telephone numbers starting with 392 were due out on the first of the month, 395 on the fifth, 397 on the thirteenth, and so on. Working as a team, they would finish 392 and then start 395 under the scheduling and direction of the supervisor. But productivity was low, due dates were missed, and overtime costs were high. Recognizing each block of billings per due date as a natural module of work, responsibility for each module was assigned to an individual. One woman was responsible for getting out 392, another for 395, and so on. The individual was responsible for the plan, do, and control functions necessary to meet deadlines. The women were making their own decisions and working out mutually supportive relationships with each other. Each could succeed or fail, but her performance and fate were under her control. Results were dramatically good: schedules were met, overtime was eliminated, and job satisfaction increased.

Other applications of the modular idea were included in Ford's studies:

- A frame man was given responsibility for handling all cross-connection work for specific groups of customers, rather than miscellaneous and unrelated wiring assignments.
- A keypunch operator was made responsible for preparing all cards from a certain geographic area or for certain kinds of reports, rather than whatever cards needed to be punched next.
- An equipment engineer was made responsible for handling all contacts from initial request to final installation in a certain area and/or for certain kinds of equipment, rather than whatever job came along next.

In each case, the key was to give each person the knowledge that he had a job to manage to satisfy "his" customer or set of customers.

The task force approach as defined above is gradually falling in disfavor, primarily as a function of the changing values in the work force, as defined on pages 22 to 33. Entrepreneurial, sociocentric and existential employees tend to resist changes wrought by management without their involvement. However, this approach may still be effective in bureaucratic organizations and among the culturally disadvantaged where values are more likely to be oriented toward conformity and tribalism.

Job Incumbent Self-Diagnosis

For many people of today's values and orientation, job enrichment is best accomplished through the active involvement of the job incumbent. Thus a group of employees may be given an opportunity to examine and evaluate their own, and other, jobs in the light of motivation theory. Such an analysis is usually preceded by an educational process which gives them a framework for making such an analysis. If they conclude, as they usually do, that their job could be improved, they are given an opportunity to recommend the inclusion of additional responsibilities to their present job.

For example, they might be shown a list of their supervisor's responsibilities with the question, "Is there anything in your boss's job that you could handle and would like to handle?" In addition, they might be given lists of responsibilities of people from other functions such as engineering, inspection, and maintenance, and asked the same question. The usual initial consequence of such an effort is to overload their own jobs. The overload may be adjusted through the subsequent involvement of job incumbents whose jobs were "plundered" in the enrichment process.

If the process were to terminate with the enrichment of jobs at the lowest level, the people whose jobs were partially annexed would feel threatened. Hence, it is usually desirable to move the process successively upward. Thus first-level supervisors may be shown the superintendent's job list of responsibilities with the same question, "Is there anything in your boss's job that you could handle and would like to handle?" This process, continued upward through superintendent, manufacturing manager, and department head, ultimately reaches the plant manager, who should also benefit from a lightened burden. Moreover, this process of moving responsibility and decision-making downward sometimes shortens communication channels by eliminating unnecessary levels of management. Incidentally, it can also reduce labor costs and thus increase productivity in the process.

If such a bottom-up process is to be initiated, it should, of course, be preceded by an orientation seminar to brief the affected management levels on the rationale of the effort and the supportive effort required of them. Otherwise, managers would be threatened by what might appear to them as intrusion into their managerial prerogatives and erosion of their responsibility.

A Multifaceted Approach

Improving a person's relationship to his or her job is not limited to one or more of the foregoing techniques of job enrichment. Sometimes a number of partial solutions or temporary techniques can be used in imaginative combination to achieve job enrichment.

Problem solving–goal setting, described on pages 138 to 143 is perhaps the most effective approach to job enrichment. The involvement of a natural work group or task force in the un-self-conscious process of solving operating problems can lead naturally to the transformation of the conformity-oriented operator in Figure 3-9 to the relationship shown in Figure 7-2.

Enrichment is in the eyes of the perceiver. Hence, people who are free to select the job they prefer have in effect enriched their job. Job posting, described on pages 227 to 231, allows dissatisfied job incumbents to seek out, perhaps by trial and error, the job most compatible with their values. Thus many routine jobs which were presumed to require redesign to make them interesting, may only require an opportunity for individuals to migrate about the organization until those suited for such jobs are able to discover them. Sometimes a routine job is made oppressive by the inability of the job incumbents to escape it. The chronic complaints of people locked into such jobs may be termed the "jailhouse syndrome." When the gates are opened and they are free to transfer out, only a few seek to do so. However, the freedom to escape a job dissipates the frustration and hostility which generated the widespread complaint syndrome within the group.

Sometimes enrichment is achieved by job rotation. For example, assemblers working along a conveyor belt assembly line were able to exchange jobs on the condition that they be accountable for the job skills of the persons replacing them. In another situation, undesirable jobs were assigned on a rotational basis to all members of a work group. Thus, in a six-person work group, each person might be required to work the job every sixth workday. Under such an arrangement, it is not unusual to find certain individuals volunteering for more than their required quota of the rotated job.

In some organizations the undesirable jobs are filled as entry jobs by new hires. Persons who might become quickly oppressed by such work are inspired by the "light at the end of the tunnel" and take the temporary assignment in stride. Such a strategy is viable, of course, only under conditions of continuous hiring. Finally, it should be noted that work itself is not the only or even the best medium for enriching jobs. In terms of a broader concept of "life enrichment" in the work place, it is necessary to give equal emphasis to peripheral systems as media for giving meaning to the job.

PERIPHERAL SYSTEMS

In every organization there are small and large systems which are peripheral to the work itself which influence the quality of work life. Peripheral systems usually do not appear in job descriptions and may serve a variety of functions which influence job incumbents directly and indirectly. Parking facilities, timekeeping methods, charity drives, company newspapers, paycheck distribution, attitude surveys, safety committees, and conflict resolution procedures are examples which illustrate the heterogeneity of peripheral systems.

In terms of the motivation and maintenance needs depicted in Fig. 1-2, peripheral systems are generally associated with the maintenance factors. As such, they have little motivational potential and are generally thought of as factors which affect the ambiance of the organization. However, many of these systems can be administered in such a way that they become media for satisfying motivation needs. Such potential is illustrated in the following example which describes the quality of work efforts of the Eaton Corporation.

The Eaton Story

The Eaton Corporation is comprised of eighty-some plants deployed worldwide, primarily in the manufacture of precision parts such as axles and transmissions. Though many jobs offer the challenge of high skills and technical competence, life in the typical factory is characterized by the usual amount of boredom, disengagement, and counterproductive behavior. As in most organizations, personnel problems were more bothersome among factory workers than among office personnel.

In 1968 the company planners saw an opportunity to revise their traditional approach to labor relations. They were planning the expansion of company operations through the opening of new plants, and sought to take advantage of the fact that it is easier to introduce new personnel practices in a start-up situation than it is to revise practices in an established operation. Start-up operations are less inhibited by the inertia of crystallized attitudes and systems which often characterize established organizations.

Noting that office personnel responded positively to personnel practices based on theory Y assumptions, they speculated that shop personnel, who were typically governed by theory X practices, might also respond better to a theory Y philosophy. Office personnel tended to enjoy the freedom of the managers with whom they worked in terms of flexibility of work rules, egalitarian practices and informal communications. Shop workers lived in a more restrictive labor-management dichotomy governed by posted work rules, which circumscribed their job roles and personal freedoms. The more reductive practices in the shop were obviously not producing the desired results and tended only to provoke creative counterproductive behavior.

They envisioned and planned for the opening of a new plant in Kearney, Nebraska, in which the traditional discriminatory practices between shop and office would be avoided. Toward that end they established a Quality of Work Life Committee composed of both union and management personnel to refine the details of such a strategy.

The implementation of these plans was sufficiently successful to encourage the extension of this philosophy to other start-up operations. Within a decade, fifteen new plants were operating with varying degrees of success in carrying this new philosophy forward. It is noteworthy that the pattern evolving in the initial plant was not crystallized and imposed by corporate authority on subsequent start-up operations. Each plant manager was encouraged to involve his own plant work force in the development of their own blueprint for implementing this philosophy. In practice, much cross-fertilization took place as managers visited each others' operations and exchanged information on their successes and failures.

Don Scobel cites the following examples as expressions of the evolving Eaton philosophy. These applications are not focused on job design or job enlargement, but, rather, on factors peripheral to work itself.

1. *Special invitation to regular meetings.* On an *ad hoc* basis, people who don't ordinarily attend are invited to sit in on such meetings as production control, supplier appraisal, engineering process, sales planning, and staff meetings. A nonsupervisory office or factory person, a union official, or a foreman might be invited.

2. *Departmental meetings.* The head of a department or operation holds periodic meetings of his people to discuss things other than immediate job projects. Meetings may be participative or have guest speakers or be led by one or more of the participants.

3. *Manager's round table.* The manager of a facility periodically meets with people randomly selected from various levels and functions (usually selected on a rotating basis) to discuss matters of importance to those attending.

4. *Supervisor's meetings.* Meetings involving supervisors from various functions—both office and factory—to share information and to coordinate the administration of personnel practices.

5. *Newspaper publication.* Volunteer reporters and editors publish the plant news sheet. Sometimes several volunteers form an editorial board which, within specific financial limits, has the full responsibility for the house organ.

6. *Hiring process.* Groups of applicants for nonsupervisory jobs are invited to informal meetings (often spouses are also invited) to discuss what the plant is all about and to meet and talk with supervisors, union representatives, and their future peers. They are given a tour of factory and office and later participate in a similarly conducted orientation process.

7. *Tour guides.* Tours for community groups, guests, job applicants, and present employees are conducted by volunteers from office and factory. Plant tours for families and friends may be totally planned by the employees themselves.

8. *Social service training.* In conjunction with local professional specialists and/or social service agency people, groups of supervisors, union representatives, and other interested employees are jointly trained in spotting employee problem situations and arranging liaison with appropriate professional counsel.

9. *Educational committee.* A committee of voluntary office and factory supervisors to analyze educational resources in the community, and to plan and recommend courses to meet employee needs at all levels.

10. *Departmental safety teams.* Each factory foreman and two or three of his people (on a rotating basis) form a departmental safety team with responsibility for safety training, accident investigation, statistical reporting, and periodic inspections. Where a plantwide safety committee exists, these local teams serve as grass-roots adjuncts to the plant committee.

11. *Recreation committee.* This committee, made up of volunteers from all levels of the organization, is given specific financial resources and entrusted with the design and implementation of the entire spectrum of recreational programs.

12. *Quality circles.* Task forces focus on quality problems and errors and find ways to improve quality and remove errors.

13. *Process improvement team.* A team composed of engineering, factory management, office, and factory personnel encourages and reviews process improvement ideas and plans. This committee solicits such ideas from the entire work force, particularly the viewpoints of the people who would be affected by changes proposed by professional systems designers.

14. *Improvement sharing plans.* The process improvement team may also provide leadership in the design of an economic sharing plan to provide earnings adjustments (for everyone) based on gains in the sales/labor ratio resulting from operational improvements.

15. *Open-floor policy.* The intent here is to consider the factory person's area a legitimate place to conduct necessary office-type business when it is effective to do so, and to encourage office personnel to make the "open floor" their natural habitat during coffee breaks, lunch periods, and routine visitations.

16. *Time recording.* Mechanical timeclocks are replaced by a time accounting report to be completed by job incumbents.

17. *Work schedules.* Work groups participate in planning regular and overtime work schedules and the use of flex-time.

18. *Absence from job.* People from all levels and functions may have paid time off for personal business and sick leave provided arrangements are made to cover absentee responsibility.

19. *Job evaluation.* A permanent part-time task force made up of representatives of various levels and functions of the organization evaluates jobs and responds to requests for clarification of job-evaluation issues.

20. *Evaluation of supervisors.* Factory and office supervisors optionally have their employees complete anonymous supervisory effectiveness rating forms.

21. *Food service committee.* A committee of volunteers administers food service activities within a prescribed budget.

22. *Disciplinary counseling.* Instead of formal Parent-Child disciplinary warnings and suspensions, supervisors are taught a more Adult-Adult counseling process for modifying behavior.

23. *Supervisor selection.* Employees have an opportunity to influence the supervisory selection process and the selection of their own supervisor.

24. *Community service activities.* Community service activities such as bond drives, Red Cross blood programs, and the United Fund are directed and coordinated by interested volunteers from throughout the work place society.

25. *Bells and buzzers.* Unnecessary and undesired sound signals to regiment employee behavior may be evaluated and discontinued.

26. *Automobile parking.* Nondiscriminatory parking may be implemented, or priority parking space may be assigned to the physically handicapped, to employees who frequently use their personal cars for company business, to ride pool cars, and to others on the basis of functional need.

27. *Attitude survey.* Employees take part in formulating the topics to be covered by the survey, refining the questionnaire, completing the survey, analyzing survey results, and formulating remedial action programs.

None of the foregoing processes, viewed singly, would substantially alter the culture or effectiveness of the organization. However, each carries with it a small positive valence for most of the people affected by it, and collectively and interactively their impact is compounded to make the Eaton plants where these ideas are implemented different and better places to work.

Don Scobel stresses the point that these processes are not standardized nor uniformly applied in all Eaton situations. His advice to managers in a public seminar is "You have to make your own road maps on where you want to go and how to get there; and you may have to modify your approaches as you go along to satisfy the different and changing needs of the participants." Much of the value of these processes derives from the fact that they are systems shaped by the systems users, and as such, they carry with them the proprietary involvement of the members of the work force. These are not "management" programs or "union" programs, but "people" programs.

A more complete list of peripheral and job systems is presented in Figure 5-1 to illustrate the rich variety of opportunities which exist in all organizations. The feasibility of activating these opportunities is, of course, a function of the governing industrial relations philosophy of the organization.

ORGANIZATIONAL CLIMATE

Every organization can be said to have a climate which colors the perceptions and feelings of people within their work environment. A company's climate is influenced by innumerable factors such as its size, the nature of its business, its age, its location, the composition of its work force, its management policies, rules and regulations, and the values and leadership styles of its supervisors. For example, the climate in Eaton plants, as described in the preceding pages, is uniquely influenced by the various peripheral systems purposely designed to minimize discriminatory practices. Many of the factors influencing an organization's climate are dynamic and interactive, resulting in ever-changing "weather" within the organization. However, some factors remain relatively constant, tending to stabilize other factors around a modal or characteristic climate for the organization. Some of these pivotal factors are defined below.

Growth Rate

Rate of growth is a climate factor. In a rapidly expanding organization, the sense of urgency and speed of change create rich opportunities for individual growth, achievement, responsibility, and recognition. Domineering supervisors who would seem oppressive in a stable organization are tolerated in the growth climate, perhaps because their roles are seen as transitory. Also, the sheer pressure of expanding responsibility reduces the authoritarian manager's ability to maintain tight controls; and delegation occurs, if only by default.

In the stabilized or retrenching organization, a condition which often coincides with economic pressures, managers frequently resort to reductive supervisory practices. Delegation is curtailed and growth opportunities are interrupted or deferred, and the more talented members of the work force become impatient and discouraged. Eager to forge ahead, they seek greener pastures and gradually abandon the organization to those who have less ability either to relocate themselves or to revive the organization. The loss of top talent to competitor organizations, of course, further handicaps the plateaued organization. Hence, growth itself helps retain the talented personnel upon whom the continuing success of the organization depends.

This is not to say that perpetual growth is necessary to retain talented personnel. The self-renewing organization, through the management of innovation, as described in Chapter 4, provides conditions attractive to high achievers, even under conditions of retrenchment.

Delegation

Delegation, as a climate factor, is expressed both through style of supervision and through organization structure. Managers operating on the basis of goal-oriented assumptions, as defined on page 43, delegate naturally and willingly—particularly managers who are themselves the recipients of delegated authority. Authority-oriented managers, in contrast, fail to delegate and do little to encourage delegation below them.

A business organized around decentralized semiautonomous product-customer centers tends to foster delegation better than the functionally layered organization. In a functionally layered organization, for example, the manager of manufacturing with five plants under his jurisdiction has limited freedom to exercise his judgment in setting goals and managing plant resources if another manager is responsible for the sale of his products and another is responsible for the research and engineering in the same five plants. In contrast, a plant manager who has the threefold responsibility of creating, making, and marketing products or income-producing services has more entrepreneurial flexibility to manage his resources and to make decisions necessary for organizational success. He is less hampered by the bureaucratic constrictions of poorly coordinated jurisdictions, and can more naturally delegate to others the freedom necessary for building synergistic empires.

Innovation

The spontaneous and constructive expression of creativity is a desirable characteristic of an organization's climate—in the management process as well as in the laboratory. Though managers readily enough accept the principle that all management is the management of innovation, few plan for it or demonstrate constructive creativity in their normal day-to-day behavior. Worse yet, official commitment to the support of innovation may foster formidable bureaucratic systems for "managing innovation" which tend to quash it. Rewards in the form of raises, bonuses, and promotions often go to those who conform to the "system," while those who might be involved in the constructive departure from the *status quo* tend to be punished or expelled from the system.

Innovation exists in great abundance in every organization, but not always to its benefit. In the democratic organization in which people at all levels have opportunity to receive information, solve problems, and set goals, innovation finds positive expression. In organizations characterized by restrictive supervision, inflexible rules, engineered labor standards, and other authority-oriented controls, creativity is usually counterproductive. The tighter the controls, the more innovative the circumventing attempts. Hence, the mission is not one of simply fostering innovation as much as it is one of providing outlets which allow it to find positive expression.

Constructive innovation is encouraged not only by style of management, but also by appropriate systems for managing innovation. The hierarchy of objectives, strategies, and tactical action programs, described on pages 150 and 155, provides a framework in which the coordinated efforts of companywide work groups and task forces can find creative expression in achieving organizational goals. The Work Simplification process, described on pages 130 to 138, teaches problem-solving–goal-setting techniques and philosophy to give expression to creativity at all levels of the organization. The task-force analysis of attitude survey results, described on pages 143 to 149, is a system for utilizing constructive talent at all levels. A climate of innovation is also enhanced by the avoidance of authority-based systems such as engineered labor standards, chain-of-command communication, defensive expense reporting, and elaborate rank-oriented status symbols.

Authority Orientation

An organization's climate may be described in terms of goal orientation or authority orientation. A person may be described as goal-oriented if he understands his job in terms of what it does for the customer, but he is authority-oriented if he performs his job in blind obedience to orders from the boss.

The reductive use of authority, as described on pages 45 to 48, is not an indictment of authority per se. Authority is freedom to act, and it is needed by every member of the organization. However, it is damaging when people at higher levels, deliberately or in ignorance, use their authority to create systems or to behave in ways that deprive others in the organization of the information and freedom necessary for goal orientation.

Without deliberate efforts to prevent it, growing organizations drift inexorably toward conformity and an authority-dominated climate. The worker parks on the company parking lot according to rules established by a nebulous "management," and the lower his rank, the farther out his parking space. His entry and departure from the plant is recorded by official timekeeping procedures, he is told by his supervisor what his job is and perhaps by his union steward what his job is not. Industrial engineering defines "correct" procedures and specifies his quantity and quality goals. A signal bell authorizes the beginning and ending of his coffee break and lunch period, and posted notices tell him he cannot eat or smoke in the hallways. Information is dispensed by management through the public-address system, official bulletins, the company newspaper, and bulletin boards. His pay is determined through the value judgment of supervision, and his paycheck is prepared by computer, minus deductions authorized by Federal and state laws, the union, and management. His supervisor may review his performance with him, detailing his strong and weak points, and prescribing remedial actions. The United Fund and Savings Bond Drives for "voluntary" participation are administered through a process which would make his nonparticipation threatening to those above him, and hence to him. His recourse in case of injustice is a grievance procedure which he hesitates to use because of the possibility of incurring reprisals from those above him. His request for time off must be justified to his supervisor by what is sometimes a humiliating detailing of personal information. When he seeks transfers and promotions or decides to terminate, his dependency on his supervisor's goodwill is inescapable. Though deliberate strategies can prevent or counter the oppressiveness of authority in an organization's climate, few large organizations have succeeded in doing so.

Goal Orientation

Goal orientation is the motivation force which gives direction to the systems and relationships defined throughout this book. It is the climate factor created by processes which make broad organizational goals comprehensible and facilitates the formation of supportive subgoals. It allows access to information and freedom to act so that individual initiative finds expression in setting goals and measuring achievements. A goal-oriented person manages his job, in contrast to the authority-oriented person who feels he is managed by his job. Goal orientation depends on an integrated balance of meaningful goals, helpful systems, and interpersonal competence, as detailed in Chapter 2. Deliberate and systematic attempts are made in goal-oriented organizations to minimize the rank-oriented status symbols which tend to make authority oppressive. Dining facilities are shared by all employees; first-name employee identification badges do not reflect rank; parking privileges, office space, and furnishings are assigned on the basis of functional criteria not necessarily related to job grade or organizational level. Mode of attire is not standardized and tends to be informal. People customarily address each other on a first-name basis and tend to communicate through the informal and fluid grapevine which exists in every organization. The unwritten, but widely understood ground rule followed by members at all levels of the organization is that individuals treat each other with the mutual respect and informality of social peers. The supervisor's influence is not a manifestation of arbitrary direction and control but, rather, reflects his role as an adviser, consultant, and coordinator. The net effect of such a system enables people to relate to each other on a competence basis in the voluntary pursuit of common goals.

Status

Climates differ with regard to the amount and kind of status afforded through organizational membership. Status may be considered as official or unofficial.

Official status is established by the bestowal of a job title and responsibility with commensurate authority, job grade, salary, and privileges. Increased official status is an incentive for personal and professional growth for those who have the talent and desire to move up the organizational hierarchy. But not every person wants a promotion in the sense of a higher job grade or the position of supervisor or plant manager. However, most people cherish the prestige of being recognized as better craftsmen and valued members of their work groups.

Unofficial status is a function of a person's role in his work group, not only in achieving production goals, but also arising from such diverse factors as his skill with certain tools and equipment, his knowledge of a particular process or technology, his generosity, his valued membership in a group, his ability to make others laugh, his contagious enthusiasm, his role as a sympathetic listener, or his willingness to accept an unpleasant task. The advantage of unofficial status is that it contains room for all; respect for a machinist does not detract from respect for a secretary, or engineer, or assembler. Nor does respect for one assembler preclude respect for another; each earns respect on the basis of unique competence factors.

Unofficial status stemming from genuine excellence leads to less rivalry and more satisfaction than official status based on power or wealth. Official status is more vulnerable to the influence of political winds and happenstance, and is at the mercy of higher authority. Unofficial status is more intrinsic to the individual, is earned through personal achievements and attributes, and tends to go with him, granting him more lasting or permanent status. Further, the perpetuation of unofficial status is not dependent on authority-oriented status symbols. For the mature and accepted member of the work group, earned status (official or unofficial) is its own reward and needs no visible symbols. The flaunting of symbols, particularly the official reminders of inequality, is symptomatic of immaturity and serves only to undermine feelings of dignity and worth in persons who have lower official status—persons on whom those of higher official status depend for their continuing success.

Most people like to be proud of their group and to be valued for their role in it. Belongingness and pride of membership constitute an opportunity and an advantage for the organization with a favorable company or product image. Attractive grounds and buildings and prestigious products are often symbols of status in a community and a source of pride at all levels of the organization. The attitude of the individual to his or her work group offers the key to filling jobs that would otherwise have low status —the key to retaining people who do the less attractive work. More important than the status of the job is the self-image of the group for which the job is done. Physicians and nurses, for example, have to do things that would disgust unskilled workers who did not see these actions in their professional context; yet the prestige of people in medicine is generally high. Hence, the prestige of the physician's work group and his needed contributions to it make the unattractive tasks acceptable. However, prestige is not limited to highly esteemed professions. The janitors cited on pages 67 to 69 enhanced their own and their company status through creative and responsible behavior. If the solidarity of a person's group is high and he earns status by his membership in it, the unpleasant aspects of the work he has to do may be taken in stride.

Communication

The type and quality of communication within an organization are usually functions of the size and predominant managerial style of the organization. One consequence of the growth of an organization is the tendency to formalize communications. In the small organization, informal face-to-face communication usually finds natural expression, and managers who do not actively prevent it have the benefit of a well-informed work force. However, as the organization expands and ages, relationships become more formalized and communications begin to lag.

A typical bureaucratic response to communication breakdown is the creation of the AVO (avoid verbal orders) and other formalized reporting processes for committing communications to paper. Though seemingly a harmless beginning, traffic in interoffice memos expands exponentially. The memo writer routinely prepares copies for his and the recipient's supervisor, and "for good measure" to others whose responsibilities are at least remotely related. These memos and their copies evoke responses in a reciprocating and exponential volume, to earn for the organization the self-imposed title of "the paper mill." The formalized communication process tends to reinforce an authority-oriented chain of command, quashing the spontaneous interactive process natural to the small organization and necessary for the functioning of a goal-oriented cohesive work force.

Apart from reasons associated with the size and complexity of the organization, communications may lose efficiency because of their defensive application against reductive managerial styles. When the interpersonal trust factor is low, "official" memos are written to provide instruction, obtain compliance, request approval, justify actions, and report progress. Informal oral commitment is no longer adequate, and rejected or unheard viewpoints find expression in the form of "letters to the file" as protective against the vagaries of the future. The massive flow of protective paperwork becomes known as the "paper umbrella."

Concomitant with organizational growth, computer technology is expanded and management systems applications are increased. The flow of memos, forms, and computer printouts increases, jamming in-baskets, filling file cabinets, and gradually encumbering the administrative process. The conformity demanded by these formalized systems takes its toll on freedom of action, administrative flexibility, and constructive expression of talent. As informal communications continue to fail, formalized communications increase in volume, only to increase the likelihood of further breakdown.

Printed media seldom solve communication problems. No matter how formalized the organization, people rely on both formal and informal communication for job information. Attempts to "manage" information by publishing more communications tend to reduce the total percentage of information assimilated. In addition, the formalized management of information evokes reactive behavior and fosters the development of a cynical and hostile grapevine.

Stability

Organizational stability is a key climate factor, particularly when it relates to the employee's security needs. Stability has many ramifications; for many employees it is freedom from the vacillating ups and downs of business, knowledge that they will have a job as long as they do good work, or confidence that they will have advance knowledge of changes that may affect them. Ability to cope with instability is often a function of a person's role in the change. Unexpected or misunderstood changes may contribute to a climate of instability and feelings of insecurity; but the same changes, when evolved through understanding participation of those who will be affected by the change, can enhance feelings of security.

So vital is employment stability to the image of an organization, and job security to the self-esteem of its members, that an organization realizes a substantial return on investment by maintaining its equilibrium through business fluctuations. Corporate planners rarely plan strategies for maintaining a stable work force. Rather, they focus strategic planning efforts on research, production, and marketing; and when business setbacks occur they will, as a last-ditch effort, pare expense, capital, and labor budgets. In labor-intensive organizations, people are usually the chief buffer for absorbing the adverse impacts of business cycles.

The long-term costs of threatened job security in terms of unfavorable public relations and employee alienation are considerable, but the cost of developing preventive strategies is relatively minor. Strategies built around an imaginative combination of the processes listed in Figure 3-12 can often eliminate or at least ameliorate the impact of business reversals.

When business turndowns seem imminent, a moratorium can be declared on hiring to allow normal turnover, consolidated operations, and reassignment to begin a natural retrenchment process. Though turnover rates vary substantially from one organization to another and generally decrease during recessions, annual turnover generally averages 20 to 25 percent. In practice, a hiring moratorium will usually yield a 25 percent reduction in personnel in 1 year and 40 percent in 2 years.

Ideally, management should maintain an early detection system to forecast business trends. Thus production demands in face of uncertain forecasts may be satisfied through temporary and part-time help, through overtime, and through the subcontracting of temporary workloads. The cutback of temporary and part-time help and the reduction of overtime at least does not undermine the security of the permanent full-time members. It is important that temporary and part-time personnel be indoctrinated at the time of hire to understand the tenuous nature of their employment.

Advance warning to the work force will often yield an abnormal flow of separations as people seek new employment to escape the crunch. Present employees can also be involved in task force efforts to brainstorm

1. Suspended hiring	12. Budget revisions
2. Normal turnover	13. Vacation scheduling
3. Consolidated operations	14. Educational leave
4. Reassignments	15. Early retirement
5. Early detection system	16. Retraining
6. Temporary employment	17. Reclassifications
7. Temporary overtime	18. Reduced hours
8. Part-time employment	19. Loan-outs
9. Subcontracting	20. Outside placement
10. Advance warning	21. New business
11. Employee involvement	

FIG. 3-12   Maintaining a stable work force.

cost-reduction strategies pertaining to expense, capital, and personnel budgets. Temporary financial gain can sometimes be realized through revised bookkeeping, amortization, and taxation procedures.

Forewarned employees can also adapt to rescheduled vacations; a few may crystallize educational leave plans, and others may opt for early retirement. Personnel transferred to fill essential positions may require retraining and reclassification as necessary and appropriate. Though some reclassifications may be promotional, most will be lateral and, under severe conditions, some may be temporarily demotional.

If further personnel budget reductions become inevitable, in spite of the foregoing measures, reductions in hours across the board may be more widely accepted than layoffs for part of the permanent work force. The more advance warning and understanding of the causal economic factors, the better will be adaptations to the cutbacks.

Other last-ditch efforts implemented by some organizations include loans of surplus personnel across departments or to outside organizations. This measure is more feasible in an industry-restricted slump than in a general economic recession. Some organizations have given employees special training and job-hunting time off to bridge their transition to a new employer. One large Canadian tobacco company avoided retrenchment by diversifying into new product lines that would absorb the slack in the tobacco business caused by new competitors and reductions in tobacco consumption.

No one of these tactics alone will maintain stability and employee job security during severe business recessions. However, various combinations of them, creatively and aggressively employed, can do much to sustain a favorable company image in the eyes of its members and the community.

Though not all people may be retained on the payroll through business recessions, if they and others in the community feel they are being treated fairly and their chances for survival are justly related to their performance, they can experience dignity as members of a company with an image in the work force and community as a good place to work. Moreover, if retrenchment squeezes them off the payroll, they leave without hostility toward the company, and can rejoin the organization when business conditions improve without loss of pride.

4

Managing Innovation

All management is the management of innovation. People who are simply perpetuating the status quo, then, are not managers but, rather, are puppets or automatons and are replaceable by programmable machines.

Creativity is a form of spontaneity which finds productive expression in a climate of freedom. Hence an effective organization enables its members to assert themselves as individuals. However, uncoordinated self-expression is anarchy. Therefore, the effective organization provides a balance of opportunities and constraints that enables individuality to coalesce in the pursuit of common goals.

People who work for themselves understand the opportunities and constraints that their self-employed status affords. Creativity can flourish in such circumstances. Unfortunately, when self-employed people prosper and their organization requires the addition of hired help, the entrepreneurs usually fail to provide their employees with the same conditions which inspired them. The key, then, to organizational leadership is to provide a data base and reward systems that unite all members in support of a common cause.

Alfred P. Sloan, in his autobiography,[1] describes the application of innovation in research and engineering, manufacturing, corporate finance, marketing, and distribution that led to the emergence of General Motors as the largest corporation in America. However, the reader comes to realize that innovation in the growing giant had been restricted to the salaried exempt people in management and technology. In terms of sheer numbers, the two-thirds of the people classified as hourly, nonexempt workers had not been part of the innovative process. Sloan referred to the "labor problems" that plagued the company after World War II as though they were the imponderable and inescapable consequences of running a company. The only application of innovation directly affecting the workers was the attempt to automate production to eliminate the wage earners or to reduce their numbers. In fairness to Sloan, it should be noted that he

[1]Alfred P. Sloan, *My Years with General Motors* (edited by John McDonald with Catharine Stevens), Doubleday, Garden City, N.Y., 1964.

endowed the Sloan School of Management at the Massachusetts Institute of Technology, and in doing so was acknowledging the need for better insights into the management of human resources.

Sloan was not alone in his perception of innovation as the exclusive realm of the managerial class. Many of his contemporaries and successors never envisioned involving workers in industrial engineering, quality control, management by objectives, and other management processes. Wasteful as this oversight was in the post-World War II era, it is exponentially more counterproductive in today's entitlement culture. Today's enlightened workers accept and expect involvement as their just due, and respond counterproductively with wrath, indignation, frustration, and disengagement to constraints which inhibit their creativity.

Attempts to control the burgeoning audacity of workers and counteract their counterproductive behavior drew hopeful attention to job enrichment as the new formula for harnessing wayward talent. Though genuine job enrichment has much potential for evoking the expression of responsible talent, as noted in the preceding chapter, its application has often been guided by unflattering assumptions about the "ungrateful wretches" that caused it to be perceived and rejected as the manipulative ploy that it sometimes proved to be.

Attempts to motivate people through circumscribed systems such as piecework incentive often fosters rebellion and counterproductive creativity aimed at "beating the system." Thus a reward system based on a prescribed method usually discourages innovation, as improved methods may lead to what is perceived as "tighter standards" and abolishment of jobs.

Like Sloan, most people associate the management of innovation with managerial and professional employees. The hourly paid workers, who have traditionally been referred to as "hired hands," usually exercise their initiative and creativity only in unofficial and informal ways, often to the detriment of the organization. If constructive creativity is latent in all individuals, then the manual workers represent the greatest reservoir of untapped resources, as in most cultures they outnumber the salaried staff at least two to one.

WORK SIMPLIFICATION

In the 1930s, Allan H. Mogensen, in the role of industrial engineer, approached workers with a clipboard and stopwatch for the purpose of establishing approved methodology and a related reward system. He found workers to be creative at thwarting his attempts to prescribe more efficient methodology and, when not under surveillance, they would develop more productive methods that would enhance their rewards. He reasoned that this creativity could be harnessed in a way that would enable every employee to be his own industrial engineer. He developed a curriculum and methodology which are generally known as "Work Simplification."[2]

In practice, Work Simplification puts the management of change into the hands of job incumbents. Many employees who would like to improve job methods fail to do so simply because they lack the knowledge and analytical skills for formulating improvements. In other cases, where they can and do recommend improvements, they may be frustrated or discouraged by supervisory apathy or hostility. Union leaders sometimes oppose methods improvement if they perceive it as managerial manipulation. If an adversary relationship exists in the organization, the union may be philosophically oriented against any effort interpreted as pro-management. Work Simplification is a natural, un-self-conscious process for endowing job incumbents and their leaders with the skills and attitudes to facilitate self-initiated change.

Employees usually learn Work Simplification through standardized company programs implemented through the guidance of Mogensen or his disciples. Because Work Simplification, as a methods-improvement process, may be perceived as a threat to industrial engineers, many companies have sent them to Mogensen's public conferences. Thus not only is their responsibility for methods improvement intact, but it is also broadened to include the encouragement of methods improvement by others. Similarly, union leaders who might otherwise oppose the process are to be involved in its planning and implementation when the concept is being introduced into the organization.

Company training programs are usually taught in two-hour blocks for a total of approximately 20 to 30 hours. Course content includes principles and techniques of motion-and-time economy, flow-process charting, cost analysis, teamwork, and on-the-job projects for applying newly learned techniques. Projects may be undertaken as an individual or group process under the guidance of either a line or staff person.

[2]Work Simplification is being applied under a variety of titles, including "job management," "operation improvement," "work improvement," "deliberate methods change," "methods change program," "improvement program," and "team improvement program." Whatever the label, many companies, including Texas Instruments, Detroit Edison, IBM, Dow Chemical Company, Canadian Industries Limited, Procter & Gamble, and Goodyear Tire and Rubber Company, are applying the principles and techniques of Work Simplification in furthering the management of innovation. At the writing of this book, Work Simplification is in its fifth decade of application, still under the guiding influence of Allan Mogensen, age seventy-nine, who still flies his own airplane and conducts conferences on the management of improvement. The evolution, definition, and application of Work Simplification are described in Auren Uris's "Mogy's Work Simplification Is Working New Miracles," *Factory*, Sept. 1965, p. 112.

AN APPLICATION OF WORK SIMPLIFICATION

A creative amalgamation of behavioral theory and technique was developed by Irving Borwick[3] and his associates in Steinberg's Limited, a major food chain headquartered in Montreal. It uniquely offers "management development" to rank-and-file employees to give substance to the concept "every employee a manager." It is probably one of the best examples of the development of wage earners so that they can assume managerial responsibility for the jobs they are now doing.

Borwick's "team improvement laboratory" (TIL), described in the following pages, is based upon principles of Work Simplification of Allan Mogensen and incorporates concepts from Blake and Mouton's "grid" program. Though subsequent applications in more than 100 stores have differed experimentally from the model described here and are implemented under different program names, the same basic principles and techniques are applied.

A typical TIL would involve about twenty persons, including the store manager, department managers, cashiers, and clerks.

Group activity is carefully scheduled for lectures and workshops:

1.   To provide an opportunity for people to make use of their capabilities and their creative and imaginative skills, in improving the work they are doing.

2.   To enrich the jobs of these employees and to give them managerial control over their areas of responsibility.

3.   To unleash the ideas and know-how of employees to bring about useful improvements in the work situation.

4.   To bring about cost savings through improvements made on the job by individual employees.

5.   To create an atmosphere conducive to open communication and mutual trust among people at various levels of the organization.

6.   To create an atmosphere and frame of mind which challenges present methods of operation and is conducive to constant change for improvement.

7.   To create project teams which provide the optimum opportunity for employees to participate in and work together on planning, controlling, doing, critiquing, and improving their work.

Following the objectives, group members are assigned the task of reaching agreement on the forty-nine questions, which they completed

[3]Irving Borwick, "Team Improvement Laboratory," *Personnel Journal*, Jan. 1969, pp. 18–24.

individually as prework, concerning the concepts of the managerial grid. An hour is allocated.

Teams adjourn to the team room to complete this task. They return to the conference room following this session and score their results.

This session is followed by a 45-minute lecture which introduces the assumptions on which Work Simplification and the TIL are based:

Assumptions

1. People do not resist change; they resist being changed.

2. Every job is capable of being improved.

3. Every employee has the basic ability to improve his job.

4. People like to improve their work, and get satisfaction from their work.

5. People like to participate in groups.

6. Improvements are best made by those who perform the job.

7. Employees should be provided with the basic skills for job improvement through an educational program.

8. The role of the supervisor is one of adviser, consultant, and coordinator.

9. The role of the employee is manager of his own area of responsibility.

Acceptance of these assumptions is the foundation for assuming managerial responsibility in their job. The first assumption, "People don't resist change; they resist being changed," emphasizes the objective of constantly changing the system rather than the person. Too often criticism of an operation is directed at, or is perceived as being directed at, the person who does the job rather than at the job itself. It is important to disassociate the two and objectify the analysis of the job. This prevents defensive behavior on the part of the operator, who is no longer the butt of adverse criticism and can willingly participate in altering the job and introducing change.

This last point is fundamental. Changes introduced by an individual not responsible for performance of the job are not likely to gain the same commitment as changes generated through employee involvement. Involvement is not a facade to suggest the illusion of reality but participation in the real sense of the word.

In the light of an understanding of assumption 1, assumption 6 becomes a corollary, "Improvements are best made by those who perform the job." Besides increasing the prospects of a committed and motivated person, such an assumption rests on the principle that he who does the job knows it best. This is not true in all cases, but it appears to be true more times than not. The person who performs a task usually has knowledge in depth not readily available to a supervisor or an outsider. With his technical proficiency and knowledge, he is the man most suited to change the job.

This assumption is tied into two other concepts, "Every job is capable of being improved" and "Every employee has the basic ability to improve his job." The latter is another case where the exceptions to the rule are minimal to such a degree as to be practically nonexistent. Any employee capable of performing a task has the capability to improve that job. The exceptions are likely to be jobs in which retarded individuals perform menial tasks under supervision. These exceptions are rare and do not invalidate the principle. On the other hand, the assumption leads one to the realization that there is a reservoir of untapped intellectual power. This tremendous reserve of people who perform rote tasks and whose energies and abilities are hardly utilized can effect a total revolution in the manner in which business is conducted.

It is important to stress this capability. Many employees, blinded to their own abilities by years of conformity to outmoded managerial practices, and blinded because of the authoritarian nature of their primary education, have lost faith in their capacity to alter the world in which they live. Allusions in the lectures and sessions to the work of Argyris, Blake, Herzberg, Likert, McGregor, Mogensen, Moore, and Myers reinforce the scientific underpinning on which such assumptions are made and give additional confidence to those small sparks of individuality that are thought to be alive in everyone, no matter how limited his or her experience.

To illustrate that every job is capable of being improved, reference is made to work experience with which the group is familiar. A classic example frequently quoted is the experience of Procter & Gamble with pallets.

Procter & Gamble used regular wooden pallets to handle its products. While there was no problem in the efficiency or capability of such pallets, there was a cost factor involved. Procter & Gamble developed the paper pallet to replace the wooden pallet and reduced operational costs while maintaining efficiency. Efficiency was improved further when the "palletless pallet" was developed, a redesigned fork truck with two broad parallel plates which lifted a load by applying pressure from the sides. This eliminated the use of pallets for approximately 90 percent of Procter & Gamble products.

This type of case history illustrates three principles in work improvement:

1. Every job is capable of being improved.

2. You do not select problem areas for improvement. It is even preferable to select jobs which are functioning well. There is no such thing as perfection.

3. The ultimate goal in improving a job is to eliminate the task altogether.

Illustrations of this type, usually selected for their relevance to the areas in which employees work, demonstrate the validity of the concept that every job is capable of being improved.

The assumption that people like to improve their work and get satisfaction from it is supported by reference to McGregor's theory X and theory Y, Herzberg's hygiene and motivation studies, and Myers' plan-do-control concept.

In the same lecture, participants are introduced to Mogensen's "five-step pattern" for problem solving:

The Five-Step Pattern

1. Select a job to improve.
2. Get all the facts.
3. Challenge every detail.
4. Develop the preferred method.
5. Install it; check results.

In conjunction with the five-step pattern, participants are also taught the rudiments of flow-process charting. This technique is an aid for analyzing their present jobs in the effort to improve what they are now doing. The teams are given a task to perform in which they apply the five-step pattern. In the case of the flow-process chart, once they have learned the rudiments of analysis, they immediately set to work using the five-step pattern and the charting technique to tackle their projects.

Teaching techniques place emphasis on team participation and direct involvement by participants. Every effort is made to avoid "telling" the student, and emphasis is placed upon students' discovering ideas for themselves. The four lectures occupy only 2 of the 38 hours normally spent in the TIL.

The teaching sequence is:

1. Assign prereading and exercises for completion before the sessions begin.

2. Task assignment is based on prework, completed first by individual and then by team.

3. Scoring of results, where appropriate, or a verbal exchange of results by a representative of each team.

4. Critique by the team of the results and their methodology in achieving these results.

The function of the laboratory leader is to coordinate these activities, act as a resource for problem situations, and deliver the four lectures. Most of the learning is done without the leader's intervention.

Films are also used during the laboratory to introduce new information not covered in the prereading and are the object of further task assignments. In this laboratory, three films are used to teach management styles, the flow-process chart, and one approach to team job improvement.

The four lectures are interspersed with laboratory experience in the following sequence:

1. Assumptions and the five-step pattern (Mogensen)
2. Managerial styles (Blake and Mouton)
3. Every employee a manager (Myers)
4. How to manage improvement (Moore)

At the end of the program, the employees, working in teams, establish an improvement program to be implemented upon their return to the work situation. The teams determine objectives, design a strategy for achieving the objectives, and then implement the tactics that will accomplish the goal.

It is made clear to employees during the lecture on change that the task of developing a program for change is a team effort and is clearly related to their new roles as managers. Through examination of the managerial functions already outlined in the lecture "Every Employee a Manager," correlation is made between the management functions (planning, doing, and controlling) and the development of a regular program of planned improvement on a systematic basis. Figure 4-1 illustrates the scope of the management functions for an enriched clerk-packer job in the supermarket.

Change should not occur as the effect of random events upon current practice, but rather as the effect of planned efforts by managers in control of their own areas of responsibility. To implement this concept, teams are asked to define operations they would like to improve in their respective work areas. This task follows immediately after they have undergone training in flow-process charting as a technique for analysis. Armed with their new knowledge of managerial responsibility, team activity, problem solving, and analysis, project teams begin a determined assault on their projects. Teams spend approximately 8 hours working on projects.

There are a number of reasons for devoting so much time to these projects. In the first place, sufficient time must be allocated for analysis and improvement. Second, the aim of the TIL is to develop every employee as a manager. It is not sufficient to "tell" employees how to manage. If they are ever to be managers, they must begin to assume managerial responsibility.

TIL graduates assume managerial responsibility for assigned areas immediately upon completion of the program. Eventually, individuals and/or teams will be responsible for scheduling, budgeting, controlling,

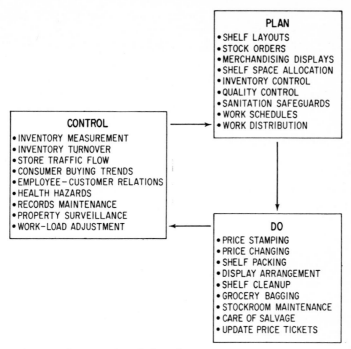

FIG. 4-1 Supermarket clerk-packer.

ordering, critiquing, and improving their own areas. They will also be provided with sales objectives, margins, product turns, and costs. The initial program has envisaged a slow development of these responsibilities based upon a growing demand by trained employees for greater managerial responsibility. Moreover, employees get additional skill training on the job and off, in order to increase their efficiency and productivity and also in order that they may assume greater responsibility.

The final session is designed to allow the employees and their senior supervisor, the store manager, to meet together and work out the details of implementing the TIL in their stores. The store manager, who has been a participant until now, becomes the discussion leader. Employees know that this program is not a one-shot affair, that following conclusion of the laboratory, they will continue to meet once a week in the same teams in their respective work areas.

Store personnel have been provided with a model of how the program should work, but every model must be altered to suit the individual circumstances of the store. The details of future meeting logistics are agreed upon before personnel return to the work situation. Together, the entire staff, including department heads, manager, and all employees, work out how the program will operate, when they will meet, and how projects will be implemented on an ongoing basis.

People who have gone through the TIL program are excited and actively participating. Employees not yet involved in the program are actively interested and excited at the possibilities of the program. When a TIL meeting was canceled because it conflicted with a union membership meeting, employees got the union to call and confirm that the meeting would be rescheduled.

Jobs have been enriched, new ideas have been unleashed, and a greater openness of communication has come about. More and more the employees are influencing the management of the operation. Improvements generated through the program include a productivity increase of more than $10 in sales per man-hour. Though other improvements are realized, it is difficult to measure improvements directly attributable to TIL efforts. For example, though observations have indicated that courtesy and concern for the customer and rise in sales were both above normal, it may be premature to assume that the results will be lasting. However, in terms of the intervening variables of improving attitudes, educating employees, developing managerial skills, and introducing the management of change, the program is already successful.

The Team Improvement Laboratory in Steinberg's Limited illustrates how Work Simplification, broadly applied in all functions and at all levels of the organization, makes "every employee a manager" in terms of the plan-do-control concept described in Chapter 3 and meets the criteria of an effective system listed in Chapter 2. It is a medium for giving people a psychological and financial stake in the organization, particularly when monetary gains are shared through processes such as profit sharing, Scanlon-type plans, and Employee Stock Ownership Plans. But most important, Work Simplification is a medium for facilitating the professional growth of people whose initiative might otherwise be quashed and opportunities limited by traditional supervisory practice, union constaints, and bureaucratic systems.

NATURAL WORK GROUPS

Natural work groups are the primary work systems through which creativity can find expression. Moreover, a natural work group, because of its established relationship to other parts of the organization, channels creativity toward the attainment of organizational goals. A department manager of 3300 people in Texas Instruments instituted a departmentwide Work Simplification program by providing trainer training for his ninety supervisors, each of whom then conducted his own Work Simplification courses for the people under his supervision.

A natural work group generally consists of a group of peers who work together with their common leader. Such groups might range in size from two to fifty members, but more commonly would have six to twelve members. Natural work groups can exist at all levels and functions of any type of organization, including, for example, the president and his vice presidents, a superintendent and his foremen, a foreman and his production operators, a laboratory head and the members of his technical staff, an office manager and his clerical staff, an infantry lieutenant and the members of his platoon, a school principal and his teaching staff, a union president and his shop stewards, a telephone crew chief and the members of his repair crew, and a maintenance supervisor and the janitorial group reporting to him.

The natural work group is potentially a ready-made task force for solving problems and setting goals. The descriptors of an effective team on pages 48 to 54 can serve as guidelines for preparing a group to function as a team.

A supervisor usually activates the problem-solving, goal-setting process by convening his or her natural work group for the purpose of dealing with specific job-related problems pertaining to quantity, quality, costs, schedules, or any other situation related to customer or client satisfaction. An actual problem need not exist to call such a meeting; the group may be convened for the purpose of improving upon a smoothly functioning process. Any process can be improved, and sometimes the anticipatory efforts of the group to reduce costs and improve quality can forestall the encroachment of competitors.

During the first meeting the supervisor should attempt to share his managerial perspective with the members of the group. People can think and act like managers only to the extent that they see the problem in the same perspective that the people above them see it. Hence, regardless of the organization's charter—be it free enterprise or public sector—the members are made to understand that they are convening to devise better ways of serving their customers or clients, and are ultimately accountable to shareholders or taxpayers. In addition, the supervisor redefines the constraints within which they are to pursue the solutions to the problem. Constraints could include, for example, budget limitations, delivery schedules, quality standards, legal restrictions, pricing targets, downtime limits, competitor performance, technical requirements, or any combination of these. All goal-setting is done within constraints, and people can be expected to set realistic goals only when they understand these constraints. Constraints cannot always be defined in advance of the problem-solving efforts, but may be introduced during the idea-evaluation stage before goal setting is completed.

Problem-solving–goal-setting meetings are held during regular working hours, when possible, but before or after the work shift (with pay) when necessary. The supervisor begins the meeting by candidly stating the problem, providing detailed information when possible in terms of history of the project (product or service), duration, delivery schedules, overhead costs, material costs, labor costs, and any of the above constraints which are relevant, so that all members of his natural work group have a full understanding of the requirements for reaching a profit-making or cost-effective level of attainment. Applying principles and techniques of transactional analysis and conference leadership, he encourages them to raise questions and discuss the problems informally. When he feels they have a good understanding of the problem, he is ready to ask for their suggestions.

Using a flip chart and brainstorming approach, the supervisor records all ideas suggested by the group, with ground rules prohibiting criticism, ridicule, and premature evaluation of the merit of any idea. When further ideas are no longer forthcoming, or when time limits are reached, the supervisor begins the evaluation phase.

In reviewing the items, the supervisor avoids statements which evoke defensiveness, such as "Let's go over the items and throw out the half-baked ones," or "Let's review and rank-order the ideas." Far better, he might say, "Let's review the items and not discard any of them, but pick out a few we can all agree with." Such a review and discussion will usually yield only a few recommendations (perhaps less than 10 percent of the items on the total list) which the members of the group at that time consider feasible and worthwhile.

Sometimes the most effective role of the supervisor at this stage is to encourage this creative process by absenting himself from the room, saying to them something to the effect, "See what you can come up with, and I'll be back in 40 minutes."

It should be noted, at this point, that asking the group to set a goal is a very essential part of this problem-solving–goal-setting process, because unless they can relate their performance to an acceptable goal, they will have no basis for evaluating their achievements. Figure 2-7 shows accomplishments of a twelve-person team through a series of problem-solving–goal-setting meetings. Their concerted efforts reduced the work-hours per unit from 138 to 41 in the year portrayed; in the following year, the rate was 32 man-hours per unit.

A problem-solving–goal-setting meeting usually starts with a natural work group but expands to include others who are not members of the natural work group, whose roles as engineers, inspectors, technicians, buyers, and other staff support personnel can influence the achievement of the mission. These additional resource people are not usually under the organizational jurisdiction of the supervisor who conducts the problem-solving–goal-setting session. In some cases, they are not even members of the organization. The criteria for including a person in the session are his or her stake in the outcome and ability to contribute to the creative process. Thus, a food chain in Canada included supermarket customers, an electronics manufacturing company included vendors, a government service group included welfare recipients, and educators in secondary schools included parents as well as students in their problem-solving–goal-setting sessions.

Outsiders to the natural work groups are not usually invited into the problem-solving–goal-setting session until the members of the natural work group are comfortable in their conference room role and until they begin to discover their own limitations. If they, themselves, see the need for and recommend the inclusion of an industrial engineer, inspector, or customer, these persons can be added without usurping and threatening the basic charter of the group. It is important that these outsiders not be perceived or allowed to act as authority figures in dominating the meeting; but, rather, as "guests" or "resources."

GUIDELINES FOR PROBLEM-SOLVING– GOAL-SETTING SESSIONS

A natural work group at its best is an effective team for achieving organizational goals. As such, it functions in accordance with the principles described on pages 48 to 54. As leader of the natural work group, the supervisor plays a key role in expediting the productivity of the group. The summarized guidelines below are provided as a supervisory guide for maximizing work team effectiveness.

1. *Size of group.* Ideally, a problem-solving group in its initial stages does not exceed twelve persons. Groups as small as two or three can be effective, but do not offer the diversity of viewpoints provided by larger groups. A supervisor with a natural work group of more than twelve members may wish to subdivide it into two or more problem-solving groups to make it possible for all to participate. Though beginning groups ideally should not exceed twelve, as members become comfortable and skillful with the group process, additional members may be added.

2. *Composition of the group.* All members of a natural work group should participate even though it may be necessary to subdivide the group to make this possible. As members of a natural work group gradually discover their limitations, resource people from other functions (engineering, quality control, vendors, customers, taxpayers, etc.) may gradually be phased into the work group meetings. Resource people should be introduced in a style which will not undermine the proprietary responsibility of the natural work group.

3. *When to hold sessions.* To the extent possible, problem-solving–goal-setting sessions are held during regular work hours and on company time. When work demands do not permit this, meetings are held on a paid overtime basis on a schedule established through advance consultation with members of the group. On-the-job meetings of this type enable people to develop a new self-image—to accept intellectual as well as manual skills as a normal part of their organizational responsibility.

4. *Starting the meeting.* The supervisor starts the meeting with an open, candid, and friendly introduction. He presents a customer requirement or organizational problem to the group and asks for their assistance in solving the problem. The novice conference leader may trap himself in a counter-productive gripe session by telling the group that this is a problem-solving session and asking them to enumerate their problems. Though the group may be productive in enumerating gripes, and the meeting may have a cathartic effect, the focus is usually on parking lots, eating facilities, air conditioning, coatracks, coffee breaks, and other maintenance problems. Their preoccupation with these dissatisfactions makes it difficult for them to focus on their purpose for being there; namely, getting a superior product or service to their customers on a cost-effective basis.

5. *Defining constraints.* All goal setting is done within constraints, and it is important that the supervisor be prepared to enumerate those applying to the group's situation. Constraints may be in the form of time limits, budgets, technology, laws, customer commitments, union agreements, company policy, skill limitations, etc. Though not all constraints can be identified in advance, the rejection of ideas is far more acceptable when it results from unchangeable constraints than when it results from the arbitrary use of authority. For instance, a recommendation for the purchase of new equipment can be evaluated by the group through a process of sharing the amortization procedure with them.

6. *Need for a goal.* The creative problem identification or brainstorming process leads to the compilation of a long list of suggestions and associated ideas. This list has little value until it is translated into one or more goals. When the list is reduced to two or three ideas judged to be workable by all concerned, the supervisor asks the group to estimate, in quantitative terms, the goals they expect to achieve from these changes, and a target date for accomplishing them. Goals are to be expressed in tangible terms such as cost reductions in dollars and cents, percentage of profit improvement, product yield in percentage points, quality standards in terms important to the customer, number of customer complaints per unit of sales, delivery schedules in terms of percent shipments on time, sales efforts in terms of net sales, or share of the available market. Sometimes goal setting is less inhibited if the supervisor absents himself from the room during the creative process.

7. *Importance of feedback.* Goals acquire their meaning through feedback. Goals expressed in tangible terms, as illustrated earlier, hold goal setters' attention only to the extent that they receive timely feedback on progress toward the goal. Traditional inspection functions sometimes fail to satisfy this requirement by delaying or distorting the feedback. People in some situations can satisfy their feedback requirements by doing their own inspection, or at least by having instant access to quality control reports.

8. *Techniques of questioning.* The appropriate use of questions serves as a stimulant to group participation. Group leaders are aided by their ability to use four types of questions: (a) overhead, (b) directed, (c) reverse, and (d) relay. The overhead question is directed to the total group, "Does anyone have a suggestion?" The directed question is addressed to a specific person, "What do you think, John?" The reverse question is returned to the questioner, "Before I try to answer your question, Bill, have you thought of a possible solution?" The relay question redirects a query to another person: "James, how would you answer Mary's question?" The experienced conference leader also finds the use of silence to be an effective pump primer. Thus, a supervisor who asks an overhead question should be prepared to wait for up to 2 minutes before interrupting the silence. In practice, such a long wait is not necessary, as few people can tolerate the ambiguity of more than 30 seconds of silence.

9. *The meeting climate.* The principles of transactional analysis, as described in pages 39 to 43 are useful for establishing a climate conducive to constructive spontaneity. Positive strokes nurture freedom of expression, while negative strokes inhibit creativity. Adult-Adult, with a sprinkling of Child-Child, transactions foster mutual respect, spontaneity, and solidarity, while Parent-Child transactions breed not-OK feelings, conformity, hostility, and dependency relationships. The supervisor does not reject an idea through the Parent-Child exercise of official authority; rather, he involves the group in evaluating an idea in terms of specific criteria so that if an idea must be rejected it is done on the basis of Adult-Adult consensus. The climate of the meeting is further enhanced by establishing group rules against ridicule or premature evaluation of suggestions. The supervisor who is sensitive to his potential Parent posture as conference leader might democratize the process by bringing additional flip charts into the conference room and asking for volunteers to help in the idea-recording process. Authentic first-name informality is, of course, supportive of a climate of friendliness and mutual respect.

10. *Job security.* Cost-reduction efforts often lead to savings in personnel costs. However, one of the quickest ways to kill creativity on the job is to lay off people made surplus by their own creativity. Therefore, it is important that people understand that they are assured of an equivalent or better job if displaced from their present assignment. For example, Donnelly Mirrors in Holland, Michigan, guarantees employees they will not lose their jobs because of procedure changes.[4] If sustained job continuity cannot be assured because of factors unrelated to the creative process, such as a market slump or contract cancellation, it is important that those affected not associate the cutback with the creative process. In some instances, group creativity can be brought to bear on anticipating and minimizing the impact of economic retrenchment.

ATTITUDE SURVEYS

Attitude surveys are feedback mechanisms traditionally used by management to take the pulse of the organization as a basis for corrective action. The development of corrective action programs requires creativity on the part of the planners. Hence attitude surveys represent another medium for managing innovation.

However, it was noted earlier that change can be threatening, particularly if the people affected by it do not understand it or if they read into it some ulterior motive. Thus attitude surveys, as traditionally administered, may have a deleterious effect on the attitudes of the very people whose attitudes are being measured. If so, such surveys actually quash creativity or evoke a counterproductive expression of it.

Methods improvement, as traditionally masterminded by industrial engineers, can be converted to a medium for managing innovation through the principles of Work Simplification. Just so, an attitude survey can also become a medium for involving a broad cross section of the work force in the creative process.

The attitude survey offers four opportunities to tap the creative potential of the work force: (1) the design of the survey instruments, (2) the completion of the survey form, (3) the analysis of survey results, and (4) the development of remedial action programs. The most benign of these is the second, the completion of the survey form; yet it is the only opportunity for involvement offered by the attitude survey in most organizations.

Applications of the attitude survey in union and nonunion situations are identical in that both cases involve task forces from all levels and functions of the organization. However, members of a nonunion organization relate their efforts to a common cause under a common charter, whereas members of the unionized work force pursue the same common cause within constraints which protect the realms of mutual independence between company and union.

Step 1: Designing the survey instrument   The subject of the sur-

[4]John F. Donnelly, "Participative Management at Work," *Harvard Business Review,* Jan.–Feb. 1977.

vey is best introduced to the members of the organization through a face-to-face group process such as a department meeting. A department head in an engineering company of 1300 employees introduced the subject by saying, "We believe our organization is a good one, but that it can be improved. The best way to improve an organization is through the help of all its members. As a starter, we'd like to find out what's right and what's wrong with our company. We need to design a survey questionnaire to get the opinions of everyone in the organization. Would each of you now spend about 10 or 15 minutes, working alone or in small groups, in listing topics that you'd like to see covered by such a survey?"

Because of the "maintenance" orientation of most work forces, people tend to write topics primarily related to maintenance factors such as parking lots, eating facilities, air conditioning, supervision, and coffee breaks. To obtain a better balance of questions in the engineering company, the eight department heads duplicated the diagram shown in Figure 1-2 so that each of the 1300 members of the company could receive a copy. The eight department heads each explained the rationale of the maintenance and motivation needs and asked employees to attempt to write topics related to each of the six maintenance and the four motivation categories.

More than 2000 suggestions were collected from the eight departments. These were given to the personnel department where they were collated, combined, condensed, and refined into approximately 200 topics. These were then written into survey format to facilitate rapid response and machine scoring, for example:

	Agree	?	Disagree
The hours of work here are OK.	( )	( )	( )
Favoritism is a problem in my area	( )	( )	( )

These 200 questions were printed in 1300 copies and distributed to all employees at the next department meeting. It was explained to the employees that this form was preliminary—that it represented an attempt by the personnel department to reduce more than 2000 items to a more manageable number. They were asked to review it for important omissions and to write these into the blank spaces provided. They were instructed not to complete the questionnaire but, in the interest of shortening the questionnaire, to select the 100 items they considered most important.

These preliminary forms were collected and subjected to an item analysis by the personnel department. The frequency count of most important items was a basis for reducing the form to 150 questions. This analysis was the basis for printing the final form for administration to the total work force.

Step 2: Completion of the survey form At the next department meeting, the final forms were distributed to all employees, who were asked to complete them at that time. They were asked to keep the questionnaire anonymous and to drop the completed form in a slotted box provided for the occasion. Administration instructions specified that participation was voluntary and that any person not wishing to complete the form could simply drop the blank form in the box upon leaving, with the assurance that nonrespondents would also be anonymous. Time to complete the questionnaire ranged from 15 to 25 minutes.

Completed forms were forwarded to data processing for keypunching. Keypunch operators were instructed to obliterate signatures or any unsolicited identifying information, on the assumption that departure from complete anonymity could ultimately inhibit candor and undermine survey validity.

In some organizations, neutral outsiders (college professors, or consultants) are chosen to administer the survey, on the assumption that their neutrality will promote greater candor. While this may be true for the initial administration, the experience of participating in an anonymous company-administered survey will do much to establish a climate of trust.

Step 3: Analysis of survey results Survey results are printed in profile form by attitude category and individual item as shown in Figure 4-2. Separate profiles are shown for the company and for each department. The department profile for the previous annual survey is shown in broken line. Each department head receives a complete set for his department and the company, in the form of transparencies suitable for projection. Department heads report the results to all employees during department meetings, candidly projecting the profiles on a screen, inviting questions and comments. Comparisons are made between departmental and total organization profiles, and when surveys are administered periodically, time trends may be identified and traced. Though the candid feedback of survey results to all members of the department is in itself an educational process, it is only a foundation for the more action-oriented diagnostic process which follows.

Task forces are organized in each department to analyze survey results and formulate remedial actions. Task forces may be nominated by peers, selected by lottery, or simply chosen through supervisory (and union leader) judgment. One of the guiding constraints in selecting task forces is the capability of the department to maintain uninterrupted productivity

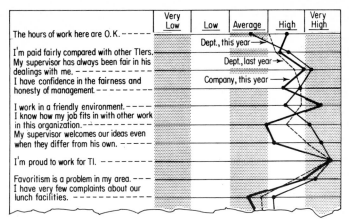

	Very Low	Low	Average	High	Very High
The hours of work here are O.K. – – – –					
		Dept., this year →			
I'm paid fairly compared with other Tlers.					
My supervisor has always been fair in his dealings with me. – – – – – – – – – –		Dept., last year →			
I have confidence in the fairness and honesty of management. – – – – – – – –		Company, this year →			
I work in a friendly environment. – – – –					
I know how my job fits in with other work in this organization. – – – – – – – – – –					
My supervisor welcomes our ideas even when they differ from his own. – – – – –					
I'm proud to work for TI. – – – – – – – –					
Favoritism is a problem in my area. – –					
I have very few complaints about our lunch facilities. – – – – – – – – – – –					

FIG. 4-2 Attitude survey profile.

while providing opportunities for the task forces to function. Task forces vary in size from two to twelve members, but five or six is usual.

Task forces are given a four-point mission:

1. To study survey results and identify what they believe to be problems or obstacles to organizational effectiveness

2. To determine the causes of these problems

3. To prescribe actions for dealing with these problems

4. To identify any pluses in the survey which show the organization to good advantage, and to explain why these favorable conditions exist

In dealing with the third point, task forces are asked to put themselves in their department head's shoes by asking themselves, "What specifically would I as department head do to resolve these problems within the constraints imposed by budgets, laws, schedules, market conditions, quality standards, prices and manpower availability?" The fourth point is included to put the total process in perspective. When the focus is placed exclusively on identifying and dealing with obstacles and problems, task forces tend to develop and present a negatively distorted impression of the organization. Thus, point 4 tends to provide a more balanced perspective as well as to identify positive features in the organization to be reinforced and perpetuated.

Task forces are given free access to any information desired, and are encouraged to consult their peers in carrying out their task-force assignments. Because group activities of this type are easily sidetracked and prolonged, the task-force mission is specifically limited to the four points enumerated above and is restricted to a prescribed time frame of 2 to 4 weeks. In a unionized organization, it may be desirable to sidestep collective bargaining issues.

In most organizations it cannot be assumed that task-force members are already skilled in participative methods. When task forces are formed, they are asked to designate a member of the group to serve as coordinator for scheduling and chairing meetings and for preparing the written report. Logistics usually do not permit the training of all task-force members in group processes; however, it is usually feasible to give special instructions to group coordinators. A half-day orientation session on conference leadership techniques, transactional analysis, decision making, and the functioning of an effective task force, as detailed in Chapter 2, usually yields a high return on investment. The use of the Group Feedback Form (Figure 2-3) enables task-force members to assess and improve upon their own group effectiveness during their assignment.

Attitude survey task forces, as described above, vary considerably in terms of number and duration of meetings required to complete their assignments. An average of five 2-hour meetings over a 3-week period is normal. The final report may be handwritten but is usually typed by a member of the task force or through typing services arranged by the department head. A report is typically eight to ten typewritten pages, but may be as long as twenty-five or as short as two pages. The quality of the final report is usually a reflection of the task force's proprietary interest in the project, and in most cases, such reports received by the department head are meticulously prepared.

Step 4: Development of action programs Upon receiving the completed report from the task force, the department head shares it with other managers in his department. In some organizations, the managerial group will suggest a tentative action plan to be reviewed and discussed with the task force. In other cases, managers and task-force members participate in joint working sessions to develop action plans. The latter approach is less likely to create or perpetuate adversary polarizations, particularly when mutually understood constraints, rather than official authority, are the basis for goal setting.

When a course of action is agreed upon, the department head shares the action plan with the balance of the work force at a department meeting. Though department meetings are typically chaired by the department head, more candid and spontaneous discussion may result if task-force coordinators make the presentation and lead the discussion. This is particularly true if coordinators include nonexempt personnel. Feedback to the total department is in terms of:

1. Results of the attitude surveys

2. Remedial actions already implemented or to be undertaken immediately

3. Actions which are to be deferred to some specific date

4. Recommendations which could not be acted on, and the reasons why not

The department meeting feedback report is ideally accomplished within 6 weeks of the administration of the questionnaire.

The engineering company mentioned earlier carried the action program planning process to the top management of the company. The president scheduled twenty-five 1-hour meetings in the boardroom to provide a 1-hour review and planning session with each of the twenty-five task forces. The president and vice presidents hosted each task force with its department head in reviewing survey results and remedial action programs. In preparation for this meeting, the task forces were asked to assess each proposed change in terms of anticipated constraints, with particular emphasis on cost of implementation and return on investment.

Emphasis in this top management review is to be given to actions which can be undertaken at the department level, and to avoid preoccupation with benefit programs and other maintenance conditions to be administered by top management. Maintenance factors cannot be ignored, of course, but if the survey process is to realize its potential as a vehicle for harnessing the creative and constructive talent of the work force, the responsible involvement of the workers in the implementation process is necessary.

In looking at the attitude survey in its total perspective, it is apparent that the survey results are not nearly as important as the process for developing and administering the survey system. Upon completion of the type of survey described herein, every member of the organization understands what an attitude survey is; how it is formulated, refined, and administered; and how these results are translated into action programs for improving the organization. In other words, the survey is a medium for getting all members of the organization on the same data base, so that all can think and act like managers. Companies that bypass their members in the development, refinement, administration, and interpretation of surveys and in the application of resultant action programs probably realize less than 10 percent of the creative potential of the attitude survey system.

In summary, the attitude survey procedure, as described above, is more than just a tool for identifying problems that need resolving or for "taking the pulse" of the organization. More important, it is a system that unites people from throughout the organization in a democratic process of problem identification and resolution. Members involved in such a process acquire a new perspective in conflict resolution not oriented around the management-labor dichotomy nor through the use of official management or union authority. Rather, the information sharing and the working through to consensus is but an extension of Mogensen's Work Simplification principles, discussed earlier in the chapter.

INSTITUTIONALIZING INNOVATION

Innovation in an organization is more than a technique or a program: It is a way of life that permeates the culture of a work place. The foregoing discussions of Work Simplification and attitude surveys are examples of vehicles or media through which creativity finds expression. Effective as they are, these programs alone cannot be expected to foster full-blown creativity throughout an organization.

Moreover, innovation is a phenomenon that cannot be engineered mechanically and created by edict. By definition, creativity is spontaneous and fragile. It thrives best in a climate of informality, open communications, trust, mutual respect, challenge, and high expectations. Unfortunately, the innovation which led to the successful growth of giant organizations was often ultimately quashed by the size and bureaucracy of the organization it fostered. Hence, the secret to preserving creativity in the giant organization is to manage it in a style that gives it the responsiveness and agility of a small young organization.

Texas Instruments has been cited as an organization that has not permitted aging and growth to undermine its viability.[5] Having achieved a size of $2.5 billion in sales and 70,000 employees, TI continues to evolve systems for stimulating and managing innovation. Moreover, it plans for no near-term plateau, but for continuing annual growth and increases in productivity of 15 percent, while improving wages and benefits by 9 percent and reducing product prices by better than 6 percent per year. TI's goal of $10 billion in sales, expected to materialize in the 1980s, is not necessarily a terminal goal. But even if company growth were to plateau at that size, it would not reduce the importance of innovation as a self-renewal process. Innovation is the lifeblood of the company, and the key to TI's success has been its network of systems to stimulate and manage innovation.

The backbone or touchstone of TI systems for managing innovation is the OST system—Objectives, Strategies and Tactical Action Programs. OST constitutes a systematically interrelated hierarchy of goals. Objectives

---

[5] "Texas Instruments shows United States business how to survive in the 1980s" (Special Report), *Business Week,* McGraw-Hill, New York, Sept. 18, 1978, pp. 66–76.

are formal statements of 10-year goals for a dozen business areas such as materials, exploration, electronic components, consumer products, or for intracompany staff functions such as personnel, facilities, and marketing. Objectives are typically pursued through about sixty supporting "strategies" which, in turn, are implemented through approximately 250 detailed 12- to 18-month "tactical action programs" (TAPs). TAPs are implemented ultimately through the goal-oriented systems at the lower levels of the organization; and of course, lower-level involvement provides a basis for TAPS development. Strategies and TAPs are the basis for managing innovation in the various create-make-market and staff support groups. This OST pyramid is overlaid across TI's operating hierarchy of thirty-some divisions (annual sales of $50 million to $150 million each) and more than 80 product-customer centers ($10 million to $100 million each). These are often self-sufficient in that many of them have their own engineering, manufacturing, and marketing units. Each product-customer center defines its long-range mission through formal strategies and, with the participation of lower levels, recommends tactics, as well as reporting progress toward the strategy on standard TAP forms for top management approval and review. The ratified TAP thus becomes a meaningful official charter for implementation at all levels.

Reviews of selected strategies and TAPs are presented monthly or quarterly to the office of the president or to the appropriate group or division vice president by strategy and TAP managers who are, in most cases, several organizational levels below the president or reviewing officer. This presentation, directly to company officers, serves several vital purposes not usually satisfied in the large organization. First, it circumvents the traditional multilayer, upward-screening process and presents the president and other senior officers with firsthand progress reports on important projects by the people who know most about them. Second, it keeps the officers updated on developing technologies. Third, it gives the project head immediate feedback, undistorted by the traditional multilayer, downward-filtering process, and enables him to align his efforts more directly to the needs of the corporation. Needless to say, the recognition afforded by this process increases the incentive and opportunity for maximum effectiveness.

In short, the OST goal-setting model is a system for managing innovation at all levels in planning, implementing, and measuring goals within the framework of a meaningful whole. Moreover, the system itself is an innovative process for bypassing the traditional impediments to communication, decision making, and involvement which quash innovation and undermine the corporation's capability for competing successfully with smaller and more agile competitors.

Annual Planning Conference

The OST system can be understood only in terms of its impact on the members of the organization through the subsystems which comprise it. For example, the annual planning conference is far more than a traditional system for reviewing plans and approving budgets. It is a system that serves at least eight important functions:

1. *Sharing information.* When 200 managers from around the world convene at corporate headquarters in December, each is prepared to make a presentation lasting from 10 to 30 minutes covering three basic points: what he said he was going to do last year, what he accomplished last year, and what he plans to achieve in the year ahead. This presentation is presented in the form of TAPs and strategies through the use of visual aids, most of which reflect sophisticated measures of financial, personnel, technological, manufacturing, and marketing accomplishments. This information is also shared with about 300 additional people who fill the remaining seats in the auditorium, and is sent through closed-circuit television to other major plant sites. The 200 managers who make presentations sit through the total conference, which generally runs from Monday till Saturday noon; however, the other 1000 or so people who attend represent an ever-changing mix of persons with a need and desire to hear the presentations and the discussions which accompany them. By the conclusion of the conference, each participant has a better understanding of the mosaic of the total organization and how and where his chunk of the business relates to it.

2. *Avoiding conflict and overlap.* Each manager of a product-customer center or division enjoys a high degree of autonomy with the provision that each avoids jurisdictional conflict and wasteful overlap. For example, managers from the several plants in the European common market are expected to coordinate their strategies so as not to be competing with each other for the same customers, and in fact may be sharing marketing and distribution facilities with each other; or a manager may adopt a uniquely different management system in his operation provided it does not undermine systems existing in other operations. During the planning conference, managers are expected to show sensitivity to this concern and to define measures taken to avoid vulnerability to conflict and wasteful overlap.

3. *Synergizing strategies.* Perhaps one of the greatest benefits derived from the widespread sharing of information during the planning conference is the opportunity for one hand to wash the other. For instance, a manager in Holland faced the problem of overproduction without the option of reducing his work force because of local laws. However, a United States manager subcontracted work to the Dutch manager, simultaneously enabling both managers to be more cost-effective in achieving their profit goals. Managers are expected to buy equipment and supplies from each other rather than from an outside vendor. If outside sources are superior or less costly, the TI source must be prepared to explain why he was not competitive with the outside supplier. To deal with peaks and valleys in manpower requirements, managers are expected to borrow and lend personnel to the mutual advantage of the employees and the organization. During the planning conference, presentations are sometimes interrupted to discuss possible synergistic relationships to be considered.

4. *Establishing priorities.* Presentations at the planning conference are often in the form of "decision packages" and are not finalized until all presentations are made and priority comparisons can be made. A decision package may be in the form of a go-no-go proposal or in the form of alternative levels of expenditure for a given project or strategy. Priorities are inevitably tied to expected return on investment. For instance, a scientist proposing a research project to develop a new product or system is expected, as part of his presentation, to indicate the probability or feasibility of making the necessary technological breakthrough, the time frame and budget required, and the served available market should the breakthrough materialize. Hence, the scientist's creativity goes beyond the laboratory and finds expression in principles of business management.

5. *Legitimizing competition.* Many organizations tend to suppress competition on the assumption that competition has a divisive effect on its members. Actually, competition cannot and should not be suppressed, particularly among high achievers. Should an organization succeed in quashing competition, it would only have thrown out the baby with the bathwater by driving the high achievers from the organization or converting them to docile conformists. The planning conference is an arena which allows individuals to display initiative, creativity, and accomplishments before those upon whom their careers depend. A manager standing before the top-management superstructure of the organization is in effect competing with company standards and with his peers. If average company growth is 15 percent, a 12 percent growth goal may not be impressive. On the other hand, a goal of 18 percent growth may appear laudable by company standards, but it may pale in comparison to a peer's goal of 22 percent. It is well known in the TI culture that the highest achievers are the ones tapped for promotions and are the recipients of higher merit increases and discretionary bonuses. People can legitimately compete in building empires provided they build them on sound foundations and don't run roughshod over their brothers in doing so.

6. *Recognizing accomplishments.* Feedback received by job incumbents in many organizations is strongly dependent on the perceptions and managerial style of the supervisor. As such, it is not standardized or even based on well-understood criteria. In contrast, the TI planning conference participant is in effect being judged by a panel composed of the top management team and his peers in terms of standardized criteria well understood in the company's culture. Because he has had a major role in establishing his own goals and criteria of achievement, his actual accomplishments as he reports them, in addition to the judgment of his supervisor, are the basis for recognition. And when failures must be reported, it is more constructive to diagnose one's own failures and prescribe remedial actions than it is to be subjected to the indignity of admonitory advice from the boss. When outstanding achievements and examples of innovation are the subject of open discussion during the conference, recognition is amplified by the importance attached to them by the large group of high-status people in attendance. Each presenter lists the contributors to his strategy or tactical action program, and since such membership is solicited based on competence, inclusion on such a list is a further form of recognition.

7. *Developing managers.* Participants in the planning conference bring to the podium the collective experience and creativity of the people who helped put the plan together. The successful manager does not sit between the four walls of his office and write his plan; rather, he involves his engineering, manufacturing, marketing, and other key personnel in developing his plan. Thus when the plan is ratified, or modified and ratified at the planning conference, the manager is in a good position to go back to the people who helped put it together and share with them the final plan, which in turn is the platform for crystallizing their own goals and tactics. Should this manager vacate his job, he doesn't leave his plant leaderless, as his lieutenants represent a cadre of experienced talent from which his replacement can be drawn. Sitting through the planning conference is also an educational experience, as it represents in effect approximately 200 lectures in business management. These are not theoretical messages; they are the hard facts of managing as presented by individuals who have earned their opportunity to appear on the podium through high achievements. The green manager in particular benefits from the experience shared by the more seasoned managers making the presentations. Managerial perspective is further broadened by discussions of unusual circumstances or innovations. Discussions might center, for example, on the merits versus demerits of licensing other manufacturers, wholly owned versus joint venture subsidiaries, hiring custodial help versus subcontracting, the pros and cons of opening a plant in a particular country, comparative analysis of union and nonunion operations, or the reasoning behind the opening of a new product line or discontinuance of an old one. The net effect of involvement in the planning conference is to endow participants with insights not attainable through formal seminars or membership in traditional organizations.

8. *Fostering goal orientation.* Planning conferences in many organizations are "show-and-tell" presentations by individuals who appear to operate under an unwritten code or gentlemen's agreement not to harass each other by asking embarrassing questions. Such presentations include a budget proposal to which management typically applies some undefined criteria which ends up in a 15 percent budget cut. The presenters, having anticipated this as standard practice, have padded their budgets by 15 percent. However, they go through the ritual of regrets and groans as they finalize their budgets. Such practices may be labeled as politically or authority oriented. The contents of the resultant official plan may have little relationship to actual operations and may reflect little sensitivity to the plans of peers. However, the plans contain the bywords and concepts known to reinforce the biases of the reviewers.

The TI OST system represents a hierarchy of goals to which all presentations are related. Objectives, strategies, and tactical action programs are objectively quantifiable realities less subject to arbitrary or capricious manipulation. Within this framework which they helped formulate, managers present goals and strategies in which they have a proprietary interest. A person pursues such goals with far more initiative and creativity than he would a goal foisted on him by official authority.

Because annual goal setting is serious business, it can easily degenerate into a somber authority-oriented ritual. TI planning conferences were often laced with levity created by practical jokes and creative humor. For instance, the head of the research laboratory made remarks about his new insights into motivation while holding an 18-inch Stilson wrench in his hand; the bald controller made a presentation wearing a dust mop for a wig; the labor relations director flashed open his coat to reveal a dozen union buttons; the president bet a division director a case of whiskey that he wouldn't achieve his goal; and the president gave a speech during a recession reminding long-faced managers that life must be fun. Informal and spontaneous expressions such as these help avoid the humorless authority orientation which can quash the creativity of a goal-oriented person.

The TI planning conference, as described above, does not end with the presentations at corporate headquarters. Each manager in turn takes information from the conference back to his department where it is shared and discussed through the medium of department meetings. The problem-solving–goal-setting sessions described earlier are extensions of the charters established at the planning conference. More than 83 percent of all TI employees are organized into what they term "people involvement teams" seeking ways to improve their own productivity.

Mindful of the stultifying potential of formal management systems in a giant organization, TI established "IDEA" programs in the early 1970s to circumvent big-company administrative constraints. An employee with an idea for process or product improvements can approach one of the forty IDEA centers and request a grant for developing his or her idea. If his idea is turned down by one IDEA representative, he can take it to another. About one-third of the ideas get funded with grants of up to $25,000, drawn from a total annual pool of $1 million. Once the grant is made, it cannot be cancelled—not even by the president. About half the ideas funded pay off, and some of the big winners were spawned by the IDEA program. TI's entry into the digital watch business, the subsequent development of electronic watch face display of traditional hands, and the low-cost voice synthesizer leading to Speak & Spell and other voice devices came out of the IDEA program.

Though TI's huge expenditures for research and development and capital improvement are essential ingredients to its success, the key to its success is its ability to develop a culture built on innovation as a cornerstone.

The TI OST system described in this chapter establishes the companywide framework on which practices and systems for innovation can be built. The following chapter focuses on the development of human resources. It will be apparent to the reader that the systems for managing innovation described in this chapter are also media for developing human resources, as described in the following chapter. Hence, the management of innovation and the development of human talent have a synergistic cause-and-effect relationship to each other.

5
Developing Human Resources

Read carefully

The development of human talent cannot be discussed separately from the process of managing an organization. Just as learning in life results from the process of living, employee development results from being a member of the organization. If every employee is a manager of his or her job, the opportunities for development are rich. But if employees are robots or automatons, little development is likely to occur.

Sometimes in an effort to give greater recognition to the importance of the human assets in an organization, a person will be designated as vice president of human resources. Such an act may boomerang if such a person is perceived by himself and others as being in charge of personnel development. He may organize the human resources department staffed by specialists who may or may not enhance the development of people in the organization. If the specialists recognize that development is best accomplished through everyday job roles and relationships in the organization, they may be successful. But if they believe that development takes place in training programs, job-enrichment projects, and attitude surveys, all administered by the human resources department, they may actually impair development. Not that such programs, per se, are damaging but, rather, these efforts often cause managers to assume that someone else is taking care of development and, hence, to neglect their responsibility for self-development and the development of others through the process of managing.

Thus, human development and organization development are inseparable. When both are being achieved well they are synergistically related to each other. People are more highly motivated in a financially viable and self-renewing organization. Organizations, in turn, prosper if their members are highly motivated. Hence, the effective organization satisfies two basic human conditions:

1. Its members are free to assert themselves as individuals.
2. All individuals are united in the pursuit of common goals.

157

In the preceding chapter on the management of innovation, it was apparent that the opportunity to be creative was supportive of both the organization and its innovators. Thus, managing innovation is also a developmental process. The discussion of training media later in this chapter illustrates the dual roles of media for furthering innovation and development.

For instance, the TI OST system described in Chapter 4, though labeled as a system for managing innovation, is simultaneously the primary vehicle for management development in the organization. Potential customers in investigating TI's capability and depth of managerial talent would sometimes express concern about the apparent absence of formalized training programs in the company. When the company was young, before its reputation was established, it was a necessary standard procedure to brief customers on the uniqueness and efficacy of the TI philosophy and management systems as media for developing managers. And because the OST system permeated the organization so thoroughly, people in all levels and functions were influenced by it. For example, when the plan-do-control concept of "every employee a manager" was first presented as part of the meaningful work strategy at the annual planning conference in 1964, the president was quick to seize on it and to give all managers the responsibility for "engineering" the concept throughout the corporation.

GRAINS OF SAND

The media in an organization through which people are influenced positively or negatively seem to be as numerous as grains of sand on a beach. Rearranging a few grains of sand will not alter the basic characteristics of a beach. However, a hurricane can rearrange enough sand to give the beach a strikingly different appearance. In the same way, the myriad of systems within an organization gives its climate a distinctive personality. Rearranging a few systems will not significantly alter the climate. But if enough of the systems are modified, an organization's climate may be substantially altered—either positively or negatively.

To borrow a term from physics, it may be said that each small system in the organization carries a small negative or positive "valence." For example, an officious, unfriendly, and insensitive security guard might represent a negative valence. A friendly and courteous guard might constitute a positive valence. Punching a time clock might represent a negative valence, whereas self-recording of time and attendance could be a positive valence. If a majority of the systems carry a positive valence, the net effect on the climate is positive, allowing people to take the relatively fewer negative valences in stride. If a preponderance of the systems carry a negative valence, the critical mass is negative, causing people to be oblivious to the few positive valences. Two factors can give a system a positive or negative valence: the design of the system itself and the manner in which it is administered. For instance, time clocks and self-recording of time represent two different systems for serving the same purpose, whereas the behavior of the two guards represents contrasting styles of implementing the same system.

Figure 5-1 lists a variety of systems affecting the attitudes and perceptions of people in the work place. The shaded blocks on the right-hand side of the table indicate the probability or likelihood that each of these systems will find expression under each of three stages of labor relations, summarized below and described in greater detail on pages 89 to 95.

Under conditions of stage 1 labor relations, where management and labor exist as adversaries, workers are shown to have little opportunity to be involved in systems that would treat them as mature, responsible adults such as planning their own work or helping plan the safety program. But they would be involved in systems exacting compliance and following instructions, such as doing their job as prescribed by their superior, following safety rules, and working according to engineered labor standards. Hence, the negative valences outweigh the positive valences, causing employees to view even positive experiences through cynical eyes.

Under stage 2 conditions, where management and labor attempt to exist as amicable adversaries, workers are occasionally involved in activities which enable them to exercise initiative and judgment, though usually under the watchful and friendly eye of their boss. The occasional opportunity to manage one's own work, to be paid according to merit, to participate in safety committees, and to evaluate working conditions represents circumstances that cause workers to begin to identify with management. Negative and positive valences tend to be rather evenly balanced when labor relations are characterized by the stage 2 conditions of détente.

Employees working in a stage 3 organization, where management-labor class distinctions are obliterated by joint concern for organizational effectiveness, are on a common data base with people of various levels and functions pulling toward common goals. They typically manage their own work, relating to a supervisor who acts as an adviser, consultant, and facilitator. They have an active role in influencing certain compensation and staffing systems and in managing safety programs, and are seldom set apart by rank-oriented status symbols. Even when people in a stage 3 environment are subject to the tedium of uninspiring and restrictive responsibilities, they can take them in stride as these negative valences are outweighed by the more numerous and influential positive valences which characterize the stage 3 climate.

	Stage 1—Win-lose adversary	Stage 2—Collaborative adversary	Stage 3—Organizational democracy
Managing one's job			
Planning	□	▨	■
Doing	■	■	■
Controlling	□	▨	■
Performance review			
Evaluation	■	■	■
Feedback	□	▨	■
Goal setting	□	▨	■
Reporting	□	▨	■
Compensation systems			
Salaried status	□	▨	■
Hourly wages	■	■	▨
Automatic pay increases	■	▨	□
Merit pay increases	□	▨	■
Piecework incentive	■	□	□
Paid suggestion plan	□	▨	□
Contributory benefits	□	▨	■
Noncontributory benefits	■	▨	▨
Discretionary bonuses	□	▨	■
Sharing plans	□	▨	■
Codetermination of pay	□	▨	■
Staffing systems			
Recruiting	□	▨	■
Interviewing	□	▨	■
Selection	□	▨	■
Orientation	□	▨	■
Placement	□	▨	■
Training	□	▨	▨
Promotions	□	▨	▨
Discharges	□	□	▨
Layoffs	□	▨	■
Health and safety			
Attend meetings	▨	■	■
Chair meetings	□	▨	■
Establish standards	□	▨	▨
Monitor compliance	□	▨	■
Investigate hazards	□	▨	■
Recommend corrections	□	▨	■
Statistical reporting	□	▨	▨
Host OSHA inspectors	□	▨	■
Safety training	□	▨	▨
Meetings and task forces			
Attend department meetings	▨	■	■
Receive information	■	■	■
Group discussion	□	▨	■
Influence meeting agenda	□	▨	■
Chair meeting	□	□	▨
Task force membership	□	▨	■

FIG. 5-1 Employee roles under three stages of labor relations.

160

	Stage 1—Win-lose adversary	Stage 2—Collaborative adversary	Stage 3—Organizational democracy
Newspaper and bulletin boards			
Receive newspaper	Usually	Usually	Usually
Write to editor	Sometimes	Usually	Usually
Place ads in newspaper	Sometimes	Usually	Usually
Report news	Seldom	Sometimes	Usually
Edit newspaper	Seldom	Sometimes	Usually
Read bulletin boards	Usually	Usually	Usually
Post bulletins	Seldom	Sometimes	Usually
Attitude surveys			
Design survey	Seldom	Sometimes	Usually
Complete questionnaire	Sometimes	Usually	Usually
Receive results	Seldom	Usually	Usually
Analyze results	Seldom	Sometimes	Usually
Prepare recommendations	Seldom	Sometimes	Usually
Participate in implementation	Seldom	Sometimes	Usually
Receive implementation feedback	Seldom	Sometimes	Usually
Rank-oriented status symbols			
Parking	Usually	Sometimes	Seldom
Furnishings	Usually	Sometimes	Seldom
Office location	Usually	Sometimes	Seldom
Dress code	Usually	Sometimes	Seldom
Signal bells	Usually	Sometimes	Seldom
Time clocks	Usually	Sometimes	Seldom
Pay schedules	Usually	Sometimes	Seldom
Eating facilities	Usually	Sometimes	Seldom
Coffee service	Usually	Sometimes	Seldom
Rank-coded ID badges	Usually	Sometimes	Seldom
Functional status symbols			
Product image	Usually	Usually	Usually
Landscaping	Usually	Usually	Usually
Architecture	Usually	Usually	Usually
Facilities maintenance	Usually	Usually	Usually
Noncoded ID badges	Seldom	Sometimes	Usually
Miscellaneous			
Access to telephone	Seldom	Sometimes	Usually
Use computer terminal	Seldom	Sometimes	Usually
Open door	Seldom	Sometimes	Usually
Open floor	Seldom	Sometimes	Usually
Access to library	Seldom	Sometimes	Usually
PA announcements	Usually	Usually	Usually
Closed-circuit TV	Sometimes	Sometimes	Sometimes
Grievance procedure	Usually	Usually	Usually
Conflict resolution	Seldom	Sometimes	Usually

■ Usually   ▨ Sometimes   ☐ Seldom

FIG. 5-1   (*Cont.*)

161

The systems listed in Figure 5-1 illustrate the high potential of the work place as a medium for facilitating the development of human resources. Stage 3 conditions provide both a philosophy and media for making every employee a manager. However, the same table indicates that most of the systems that give meaning to the work place do not exist under stage 1 conditions. Stage 1 philosophy, then, reflects insensitivity to human needs, and in doing so, it fails to excite the motivation essential to organizational excellence and development.

TRAINING

The term "training" reflects a process that is intrinsically unsound as a strategy for changing people. Most learning and growth result not from training programs but, rather, from living itself, particularly in those life roles directed toward the attainment of personal goals.

People are motivated primarily by their personal goals, and will take the initiative in acquiring knowledge and skills necessary to attain them. They are motivated by organization goals only if they feel that attainment of them will result in the achievement of their personal goals. Beyond the subsistence level, the attainment of most personal goals leads to the satisfaction of growth, achievement, responsibility, and recognition needs. In the work place, these needs are satisfied through the guiding principles and strategies outlined in Chapter 2. Training, within this context, is not a program, but a variety of job-related activities supporting a way of life at work.

The Changing Focus of Training

The knowledge explosion, which has accelerated change in technology and human values, has placed a two-pronged focus on technical training and managerial effectiveness. In regard to technical training, for example, engineers and technicians, whose technology once served a lifetime, now require constant updating just to stay employable. Large blocks of skilled and semiskilled workers are continuously rendered temporarily obsolete by product and process evolution. Similarly, the manager's competence requires continuous updating to keep abreast of changing systems technology.

The philosophical underpinnings of scientific management are also changing to give managerial competence a new meaning. Since increasing numbers of people in business organizations are reacting adversely to direction and control by authority, and are expecting and seeking opportunity to influence their organizational goals and the methods for achieving them, managerial training to guide this initiative must now apply to every member of the work force. If every employee is to be a manager of his job, he or she must be granted much of the same knowledge and freedom previously reserved for top-echelon people who formerly assumed the full burden of organizational responsibility. The focus of training, then, is on both technical and managerial training, and is for all levels of the organization.

A Pitfall of Paternalism

If individuals are to experience sustained growth and maturity, their training must result from their own initiative. A trend has developed, however, particularly in the public sector and in big industry, which has gradually conditioned people to look to the organization for guidance and support in furthering their careers. It is not uncommon to find massive training programs which routinely schedule people at all levels of the organization, from top management through semiskilled ranks, for participation in courses prescribed by someone in line or staff management. The fault with such a system lies not so much in the content of the courses as with the source of initiative it represents. In essence, it undermines self-responsibility by conditioning people to be outer-directed, to wait for directives and cues from authority figures. It leads to dependency relationships and complacency based on the feeling that "management" knows what is best for them and will see to it that they are trained and utilized effectively. The duplicity of such a system is discovered by many individuals late in their careers when they awaken abruptly to the realization that life has passed them by and that retirement is around the corner. Only then do they discover their own dereliction in abandoning self-responsibility and their company's dereliction in encouraging them to do so. Hence, paternalism is an insidious, though innocently set, trap which takes the initiative away from the individual, but fails to replace it with an alternative that satisfies his long-range goals.

Learning Processes

Activities which cast participants in passive listening roles, such as films and uninterrupted lectures, are less likely to result in change than processes employing active learning techniques, such as those listed in Figure 5-2. Most effective training programs are not training programs as such but, rather, are processes which involve individuals in the pursuit of meaningful goals. The developmental roles of a number of these systems or processes are summarized below with page references, where relevant, for more complete descriptions of the systems themselves.

- The *planning process* described on pages 151 to 155 offers rich opportunity for managerial development. Not only does it perpetuate the development of upper and middle managers, but its involvement of man-

1 - In-basket. Situational test for simulating a person's responsibility in handling letters, memoranda, phone calls and other material collected in his in-basket.

2 - Role playing. Real or hypothetical problem-solving by a number of individuals in simulated roles.

3 - Management games. Teaching of business strategy and counter-strategy by involving small teams of players in competitive manipulation of business variables.

4 - Sensitivity training. Small trainee-centered groups in permissive atmosphere coping with frustration and interpersonal processes through unstructured methods, usually with occasional intervention by skilled observer-trainer.

5 - Programmed instruction. Individual self-instruction through machines or textbooks which present organized instructional material requiring responses and feedback.

6 - Group discussion. Used in conjunction with lectures, films, readings and day-to-day job activities for developing better understanding, acceptance and application of subject matter; usually stimulated by the use of overhead, directed, relay and reverse questions.

7 - Task force. Small groups of persons, usually representing a variety of relevant functional skills and responsibilities, in pursuit of specific organizational goals.

8 - Problem analysis. Involvement of individuals in identifying and defining barriers to organizational effectiveness and prescribing remedial action.

9 - Listening. The practice of showing courtesy, respect and acceptance in providing time and opportunity for individuals to be heard.

FIG. 5-2   Active learning techniques.

agers at lower levels in defining goals, strategies, and budgets prepares them for advancement and determines their candidacy for promotion. Moreover, their participation in the formulation and implementation of higher-level goals provides a model for involving their natural work groups in similar problem-solving–goal-setting strategies. Planning-conference presentations of the open-forum type dispense information that enables conference participants to avoid conflict and overlap and to discover opportunities for mutual support. The public presentation, in terms of performance against last year's goals and the definition of new goals, places the responsibility for establishing goals and strategies and assessing achievements on the shoulders of the goal setter. The presentation is a timely and original "lecture" on innovativeness in strategic planning, organization of resources, and control processes, offering learning opportunity to conference participants. Hence, the planning process leads to the development of managerial skills and knowledge, and in itself represents diverse models for managerial effectiveness.

- *Strategy management,* defined on page 150, offers managerial training to task-force leaders whose strategies support broad business objectives defined in the long-range planning conference. A strategy manager's competence is a function of his ability to identify and influence the resource personnel throughout the organization, whose combined talent will enable him to define and implement strategies for supporting longer-range objectives. Perhaps the most developmental aspect of the strategy manager's assignment is the requirement that he organize and gain commitment from human resources without the use of official authority. Since his strategy teams cut across organizational lines, he cannot exercise organizational control over them. Hence, his successful attainment of strategy goals requires the development of leadership skills.

- *Attitude surveys,* conducted along the lines described on pages 143 to 149, offers a multifaceted opportunity for employee development. Management development in its broadest sense results from employee involvement in suggesting questions for the survey, refining the questionnaire, administering the survey, completing the questionnaire, interpreting survey results, and translating them into applications. Unlike the traditional approach which involves people only in completing questionnaires and receiving survey feedback, the survey described herein involves employees in the total creative, diagnostic, and managerial process which enables them to think and act like managers. Though task-force membership directly involves only a small percentage of the work force, their informal impact on the grapevine evokes the involvement of most of their peers. Hence, this program broadens employees' management perspective and develops a greater sense of responsibility at the lower levels. In short, the process of creating and applying the survey system has far more developmental influence than the action plans spawned by the survey. Thus, companies which hire an outside consultant to provide, administer, and interpret a survey fail to realize at least 90 percent of the potential developmental value of the survey. The role of an outside consultant in connection with an attitude survey would more appropriately be that of guiding an organization in learning how to develop and administer surveys through the use of its own internal resources.

- *Job posting,* described in greater detail on pages 72 to 76, is another example of a system with developmental potential extending beyond its original or intended purpose. Properly administered, job posting gives people the information, freedom, and incentive to take charge of their own careers. Rather than waiting around for a mentor or other authority figure to discover them and prescribe their advancement plan, they learn to be on the lookout for opportunities which fit their own unique qualifications and aspirations. Feedback from the system alerts bidders to the knowledge, skill, and experience requirements for posted jobs, thus activating their involvement in the tuition refund program. The developmental value of the job-posting system is proportional to its availability to all members of the organization under ground rules that satisfy the characteristics of an effective system, as described on pages 76 and 77.

- *Work Simplification,* described on pages 130 to 138, is the downward extension of planning, organizing, and control functions which enables people at lower levels to apply their talents, individually and collectively, in managing their own jobs. It replaces traditional time and motion study on the assumptions that:

  1. Most people have creative potential for improving their own jobs.

  2. Improvements are best made by those who perform the job.

  3. Self-initiated change is positively motivational, while change imposed by authority is usually resented and opposed.

  4. People satisfy social and achievement needs through cooperative work-improvement activities.

  Employees learn Work Simplification through standardized company programs, taught by professional trainers or their own supervisors. Classroom sessions, which usually total about 20 hours, provide principles and techniques of time-and-motion economy, flow-process charting, cost analysis, human relations, and an on-the-job project for applying newly learned techniques. Development occurring through Work Simplification broadens employees' perspectives to enable them to exercise initiative in the management of change and, thus, to perceive their job and the organization through the eyes of a responsible manager.

- *Problem solving–goal setting,* defined on pages 138 to 143 as a process for managing innovation, is an evolutionary outgrowth of the Work Simplification process and, in many respects, duplicates the corporate planning model. The problem-solving–goal-setting process on the production line, for example, is initiated for specific purposes, such as reducing costs, increasing quality, and shortening schedules. It involves natural team members such as operators, engineers, inspectors, and foremen. Participants gain a better understanding of their goals, their problems, and their interdependent relationships, and work cooperatively in solving problems and setting goals. The process develops interpersonal competence and responsible behavior across all functions and levels of the organization.

- *After-hours training opportunity* offered through company education assistance programs enables individuals to assume the initiative for their own development. The pursuit of specific knowledge and skills, a general education, or a college degree requires the definition of career goals by the individual and his commitment in time, effort, and finances to the attainment of these goals. Self-initiated after-hours activities, whether in the classroom or through correspondence courses, are reinforced in an environment of promotional opportunity, as offered by the internal staffing strategy defined on pages 227 to 231. Apart from the doors opened by improved educational credentials, the intellectual messages received from textbooks and lectures may ultimately have a profound impact on behavior, but usually by a process so subtle and delayed that cause-and-effect relationships are difficult to establish.

- *Preemployment training* is becoming increasingly important, particularly at the lower levels, for bridging the gap between the requirements of technology-based organizations and the qualifications of the culturally disadvantaged recruited for entry occupations. Many industrial organizations, in collaboration with the U.S. Department of Labor, have undertaken projects for preparing the disadvantaged for responsible job roles and citizenship. For example, 400 participants in one of Texas Instruments' contracted preemployment programs were exposed to varied experiences designed to enable them to overcome obstacles—social, psychological, and educational skill deficiencies—which had deprived them of meaningful employment. In addition to socialization opportunities provided by the preemployment training environment, they receive up to 280 hours of remedial academic instruction and world-of-work orientation. The educational foundation includes spelling and grammar; reading fluency, comprehension, and analysis; fundamental arithmetic skills; and application of math skills to work-related problems in measurement and decimal conversions. Reading assignments and discussion encompass history, civics, basic science, and job-related materials. The goal is to raise the minimum academic achievement level to that of the eighth grade. The world-of-work orientation covers concepts of getting, holding, and advancing on a job; basic economics of family budgeting and planning; and how to use credit intelligently, and to understand employee benefits, taxes, and payroll deductions. Persons entering the work force after completing this training program are, on an average, superior to those hired through the normal selection and placement process, particularly in regard to self-responsible behavior.

- *Laboratory experiences,* particularly off-site, are sometimes desirable if for no other reason than to disengage people from the cultural entrapments within the organization. Laboratory experiences have many forms, but always employ some aspect of sensitivity training. Training groups may be composed of members of separate organizations (strangers), members of the same organization, not closely related in function or chain of command (cousins), or members of natural work groups (family). The sensitivity process is guided by ground rules against use of criticism and places the emphasis on understanding and accepting self and others. The trainer's role is largely one of observing and intervening when appropriate to sensitize members to group processes. A successful laboratory generates a climate conducive to interpersonal competence, in which candor and spontaneity have an affirming rather than a threatening impact on participants. The assumptions underlying this process are that self-understanding and self-acceptance are keys to eliminating the protective facades which prevent authentic human interaction, and that the results of laboratory experiences will be transferred to the work situation to improve organizational effectiveness. In industry it is found that laboratory experiences become more relevant to the job situation when combined with intellectual messages and goal-oriented exercises such as the team improvement laboratory described on pages 132 to 138, the managerial grid described on pages 19 and 20, or the power structure workshop described on pages 20 to 22. Though candor or leveling may occur more easily in stranger labs because of the absence of established social or authority relationships which sometimes inhibit progress in family or cousin labs, the ideal in terms of ultimate job success is the development of interpersonal competence within and between natural work groups.

• *Supervisory skills* training is becoming increasingly critical as rapidly changing technology-based organizations promote technically trained personnel into supervisory responsibilities. Ideally, supervisors should have at least basic orientation in planning, organizing, and control functions, along with principles of human relations and techniques of supervision before assuming their new supervisory roles. However, in practice, this orientation is usually not undertaken until after the supervisory appointment. If not delayed too long, learning while supervising can provide more realistic training, as it enables the individual to reinforce his learning through immediate application of theory.

An innovative program for training new supervisors was instituted by a department manager in Texas Instruments who trained operators to train new supervisors in their department.[1] Some of the first-line supervisory positions were filled by promotion and transfer, but approximately 60

---

[1]Earl R. Gomersall and M. Scott Myers, "Breakthrough in On-the-job Training," *Harvard Business Review*, July–Aug. 1966, pp. 62–72.

percent of them were filled by new college graduates. Preemployment conditioning of new supervisors in parent-child, teacher-student, officer-enlisted man relationships caused many of them to approach their first supervisory jobs with the traditional notion that a leader is a person with authority who "can do everything his subordinates can, only better."

Because of his desire to be the infallible leader, the new supervisor understandably felt inadequate in his new role of supervising large numbers of individuals, most of whom knew the operations better than he did. He did not realize that the operators recognized and accepted his limitations and that it would be futile and self-defeating for him to try to conceal them.

To help new supervisors gain early acceptance of their limitations and a better understanding of their supervisory role, a plan was developed for having operators train the supervisor. Working in pairs, operators (who had received trainer training) gave the new or transferred supervisor his first orientation to their assembly line, acquainting him with the pitfalls traditionally encountered by new supervisors and defining his role as it is perceived by the operators. This innovative approach serves three basic purposes:

1. It provides a supervisor with valid information directly from the persons who have the most detailed knowledge of the operations.

2. It provides assurance to the operators that the supervisor is properly qualified and acquainted with their problems. Because they get personally involved in this training, they will seek to make him successful.

3. Most important, it reorients the values of the supervisor and lessens the likelihood of his drifting into authority-oriented supervisory behavior. A supervisor who, in his first experience as a leader, learns to expect and seek information from subordinates, and discovers that they are creative and responsible, is favorably conditioned or "reprogrammed" to look to, and rely on, people under his supervision for assistance in solving problems.

- *Job skill training,* because of the accelerating rate of technological change, is placing increasingly heavy demands on the organization and the resourcefulness of trainers. Training functions which attempt to provide skills training for the organization find that the staff trainer usually has neither the technical background to cope with diversifying technologies nor the resources to cope with logistics problems stemming from the combination of increasing numbers, changing technologies, and geographical dispersion. Increasingly, then, the professional trainer's role must be that of training line people to become trainers.

A professional trainer in Texas Instruments provided a good example of this more effective role when he was asked by the head of a drafting department to provide a training program for sixty of his draftsmen. The staff trainer involved the department head and his supervisors in the training-needs analysis by asking them to define the drafting skills and knowledge in which the draftsmen were most deficient. When the line managers had completed this preliminary analysis, the training manager taught them how to write multiple-choice test questions covering the areas of deficiency. A test of approximately 100 multiple-choice test questions was developed and administered to all draftsmen in the department. An item analysis of test results showed the primary areas of deficiency for the total department and specific areas for each draftsman. The curriculum for the training program was designed to emphasize areas of deficiency.

In planning the implementation of the training program, the search for technically qualified trainers led back to the supervisors themselves, who after being briefed in training techniques, were the persons best qualified to conduct the training programs within their own departments. Upon completion of the training program, the same multiple-choice test was used again, this time to measure the success of the training program. Draftsmen who failed to meet standards, as measured by the test, were given additional training. Not only did this training program give the draftsmen more valid training, but more importantly, it familiarized the supervisors with the levels of competence and talent in their department, and prepared them for future trainer roles.

• *Job orientation* is becoming an increasingly critical requirement as people seek to adapt to the complex systems, restrictive legislation, and rapidly changing job requirements of large organizations. Many new employees unquestioningly accept conformity roles simply because they have no realistic expectation of being able to exercise initiative and creativity in the overwhelming environment which characterizes the new world of work. For many, work is expected to be unpleasant and meaningless, having value only as a source of money for buying necessities. Therefore, to say the least, creativity and self-confidence cannot be expected from people conforming to the requirements of what they perceive as an alien and sometimes threatening environment.

A Case Study in Job Orientation

Recognizing the problem of alienation noted above, a manager in Texas Instruments initiated an innovative process for orienting people to their world of work which could serve as a job orientation model for almost any type of organization. The study[2] was made in a rapidly growing electronics manufacturing department of Texas Instruments which included more

[2]Earl R. Gomersall and M. Scott Myers, "Breakthrough in On-the-Job Training," *Harvard Business Review*, July–Aug. 1966, pp. 62–72.

than 1400 women operators who collectively performed approximately 1850 different operations on three shifts (the most numerously replicated of these operations having only seventy operators per shift). Approximately 57 percent of the operators worked with microscopes, and all jobs placed a premium on visual acuity, eye-hand coordination, and manual dexterity.

The staffing of operations required a continuous training process: training new people hired for expansion and replacement purposes, and retraining transferees and the technologically displaced. The learning curve of ball bonders, as shown in Figure 5-3, was fairly typical for production operators in the department.

Ball bonders required approximately 3 months to reach the "competence" level, at which stage they could independently perform the operation but had not achieved the speed and accuracy ultimately expected of them to reach performance standards established by industrial engineering. The competence level would be about 85 percent of labor standards, while in this department about 115 percent of standard was termed the "mastery" level.

In a process initially unrelated to the training effort described here, the department manager had, during the preceding year, followed a systematic program for interviewing individuals during the morning coffee break. The results of 135 interviews with 405 operators yielded the following facts:

• Their first days on the job were anxious and disturbing ones.

• "New-employee initiation practices" by peers intensified anxiety.

• Anxiety interfered with the training process.

• Turnover of newly hired employees was caused primarily by anxiety.

• The new operators were reluctant to discuss problems with their supervisors.

• The supervisors had been successful in translating motivation theory into practice.

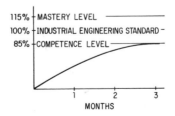

FIG. 5-3 Learning curve for ball bonders.

Facts uncovered through these interviews underscored the impact of anxiety in inhibiting job effectiveness of operators. It seemed obvious that anxiety dropped as competence was achieved. The relationship between the learning curve and what was believed to be the anxiety curve of operators is illustrated in Figure 5-4.

To supplement information obtained through personal interviews and to gain a better understanding of the characteristics of the anxiety to be reduced, a 92-item questionnaire was developed to measure the following possible causes of tension or anxiety: supervision; job knowledge and skill; social acceptance; physical conditions; orientation; job pressure; regimentation; vocational adjustment; personal problems; financial worries; outside social factors; and opportunities for the satisfaction of growth, achievement, responsibility, and recognition needs.

Administration of this questionnaire to short-tenure and seasoned employees identified three types of tension in the job situation—the first two harmful and the third potentially helpful:

1.   The primary source of anxiety, mentioned previously, stemmed from the unpredictable, overwhelming, and sometimes threatening new world of work. This anxiety was higher among new trainees and, according to the manager's interview results, appeared to diminish as competence was gained, as hypothesized in Figure 5-4.

2.   Another type of tension, largely unrelated to job tenure, resulted from anxieties about nonjob factors such as personal finances, domestic problems, professional status, and outside social relationships.

3.   The third type of tension was identified as a positive, inner-directed desire for constructive self-expression. This creative tension is the type observed in the job situation that finds expression after job competence is reached either in constructive job-improvement activities or in counterproductive behavior.

Assuming the validity of Figure 5-4, the manager questioned the presumed cause-and-effect relationship between competence and anxiety.

FIG. 5-4   Relationship of anxiety to competence.

Anxiety on the job is characteristically assumed to be the dependent variable, gradually dropping as competence is acquired. Might not the reverse be true? And if so, is it possible to accelerate achievement to the competence level by reducing anxiety at a faster rate? With this question in mind, he developed an orientation program to reduce the anxieties of experimental groups of new employees. Experimental groups were selected from the second shift and control groups from the first and third shifts. Precautions were taken to avoid the "Hawthorne effect" of influencing behavior through special attention.

Control groups went through the usual first-day orientation, which consisted of a 2-hour briefing by Personnel on hours of work, insurance, parking, work rules, and employee services. This session included warnings of the consequences of failure to conform to organizational expectations and, though not intended as a threat, tended to raise rather than reduce anxieties.

Following this orientation, it was customary for a bonder to be introduced to her friendly but very busy supervisor, who gave her further orientation and job instruction. Unfortunately, the supervisor's detailed familiarity with the operations often desensitized him to the technical gap between them, and the following might be typical of what the operator might hear him say:

> Alice, I would like you to take the sixth yellow chair on this assembly line, which is in front of bonding machine 14. On the left side of your machine you will find a wiring diagram indicating where you should bond your units. On the right-hand side of your machine you will find a carrying tray full of 14-lead packages. Pick up the headers, one at a time, using your 3-C tweezers and place them on the substrate below the capillary head. Grasp the cam actuator on the right-hand side of the machine and lower the hot capillary over the first bonding pad indicated by the diagram. Ball bond to the pad and, by moving the hot substrate, loop the wire to the pin indicated by the diagram. Stitch bond to this lead, raise the capillary, and check for pigtails. When you have completed all leads, put the unit back in the carrying tray.
>
> Your training operator will be around to help you with other details. Do you have any questions?

Overwhelmed by these instructions and not wanting to offend this polite and friendly supervisor or look stupid by telling him she did not understand the instructions, the operator would go to her work station and try to learn by furtively observing assemblers on either side of her. But they, in pursuit of operating goals, had little time to assist the new worker. Needless to say, her anxieties were increased and her learning ability was impaired. And the longer she remained unproductive, the more reluctant she was to disclose her wasted effort to her supervisor and the more threatening the job situation became.

Experimental groups participated in a one-day program especially designed to overcome anxieties not eliminated by the usual process of job orientation. Following the 2-hour orientation by Personnel, they were isolated in a conference room before they could be "initiated" by their peers. They were told there would be no work the first day and they should relax, sit back, have a coke or cigarette, and use this time to get acquainted with the organization and each other, and to ask questions. Throughout this 1-day anxiety-reduction session, questions were encouraged and answered. This orientation emphasized four points:

1.   "Your opportunity to succeed is very good." Company records disclosed that 99.6 percent of all persons hired or transferred into this job were eventually successful in terms of their ability to learn the necessary skills. Trainees were shown learning curves illustrating the gradual buildup of competence over the learning period. They were told five or six times during the day that all members of this group could expect to be successful on the job.

2.   "Disregard 'hall talk.' " Trainees were told of the hazing game that old employees played—scaring newcomers with exaggerated allegations about work rules, standards, disciplinary actions, and other job factors—to make the job as frightening to the newcomers as it had been for them. To prevent these distortions by peers, the trainees were given facts about both the good and the bad aspects of the job and exactly what was expected of them.

The basis for "hall-talk" rumors was explained. For example, rumor stated that more than one-half of the people who terminated had been fired for poor performance. The interviews mentioned earlier disclosed the fact that supervisors themselves unintentionally caused this rumor by intimating to operators that voluntary terminations (marriage, pregnancy, leaving town) were really performance terminations. Many supervisors felt this was a good negative incentive to pull up the low performers.

3.   "Take the initiative in communication." The new operators were told of the natural reluctance of many supervisors to be talkative and that it was easier for the supervisor to do his job if they asked him questions. They were told that supervisors realized that trainees needed continuous instruction at first, that they would not understand technical terminology for a while, that they were expected to ask questions, and that supervisors would not consider them dumb for asking questions.

4.   "Get to know your supervisor." The personality of the supervisor was described in detail. Candor was the rule. A description might reveal that:

- The supervisor is strict, but friendly.
- His hobbies are fishing and ham radio operation.
- He tends to be shy sometimes, but he really likes to talk to you if you want to.
- He would like you to check with him before you go on a personal break, just so he knows where you are.

Following this special day-long orientation session, members of experimental groups were introduced to their supervisors and their training operators in accordance with standard practice. Training commenced as usual, and eventually all operators were given regular production assignments.

A difference in attitude and learning rate was apparent from the beginning in the progress of the two groups. By the end of 4 weeks, experimental groups in ball bonding were significantly outperforming control groups, as reflected in Figure 5-5.

Figure 5-6 shows performance curves reflecting results for over 200 members of additional experimental and control groups for assembling, welding, and inspection, along with their absenteeism rates.

A significant effect of the new orientation program is the encouragement of upward communication. Sensitivity of the supervisors is a key ingredient of a climate conducive to natural and informal exchange of information. It was as a result of sensitizing supervisors to the importance of listening and maintaining fluid communication channels at all levels that the following incident took place:

An operator approached a supervisor during coffee break and casually struck up a conversation about the "units with little white specks on them that leaked after welding." The supervisor asked, "What little white specks?" The operator pointed out that almost all of the units that leaked after welding had little specks on them, a fact unnoted by the supervisor before. Verifying and investigating this fact revealed that units were placed

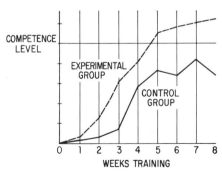

FIG. 5-5 Learning curves of experimental and control groups—ball bonding.

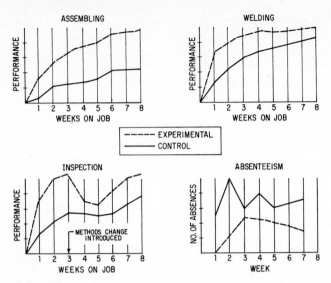

FIG. 5-6 Further comparisons of experimental and control groups.

in plastic trays while still hot from a previous process; their heat caused many of them to fuse to the plastic container. Removing them from the container caused the units to pull away a small amount of plastic, thus insulating them during the welding process.

Once this was discovered, the problem was solved simply by delaying the placing of units in the plastic trays until they had cooled sufficiently. This single suggestion reduced rejects to less than one-fourth their previous level for this product—a projected cost prevention of hundreds of thousands of dollars.

The point emphasized here is that casual questions and observations of the type described take place only in an atmosphere of approval, genuine respect, and interest.

On the basis of increased production, reduced turnover, absenteeism, and training time, annual departmental savings in excess of $50,000 were realized. Moreover, as trainees with less anxiety gradually became members of the regular work force, their attitudes began influencing the performance of the work groups they joined. The greater confidence of the new members seemed to inspire greater confidence among their older peers. Their higher performance established new reference points for stimulating competitiveness, and old peers were sometimes hard pressed to maintain a superiority margin between themselves and the newcomers. There was evidence of improvements in quality and quantity, not only among immediate peer groups but also among adjacent work groups who were influenced through the informal social system in the plant.

6
Compensation

Pay commonly serves the following functions, arranged to correspond roughly with man's hierarchy of needs.

- Pay satisfies maintenance needs.
- It is a measure of status.
- It is a scorekeeping system.
- It buys freedom and opportunity.

As a *maintenance factor*, money pays for food, shelter, clothing, education, transportation, and the costs of government. As a society's affluence increases, its citizens' maintenance needs are broadened to include a myriad of leisure-time pursuits, supplemental benefits, services, and symbols of status. The maintenance needs of an individual are sometimes defined as the goods and services that enable him to keep up with the Joneses. The illiterate farmer in the isolated Iranian village was not dissatisfied, until he visited Tehran. Similarly, an underprivileged American finds little consolation in the fact that he is living better than the middle class in an undeveloped country; he measures his maintenance needs according to standards surrounding him and made visible by television and other media. Labor unions, through collective bargaining, have stressed "equal treatment" and reinforced the role of compensation as a maintenance factor in providing adequate wages, hours, and working conditions.

Pay is a *measure of status*—personally, vocationally, and socially. Engineers, scientists, managers, college professors, and other professionals scan salary survey data to determine their vocational progress and status, within and outside the organization. Individuals in work groups may gain or lose prestige, if only in self-image, according to their relative standing in the group in regard to monetary increases, awards and penalties, and pay level. Organizational status is reflected as a gross dichotomy in differential pay systems for hourly and salaried employees, and is a function of job grade at all levels. Social relationships and pay status are inextricably related in the community.

Money is a *scorekeeping system*, particularly for those who have no more tangible measure of achievement. The loss of one-half his fortune would not be felt by the multibillionaire, unless he was informed of his loss. Yet, the name of his game is making another million—much as the checker player uses checkers for scorekeeping. Silas Marner had no plan for converting his gold into goods or services, but the money itself afforded him a measure of achievement and satisfaction, and the gold coins were the units for measuring his most prized possession. Employees on piecework quickly learn to translate labor standards into monetary equivalents as a basis for measuring job performance. For employees whose impact on job goals is otherwise obscured, the pay increase, or lack of it, determined through the judgment of the supervisor may be the only feedback received. Pay is often the scorekeeping system for giving substance to allegations of favoritism or feelings of justice.

Some desire money for the *freedom and opportunity* it buys. Money provides freedom from drudgery, monotony, pettiness, fear, subservience, and other conditions that are seemingly unbearable and are otherwise inescapable. Money provides opportunity to seek higher goals, multiply achievements, buy power or influence, grow personally and professionally, and realize the American dream. The risk takers—mineral explorers, stock market or real estate speculators, gamblers, inventors, entrepreneurs— when their goal is spectacular financial gain, are often seeking or experiencing freedom and opportunity.

The above categorization of pay is primarily a system of emphasis, as money in any given instance might serve any or all of the four functions described. In addition, it must be recognized that these categories are somewhat arbitrary and oversimplified. Almost every individual becomes highly motivated by the prospect of acquiring a large amount of money— and he does not need to analyze his motives for wanting it. Money itself has come to symbolize all that money can buy and is sometimes a substitute for what money can't buy, as there is a bit of Silas Marner in most of us. But this classification system underscores the fact that money does not serve the single, simple function that seems to be implied in traditional approaches to wage and salary administration.

Compensation, in the form of both pay and supplemental benefits, is often more potent as a dissatisfier than as a reinforcement of motivation. Dissatisfaction with compensation arises more often from the pay system itself than from the amount of pay. A pay system based on merit is preferred to one based on tenure, but only if the merit system is understood and equitably administered. Hence, pay is a dissatisfier when it fails to satisfy the purpose for which it is sought, particularly if the pay system lacks the characteristics of an effective system as defined on pages 76 and 77.

MERIT PAY

The concept of merit pay reflects an attempt to discriminately reward members of the organization according to their effectiveness in supporting organizational goals. Outside the job situation, this concept widely permeates the culture: good children get more favorable recognition at home and in school, better students receive higher marks and land better-paying jobs, better tennis players and golfers win more trophies, popular people win the most desirable mates, charismatic politicians win more elections, successful business organizations survive and prosper, alert shoppers grab the best deals in bargain basements, wily crooks make the biggest hauls, competitive persons are first through traffic signals and check-out lines, and effective union campaigners are elected to union offices. Hence, negation of the merit pay concept is inconsistent with universal motivation theory.

Dissatisfaction with merit pay systems is minimized when *pay increases* and *pay levels* are perceived to be equitably related to performance. However, when majority rules, as it often does, particularly when collective bargaining is the medium of leverage, automatic progression is the usual result. This deemphasis of merit in favor of tenure usually reflects a lack of confidence in the merit system, or the people who administer it. Dissatisfactions arising from automatic progression are probably no more numerous than the dissatisfactions stemming from a merit system. When merit pay schemes fail, it is not because they reflect merit but, rather, because they fail to reward merit at all levels of the organization or their merit features have become encumbered with, and overshadowed by, bureaucratic dissatisfiers. For instance, unions customarily oppose merit pay concepts in favor of seniority—primarily because of their mistrust of management's definition of merit. But when union representatives have a hand in defining the criteria, merit itself is not an objectionable concept.

Some organizations, in attempting to remain union-free, fallaciously assume that unions can be best kept at bay by emulating the equal-pay strategy of unionized work forces. But this only increases their vulnerability to unionism, as merit pay satisfies high achievers and dissatisfies low achievers, whereas uniform pay, or pay based on seniority, tends to satisfy low achievers and dissatisfy high achievers whose leadership organizes labor unions.

Dissatisfied high achievers tend either to leave the organization or to find outlets for their talent in counterproductive ways such as assuming leadership roles in union drives. Low achievers, disappointed through the merit system, have incentive to become high achievers or to leave the organization—either alternative beneficial to the organization, to the individual himself, and in turn, to society.

Therefore, the soundest long-range strategy is to develop an equitable merit pay system that is widely understood and accepted throughout the work force. However, not all incentive pay systems are effective. Mechanistic methods of awarding merit pay, such as individual piecework incentive or traditional paid suggestion systems, are potent dissatisfiers for reasons detailed later. Moreover, people whose performance is limited by paced systems and dependence on others have little realistic opportunity to demonstrate meritorious performance. Therefore, implementation of the merit pay concept must, of necessity, involve job incumbents (and their union if they have one), industrial engineers, and other system designers to provide the degrees of freedom necessary for high achievers.

In practice, the most effective merit pay system is based on a person-to-person comparative rating system in which individuals are classified into merit categories according to their overall contribution to the success of their organizational unit. Obviously confidence in such a system depends to a high degree on the climate of trust in the organization in general and trust in the competence and fairness of supervision in particular. Such a system has greater credibility when more than one level of supervision has a hand in the merit judgment process. Moreover, people affected by the process must be able to receive an explanation of the factors contributing to the overall rating—which should be keyed as closely as possible to the attainment of tangible goals, but might include diverse criteria such as quantity, quality, initiative, creativity, dependability, interpersonal relationships, and cost effectiveness. Ideally, members of the work group should have a hand in defining the criteria of job effectiveness.

No matter how carefully a merit pay scheme is administered through the joint efforts of management and the affected job incumbents (and their union), it has a potentially dissatisfying characteristic—particularly for the enlightened members of the new work ethic. It still depends on judgmental inputs which may appear arbitrary to those affected by it. This characteristic need not disqualify it, provided it is based on describable criteria of merit in particular and takes place in a climate of mutual trust. A climate of trust is developed, of course, by trustworthiness in the company and the supervisors (and union leaders) on whom people depend for the satisfaction of their psychological and financial needs in the organization.

When the members of an organization have a significant financial and psychological stake in its success, they are not likely to strike against it or to undermine it through other counterproductive activities. However, high pay and supplemental benefits do not necessarily create a motivated and responsible work force. The concept of joint stake is rarely created by paternalism, but rather by conditions which create a team spirit and the opportunity to influence and share in the fate of the team.

Some managers and union leaders scoff at the notion that employees would be willing to share in anything but gain. They say that employees are fair-weather friends who turn against their employer or their union during an economic recession. Such an assumption is valid, of course, when compensation practices are based on the jellybean philosophy lampooned in Figure 6-1.

OTHER MERIT SYSTEMS

Merit pay can be earned in forms other than wages and salaries. Discretionary bonuses, piecework incentive, paid suggestion systems, stock purchase plans, and even sharing systems represent merit compensation if appropriately designed and administered.

Bonuses

Bonuses function as dissatisfiers or motivators, depending on how and to whom they are distributed. When distributed only to people in upper job grades, they dissatisfy people in the lower job grades. If bonuses are proportional to base salaries, the lower salaried are again dissatisfied. If bonuses are distributed according to merit criteria, the lower achievers are dissatisfied. If bonuses are distributed without regard for merit, the high achievers are dissatisfied.

Unfortunately, most bonus plans are not appropriately keyed to the psychological needs of the people and, even when technically equitable, they are rarely understood. The major shortcoming of bonus plans, however, is that they usually bypass the wage-roll people and, hence, reinforce the traditional two-class system. Unions can point to most bonus plans as valid indicators of social and economic injustice.

However, like other forms of merit pay, they also have potential for rewarding high achievers and increasing their psychological stake in the success of the organization. The knowledge explosion and the increasing enlightenment of wage-roll people make it correspondingly important that achievement be recognized at all levels of the organization. Therefore, a merit bonus system which extends through all organizational levels will do much to reinforce the joint stake feelings of high achievers and help prevent the crystallization of a management-labor dichotomy. A bonus committee, in implementing a plan which will be seen as equitable to high

FIG. 6-1 Pavlov and the bear. (M. Scott Myers, *Managing Without Unions*, Addison-Wesley Publishing Company, Reading, Mass., 1976, pp. iii–xxvii.)

FIG. 6-1 *(Cont.)*

achievers at all levels of the organization, is one which periodically (usually annually) identifies a meritorious percentage slice of every job grade level to be recipients of discretionary bonuses.

Piecework

Emphasis on merit pay based on productivity pleases the high achievers and threatens the low achievers—the people whom management would most like to motivate to produce more or to abandon the organization. Unfortunately, the piecework incentive—the most commonly accepted merit pay scheme among unionized organizations—also leads ultimately to mediocrity.

When unions accept piecework incentives based on engineered labor standards, they may do so because they are based on tangible and measurable criteria which can be monitored by union leaders and job incumbents. However, piece rates ultimately become unmanageable because of the real or imagined inequities which exist among jobs. When a few become satisfied with their labor standards, which are the basis for production bonuses, others whose tight standards don't permit comparable earnings are dissatisfied. But when methods improvements require the engineers to change standards for the high performers in the interest of equitability, the high achievers become dissatisfied. They learn to thwart the intervention of the industrial engineers by opposing methods changes and by limiting productivity. Members of a natural work group would understandably oppose the formation of creative problem-solving groups because of its interference with their output and because of the anticipated changes in standards. Hence, not only does the piecework incentive fail to increase productivity, but also it usually serves to inhibit creativity and put a ceiling on, or lower, productivity.

Paid Suggestions

The typical paid suggestion plan is another incentive system which usually becomes more potent as a dissatisfier than as a motivator. Dissatisfactions arise from the slow processing of suggestions, the rejection of suggestions, and what is perceived as miserly payback to the suggester. Dissatisfactions also arise from the unequal opportunity to participate in the plan. For example, most plans exclude engineers, supervisors, and other professional personnel. Apart from being a dissatisfier, this type of discrimination encourages the unethical and covert channeling of ideas through eligible participants to the mutual, though secret, advantage of the collaborators.

Unfairness is often perceived by members of the old production line who note the greater frequency of payoff in the new production facilities which are still undergoing major debugging adjustments. Allegations of unfairness also come from people in staff functions such as accounting or personnel who accurately perceive that payback for their ideas is usually not as generous as it is for people in mainstream operations.

Paid suggestion plans tend to inhibit group problem-solving–goal-setting efforts. If a participant in a creativity task force experiences a brilliant insight as a result of group interaction, it is understandable, though not laudable, if the employee withholds an idea from the group and covertly drops it in the suggestion box. Though the person's financial payback is increased, collaborative effort and solidarity is undermined, and thus, the flames of dissention are fed, which become easily translated into an image of unfair or inept management.

Further, it should be noted that a paid suggestion plan represents a "language of action" which says, "Salaried people are creative, responsible and intelligent; but hourly people work with their hands; but if they should happen to think, we'll pay them for it." Thus, the typical paid suggestion plan is one of the many systems in the traditional organization which reinforces the cleavage between management and labor.

Though the paid suggestion system may evoke collaborative efforts to beat the system, as noted above, it tends to quash group collaboration in problem solving. Because the system is designed to reward *individual* creativity, individuals understandably protect their ideas by concealing them from others. A paid suggestion system can be designed to encourage both individual and group effort by giving it some of the characteristics of a group-sharing plan. If all suggestion awards were placed in a common pool and distributed as a flat percentage of base rate to all in the group, individuals would have a natural incentive to see their ideas elaborated and improved through the efforts of others. Peer pressures thus would not be directed aggressively against the system; but, rather, constructively toward enlarging the fund, thereby adding synergistic support to organizational goals. Though such a sharing plan has potential for dissatisfying the frequent contributors, high achievers can be separately recognized through discretionary bonuses and merit pay.

Stock Options

Stock options have long been awarded to employees, primarily at the upper levels, as a form of compensation presumed to increase the recipient's proprietary commitment to the success of the organization. Also, stock options, until modified by Federal legislation, offered tax advantages, particularly at the upper levels where increasing tax rates diminished the incentive value of salary increases.

Stock options have not commonly been made available to people at the lower levels, apparently as a result of two implicit assumptions. It is traditionally assumed that, since the reins of the organization are in the hands of the managers who occupy the drivers' seats, managers are the ones who must be motivated. After all, they are the decision makers who make things happen, and it is natural for them to identify with the success of the organization. In contrast, it is reasoned that people at the lower levels of the organization are pretty much limited to what they are told to do, and stock options would have little value in changing their perspective and commitment. Further, it is assumed that people at the lower levels are not sophisticated enough to comprehend the vagaries of the stock market, or that they are not able to afford, or willing to accept, adverse price fluctuations.

These assumptions are partly valid and are understandable consequences of the tradition that has circumscribed the responsibility, perspective, and security of people at the lower levels of the organization. However, these assumptions are being invalidated by the efforts of enlightened managers who are releasing more constructive expression of talent and commitment through job enrichment and goal-oriented supervision, and by the impact of increasingly affluent cultures, which are providing better-informed and more self-reliant job candidates. Whatever value stock options may have at upper levels can now be realized as well at the lower levels.

One successful and progressive corporation has made stock options available to all employees through payroll deductions—stock certificates to be delivered when paid for, at the market price in effect when payroll deductions were authorized. As a hedge against price decline or urgent need of cash, the plan permits the individual to receive his deductions plus interest instead of stock certificates. To the extent that stock ownership increases proprietary commitment, and to the extent that this commitment is permitted to find constructive expression, stock options can yield a better return to the organization.

The potential of stock ownership for inspiring commitment is discussed more fully in the description of ESOPs later in this chapter.

Sharing Plans

Compensation schemes that reward individuals in a group for their collective efforts are referred to by Bert Metzger, president of the Profit Sharing Research Foundation, as "total systems incentives."[1] Under such plans, members of a total group share in benefits derived from cost savings, sales increases, productivity gains, and improved profits.

Profit sharing is one of the more commonly used total system plans, found in approximately one of three companies in American industry. The

[1] Bert L. Metzger, "Profit Sharing—One of the New Breed of Total Systems Incentives," *Atlanta Economic Review*, May–June 1974, pp. 60–62.

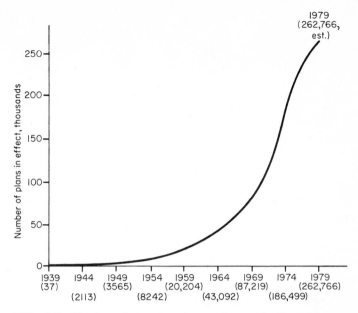

FIG. 6-2   Number of corporate sharing plans in the United States. (Qualified deferred profit sharing and stock bonus plans in the United States, Profit Sharing Research Foundation calculations based on U.S. Treasury Department reports on new corporate plan approvals and terminations; from Bert L. Metzger, *Profit Sharing in 38 Large Companies*, Profit Sharing Research Foundation, Evanston, Illinois, 1978, p. 3.)

dramatic growth of sharing plans since 1939 is portrayed in Figure 6-2. Though profit-sharing plans differ significantly in administrative details and can work in either union or nonunion situations, they have in common the sharing of a portion of the company profits with members of the work force. The most effective sharing plans have the following characteristics:

1.   They apply to all members of the work force, both hourly paid and salaried.

2.   All members benefit equitably in the distribution of the shared pool, in most cases as a percentage of the base pay, but occasionally in equal amounts. In cases where other compensation plans remunerate people in higher job grades adequately for their greater accountability, more mileage might be obtained by distributing the fund in equal shares to all members of the organization. However, care must be exercised to make sure that total compensation packages proportionately reflect contribution to organizational performance.

3.   The amount allocated for profit sharing is enough to make it seem worthwhile to the members and is realistically related to company success. Though small or zero profit sharing can be understandable and acceptable in lean years, higher payout is expected when profits are up. Consistently small payouts, particularly when members don't understand the formula, are often perceived as tokenism or managerial manipulation.

4.   Members of the organization understand the formula through which the profit-sharing fund is determined. Though the amount set aside for distribution to members is typically discretionary with top management (along with allocations for stock dividends, facilities maintenance and expansion, research, and engineering, etc.), it is important that the members who wish to know can understand the logic which creates the profit-sharing fund and that union leaders, in particular, understand and accept the formula and be prepared, if necessary, to explain it to their members. Some organizations publish formulas to enable members to make current estimates of future profit-sharing payouts.

5.   Feedback on benefits is frequent and timely. Plans that give members prompt quarterly or monthly status reports are more effective than those that present only a year-end annual report, particularly if the annual report is delayed a few months. Frequent and current reporting keeps people "in on the know" and enables them to respond responsibly to business fluctuations.

6.   Members have a hand in managing their individual profit-sharing accounts. For example, options might include annual or semiannual decisions on how individual accounts should be invested and how much of the account is to be received in cash and how much is to be deferred. A plan that permits monthly or quarterly payout of one-half the estimated ultimate benefit provide tangible feedback and still provides an annual contribution to the deferred account for discretionary investing.

The Employee Retirement Income Security Act (ERISA) of 1974 was intended to protect employee rights under qualified retirement income plans but, unfortunately, it imposed new constraints regarding participation, vesting, funding, fiduciary standards, reporting/disclosure, and plan termination insurance. These are not insurmountable constraints provided employees are made aware of the details of the legal framework under which their plan functions.

7.   Participants should also be protected against bureaucratic inflexibilities which defeat the purpose and spirit of the plan. For example, safeguards should be provided against the mandatory payout of a depressed profit-sharing account resulting from retirement during a business recession. Sometimes the only safeguard that can be provided is to inform employees in advance of retirement of the various options available to them.

8. Members are prepared financially and psychologically to take the lean periods in stride. In plans providing for periodic cash payouts, for example, members of the plan could reach agreement on a formula for both profit sharing and "loss sharing." They might, for example, agree to hold 15 percent of the quarterly payout in escrow as a hedge against lean periods. Obviously, the more that people understand about corporate finance in general and their specific plan in particular, the more likely they are to respond maturely to fluctuations in shared benefits.

9. Members have an opportunity to apply their talents and efforts in tangible ways to influence organizational cost effectiveness. People who are active in improving methods; participating in problem-solving–goal-setting; and cost reduction, quality improvement, productivity acceleration, and preventive maintenance feel a greater proprietary interest in their profit-sharing plan than do employees whose roles are circumscribed by company procedures, union by-laws, and routinized systems.

Other well-known sharing plans which usually pay off on improvements in the ratio of payroll costs to sales value or production value are known as Scanlon or Rucker plans.[2] Conceived in principle by Joseph N. Scanlon in the 1930s, Scanlon plans are based on a philosophy and techniques which enable people to benefit from their joint efforts in operations improvements. Though Scanlon plans are being applied successfully in nonunion organizations, they probably could find more widespread application than they actually do were it not for the fact that they have been applied more commonly in unionized organizations. This is probably due to the fact that Scanlon himself and most of his disciple-consultants were former union leaders who perhaps subconsciously bring the "management-labor" orientation into the administration of their plans. Since three out of four members of the work forces of the United States and Canada are not unionized, rich opportunity exists for the application of Scanlon plans which are not based on the two-class concept. In fact, the Donnelly Mirrors[3] experience demonstrates the potential of the Scanlon plan for abolishing the two-class system. Moreover, such plans also have potential for application in the public sector.

ESOPs

An innovative sharing plan is being introduced into increasing numbers of American organizations under the label of ESOP (Employee Stock

[2]Frederick G. Lesieur and Elbridge S. Puckett, "The Scanlon Plan Has Proved Itself," *Harvard Business Review*, Sept.–Oct. 1969. Robert C. Scott, "Rucker Plan of Group Incentives," in *The Encyclopedia of Management*, 2d ed., Van Nostrand Reinhold, New York, 1973, pp. 895–900.

[3]John F. Donnelly (interview), "Participative Management at Work," *Harvard Business Review*, Jan.–Feb. 1977, pp. 117–127.

Ownership Plan). Developed by lawyer-economist Louis O. Kelso over the last two decades, the plan is finding widespread acceptance by conservatives and liberals alike. The ESOP offers an opportunity to engender an entrepreneurial spirit in society by evoking a proprietary interest in the success of the organizations that offer them.

As noted earlier, self-employed people are highly motivated and by definition, are working under a compensation plan which inspires commitment, productivity, and innovation. However, most workers in American industry don't work for themselves; they work for the shareholders, who own all or most of the stock of the companies that employ them. Because most of these absentee owners are not on the payrolls of the companies whose shares they own, they have little opportunity to influence productivity within these organizations. Employees who work for governmental agencies are no better off, as relatively few American taxpayers are inspired to higher productivity simply because a small slice of their taxes supports the organization that employs them. Thus, except for the small percentage of people who are actually self-employed or have a significant ownership in their employing organizations, American workers are working for someone else. As has already been discussed, however, people are motivated by their own goals, not the goals of others.

The ESOP is described diagrammatically in the solid lines in Figure 6-3. Kelso has described this plan and its ramifications in several books and articles, and the concept has been evaluated in numerous trade journals and management periodicals.[4]

ESOP combines employee-benefits plans with corporate financing to the mutual benefit of the corporation and its members. A company sells stock to the ESOP trust for the purpose of raising operating capital and/or inspiring productivity or creating a viable retirement plan. The ESOP trust borrows money to buy the stock and may pledge stock and/or use company guarantee as security. Within specified limits, employer contributions to qualified ESOPs are tax deductible, and bank debts (both principal and interest) are repaid with pretax earnings.

Employees receive ownership in company stock proportional to their cumulative gross income. Hence, both income level and company tenure influence the amount of a second income they collect when they leave the organization. Individuals pay no tax on their stock ownership until they leave the organization, at which time it is taxed at a lower retirement income rate as permitted by the Internal Revenue Code.

[4]Louis O. Kelso and Mortimer J. Adler, *The Capitalist Manifesto*, Random House, New York, 1958; Louis O. Kelso and Patricia Hetter, *Two-Factor Theory: The Economics of Reality*, Random House, New York. 1967; W. Robert Reum and Sherry Milliken Reum, "Employee Stock Ownership Plans: Pluses and Minuses," *Harvard Business Review*, July–Aug. 1976, pp. 133–143; Charles G. Burke, "There's More to ESOP than Meets the Eye," *Fortune*, Mar. 1976, p. 128.

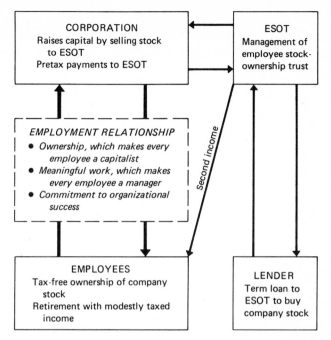

FIG. 6-3 Employee stock-ownership plan. (M. Scott Myers, *Managing With Unions*, Addison-Wesley Publishing Company, Reading, Mass., 1978, p. 53.)

Critics of the plan have made their assessments almost exclusively on the basis of the ESOP as a process for raising money and/or as a method of financing a retirement plan—that is, the solid-line portion of Figure 6-3. This viewpoint does not give adequate recognition to the plan's potential for enhancing the motivation of the work force—as described in italics within the dotted lines in Figure 6-3.

The employment relationship portrayed in this diagram underscores the importance of synergizing meaningful work concepts with capital ownership to obtain proprietary commitment to organizational goals. From the perspective of enlightened workers, the plan creates economic justice with a motive for high achievement. The ESOP represents one of the rare situations in which people can receive a free benefit without its being perceived as a jellybean. The reason, of course, is that the value of the stock is, or becomes, a function of employee productivity. Therefore, the payout from ESOP is an earned reward rather than a manifestation of paternalism.

The compulsion to work, once created by the Protestant ethic, is now being replaced by a joint-stake reason to work. People who manage challenging jobs and receive financial feedback proportional to their accomplishments can experience dignity and self-reliance.

Unlike socialism, which tends to quash incentive and to equate incomes, the ESOP reinforces initiative by rewarding high achievers. For instance, the higher merit pay and discretionary bonuses of higher achievers are reflected in their greater ownership of ESOP. Increased productivity renders an organization more competitive and profitable, further increasing the cash value of the ESOP. Moreover, the joint financial stake which people share with the company and one another tends to bring peer pressure to bear on counterproductive members. The philosopher-educator, Mortimer J. Adler, says of the ESOP:

> According to Mr. Kelso's theory, capitalism perfected in the line of its own principles, and without any admixture of socialism, can create the economically free and classless society which will support political democracy and which, above all, will help us to preserve the institutions of a free society. In what we have become accustomed to call "the world-wide struggle for men's minds," this conception of capitalism offers the only real alternative to communism, for our partly socialized capitalism is an unstable mixture of conflicting principles, a halfway house from which we must go forward in one direction or the other.[5]

Second incomes derived from stock ownership render retirees less dependent on social security and in some cases might even displace it. Unlike social security, which punishes the fiscally responsible by depriving them of the annuity to which they contributed, ESOP also rewards retirees who continue to be high achievers.

For some organizations, the greatest value of the ESOP is its potential for redirecting the human energy now being dissipated in adversary relationships. As long as management is composed of the "haves" and labor of the "have-nots," win-lose strategies will be perpetuated between company and union over bigger shares of a diminishing pie. Under ESOP, in which all employees are part owners, union leaders on the board of ESOP represent employees as shareholders rather than as adversaries. People working for themselves strive to increase the size of the pie and do not strike against themselves or engage in other counterproductive measures.

The fruition of ESOP in the United States, as envisioned by Kelso, required the legislative changes already enacted and perhaps further changes in the law. However, with facilitative legislation already enacted, ESOP has much to offer to support the cause of social and economic justice and to preserve capitalism and the free-enterprise system. Countries

---

[5] Kelso and Adler, op. cit., p. xvi. Reprinted by permission.

that at present do not offer financial incentive for the ESOP may capitalize on the potential it offers simply by enacting facilitative legislation.

The ESOP concept has potential for solving or ameliorating a number of interdependent societal problems:

1. Enlightened members of American work forces are becoming increasingly dissatisfied with traditional wage systems in general and paternalism in particular. Their broader perspective enables them to see the merits of an ESOP, which gives them a joint financial stake in the success of the organization.

2. The compulsion to work, based on the Protestant ethic, is giving way to the quest for meaningful work. For many, being on relief is no less demeaning than being a highly paid automaton. The ESOP fosters a new work ethic, but on a rational foundation of productivity and responsibility.

3. Per capita productivity is gradually declining across the nation, resulting in inflation, competitive disadvantage in the world market, and balance-of-trade deficits. Though Federal treasury receipts are temporarily reduced by the tax breaks offered by ESOPs, less tax revenue is needed to finance relief programs. Actually the accelerated cash flow activated by increased discretionary income of retirees has potential for maintaining tax revenues. Hence the reward system of ESOP increases productivity and thus benefits the nation, as well as organizations and their members.

4. Leaders in government and business are increasingly concerned that recent trends can lead America into socialism and the debilitating bureaucracy now being experienced in Great Britain. Managers recognize the need to improve the economic status of workers, but are deathly afraid of giving the company away. ESOP at once improves worker status and bolsters the free-enterprise system. Though originally designed for profit-making organizations, the ESOP can be adapted to the public sector to apply, for example, to postal services, universities, and municipal administration.

5. The social security retirement system is near bankruptcy, and the income needs and expectations of retirees are accelerating at a faster rate than contemporary taxpayers are willing to support. The second income created by an ESOP constitutes a supplement which can reduce tax burdens and increase retirement incomes.

6. Unions are making inroads into the public sector and what were heretofore recognized as the ranks of management—unionism is becoming less of a white-collar/blue-collar dichotomy. Traditional unionism, basing its existence on adversary relationships, tends to convert people into opponents squabbling over greater shares of a shrinking pie. ESOP has the potential for converting the win-lose mentality of labor relations into collaborative win-win strategies through which people increase the size of the pie.

Supplemental Benefit Systems

Supplemental benefits include various forms of compensation not specifically related to the work itself, but received just for being a member of the work force—benefits such as holiday pay, vacations, retirement plans, sick leave, rest periods, free coffee, and the Christmas turkey. These benefits are maintenance factors, as described in Figure 1-2, and have more potential for dissatisfaction than they have for motivation. However, some supplemental benefits, such as profit sharing, Scanlon-type suggestion plans, educational assistance, stock-ownership plans, and professional society memberships also have potential for satisfying motivation needs.

The latter types are better investments for both the company and its members. The company benefits from the increased commitment of people with greater psychological and financial stake in the organization. Its members gain from the intrinsic value of these benefits and from the increased self-respect resulting from these nonpaternalistic programs.

During the first half of the twentieth century in the United States, the cost of supplemental benefits as a percentage of total compensation has risen from less than 10 percent to more than 30 percent. Some of these benefits are required by law, some were won through collective bargaining, many were granted through paternalism, and others were provided by enlightened management. Though aimed initially at remedying deficiencies in wages, hours, and working conditions, they have been increasingly broadened to support the expanding maintenance needs of an affluent society. Increasing costs of supplemental benefits, unless they are productivity oriented, ultimately work to the detriment of employees as they reduce the organization's ability to compete in the world market.

The evolution of supplemental benefits illustrates the overriding strength of tradition in blinding management to the changing needs of people. In earlier decades, when many people did in fact suffer from thwarted maintenance needs, management learned that satisfying these was a sound business investment. To many managers, supplemental benefits are still seen as key incentives in stimulating effectiveness. Employees are often blamed for their seemingly insatiable demands for increased supplemental benefits, when it was and is management's perceptions and invalid assumptions about people that escalated these benefits to their excessively high levels. As noted earlier, preoccupation with maintenance factors in today's society is more often a symptom of thwarted motivation needs than of unsatisfied maintenance needs. But most managers do not know how to provide the conditions necessary for satisfying motivation needs. Though the motivation needs of people are best satisfied through the medium of meaningful work itself, these needs can also be partially satisfied through people's involvement in the management of their supplemental benefit systems.

Consider *group insurance* as a specimen supplemental benefit. Traditionally, a group insurance system is masterminded by personnel experts within constraints designated by top management. The mission is to provide the most attractive program for the greatest number at the lowest cost. In effect, Personnel, through armchair logic, evolves a system to satisfy the presumed needs of their customers—the employees of the organization. Following the development and ratification of the program by top management, it is given the hard sell by the personnel department, who point out to the people the benefits and advantages of the new system over others. Though inflationary trends may have increased the price of the package, they are assured that they are getting more for the price than before. The ardor and eloquence of management in selling this system usually makes it suspect. The system might in fact be superior, but employees feel a vague suspicion about management's need to convince them of its merits. They have learned that "The big print giveth and the little print taketh away." They are hearing the "big print" and wondering about the unspoken "little print." The greater the gap between management and labor, the less likely employees are to believe that management is acting in their behalf. It is understandable that a group insurance program is often the issue of collective bargaining where the employees feel that their rights are being protected by their peers in the bargaining process. In short, it can be said that employees typically do not see the group insurance program as their program simply because it is labeled "employees insurance plan." Employees are both the customer and the user of the group insurance program and, therefore, the system will succeed or fail according to the criteria listed on page 77. As the customer, employees must have an opportunity to define the purpose of the group insurance system; they will then understand and agree with its purpose. They must know how to use the system and apply it to their own situations. They must receive timely feedback when they activate the system and be able to initiate actions to adapt or revise the system to increase its effectiveness. The primary system user thus has the opportunity to influence the development, administration, and revision of a system designed to service him as a customer. To do this responsibly, he must, of course, be fully informed on matters pertaining to policy and legal guidelines, economic trends, and financial and service resources available for this system.

A group insurance system that will minimize dissatisfactions and satisfy the needs of the largest number is evolved through participation by panels of employee representatives, as illustrated in Figure 6-4. If possible, these

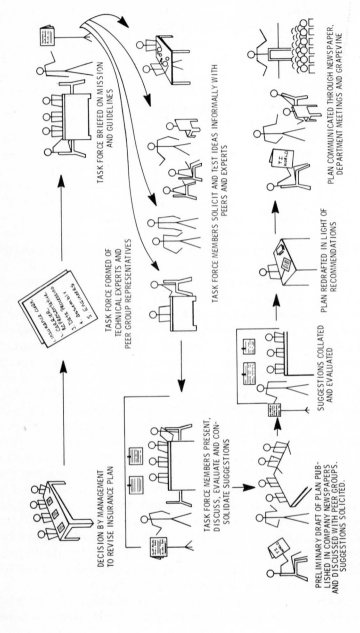

DECISION BY MANAGEMENT TO REVISE INSURANCE PLAN

TASK FORCE FORMED OF TECHNICAL EXPERTS AND PEER GROUP REPRESENTATIVES

TASK FORCE BRIEFED ON MISSION AND GUIDELINES

TASK FORCE MEMBERS SOLICIT AND TEST IDEAS INFORMALLY WITH PEERS AND EXPERTS

TASK FORCE MEMBERS PRESENT, DISCUSS, EVALUATE AND CON-SOLIDATE SUGGESTIONS

PRELIMINARY DRAFT OF PLAN PUB-LISHED IN COMPANY NEWSPAPERS AND DISCUSSED WITH PEER GROUPS. SUGGESTIONS SOLICITED.

SUGGESTIONS COLLATED AND EVALUATED

PLAN REDRAFTED IN LIGHT OF RECOMMENDATIONS

PLAN COMMUNICATED THROUGH NEWSPAPER, DEPARTMENT MEETINGS AND GRAPEVINE

FIG. 6-4 Development of group insurance system.

196

panels should be selected by a flexible process that taps groups naturally related through work roles, union membership, or fluid communication channels. Perhaps the first assignment of the panel is to evaluate the membership in the light of the assignment and to suggest revisions. Though panels will naturally include professional, managerial, and wage-roll personnel, their membership involves them not as agents of management or labor but, rather, as concerned system users.

Qualification for panel membership is based on either technical competence needed for designing and administering the system, or ability to represent the members of natural work groups or segments of the organization. Technical competence factors, for example, would draw membership from systems designers, carrier representatives, data processors, legal staff, and particularly the company insurance clerks who have day-to-day contact with the users. Employee representation considerations would include members who would represent the interests of different age groups, married and single, male and female, unskilled and skilled, professional and managerial individuals, who collectively compose the work force and are to be served through the system.

The selection of panel members is an important key to the successful development of a system to serve the entire population. All organizations have bellwethers who are pivotal to the fluid communication process because their personality characteristics make them the natural, informal, and trusted unifying agents of informal peer groups. To prescribe membership simply through prescheduled and formalized appointments, elections, rotation, or lottery would not usually achieve representativeness. The informal nomination and election process, with flexible guidelines for periodic review and revision, is more likely to keep the panel attuned to its constituency's grapevine.

The effectiveness of such a working task force depends on open access to all information that would be available to corporate systems planners. The first meeting of the panel task force should be a briefing session, to define the mission and administrative guidelines, and to determine the adequacy of panel membership with respect to technical know-how and work-force representation. The briefing session is conducted informally by the panel itself, drawing on the heterogeneous talent represented in the group.

Orientation should include brief reviews of historical data, economic trends, experience with previous plans, comparative survey data, reasons for developing a new plan, reasons for working through panels, support services available, and budgetary guidelines.

The group is goal-oriented rather than authority-directed, functioning as an effective team as defined on pages 48 to 51. The chairman of the task force is usually a corporate insurance administrator, but chairmanship may be transferred or rotated to other members at the group's option.

The panel should conclude the first meeting with a clear understanding that they are responsible for building the company group insurance package, with the freedom and responsibility to discuss the issues informally with their peers on the job. Though no group insurance plan would ever satisfy all members equally, this process is better for four reasons:

1. It is more likely to result in a system attuned to the most important needs of the greatest number of users.

2. Work-force representation through panel membership increases employee identification with the system.

3. The resultant evolutionary, self-correcting system places little dependency on high-level administrators who may be unresponsive to desired program modifications.

4. The group insurance system, being widely visible throughout the organization, is a language of action symbolizing management by competence rather than management by authority.

PAY SYSTEMS AS DISSATISFIERS

Apart from the roles of pay itself discussed earlier, pay systems, like supplemental benefit systems, have potential as either detractors or reinforcers of satisfaction derived from work itself. Take-home pay is generally influenced directly or indirectly by the following factors:

1. Financial reviews

2. Job evaluation

3. Performance appraisal

4. Wage and salary surveys

5. Cost-of-living index (Bureau of Labor Statistics)

6. Federal income tax (Internal Revenue Service)

7. Social security (Department of Health and Human Services)

The first four systems are usually designed and administered by the employer, and the last three by arms of the Federal government. All these systems have potential for dissatisfaction, but the employing organization can influence their administration to reduce or eliminate their negative impact on employees—certainly the first four more than the last three, but all can be influenced.

Typically, these seven systems impact the paycheck in the following manner. Top management of the organization during the year-end *financial review* makes a forecast of profits for the coming year. This forecast is a partial basis for allocating funds for pay increases throughout the year. However, before funds are finally allocated, consideration is given to the results of the company *survey of wages and salaries* in comparable industries and communities, and any changes in the *cost-of-living index* published by the Bureau of Labor Statistics. Considering these three inputs, management allocates a fund that the company can afford, usually expressed as a percentage of total payroll—such as "an average of 5 percent increase across the board." The actual distribution of this average percentage is, of course, delegated to successive levels of supervision down the line so that actual increases range from zero (or perhaps a reduction in pay) to varying amounts above 5 percent.

The distribution of pay to individuals is influenced by *job evaluation* and *performance appraisal.* Job-evaluation systems establish pay levels or rate ranges for each job, based on comparative analyses of jobs in terms of a wide variety of factors, such as skill and knowledge requirements, accountability, creativity, health hazards, and amount of supervision required. Job evaluations determine the relative values of jobs within the company, and these evaluations are in turn coupled with rate surveys to establish the actual rate range for the job. Once a rate range is established through job evaluation, an individual's personal rate within that range and any subsequent increases are usually established by the judgment of his supervisor who typically compares him with his peers in terms of preselected factors such as quantity and quality of work, initiative, creativity, cooperativeness, and responsibility.

Finally, the individual receives his paycheck from his supervisor and notices on the check stub that the payroll department has deducted amounts for Federal income tax and social security, as required by law. These are the minimum deductions; he may have his paycheck further diminished by payroll deductions for state taxes, union dues, charity donations, savings bonds, insurance premiums, retirement pension, and credit union loans. And though most of the items in this expanded list of deductions are authorized and theoretically optional, in practice they are to him as inescapable as the legally required deductions.

Thus the average employee perceives his paycheck as a residual of insidious processes controlled by unknown, arbitary authority figures in Federal and state governments, management and supervision, payroll and personnel departments, and the union. In a climate of security and trust, his dependency relationship is bearable, but in a climate of insecurity and deception, he responds with apathy or hostility.

WHY PAY SYSTEMS FAIL

Dissatisfactions arising from pay stem largely from ineffective application of systems that influence pay. No matter how intrinsically well-designed the system, if it does not satisfy the conditions of effective systems, as defined on page 77, it will not win acceptance and satisfaction.

In reviewing the foregoing seven systems affecting the paycheck, it is apparent that not all conditions for effectiveness can be satisfied directly for each system. However, three conditions are satisfied for all seven systems if people understand and agree with the systems and receive timely feedback from them. The other conditions (which enable individuals to use, control, and adapt the systems), usually cannot be satisfied directly, but this is not always necessary as long as individuals know how the system is used, how and who controls it, and when and why it is adapted to new situations.

The financial review deals with data traditionally treated as top management proprietary information. The logic defending this practice reflects the assumptions that people at the lower levels are not responsible, honest, and reasonable—that they will use the information inadvertently or maliciously to the detriment of the organization. Management will cite cases in point where individuals have surreptitiously gained and misused information—or where rumors based on mismanaged information have resulted in morale problems, disruption of work, and disaffection.

The withholding of such information reflects a lack of trust; and the evasiveness of managers when asked for information is often perceived as deception, thereby reinforcing the management-labor, two-class system. Since job success requires access to relevant information, unofficial channels are developed by lower levels. This, of course, causes management to tighten controls on company information. The ultimate and often unrecognized consequence of this circular process is that much of the energy at the lower levels of the organization is dissipated through unofficial pursuit of forbidden information.

Thus, when top management announces the amount of funds available for pay increases, the climate is rife with suspicion, cynicism, and a readiness to challenge the decision and to demand more. It may be that management has strained company resources to make the allocation, but in a climate of mutual mistrust where deception is presumed, truth evokes suspicion. Hence, a well-meant change in policy to disclose financial information to explain the allocation of funds for pay increases does not immediately win the understanding support of the people influenced by the allocation.

But the scope of the financial review is broader than the compensation system. It is also the basis for planning company growth, developing marketing strategies, discontinuing or adding products and services, investing in buildings and equipment, financing research, planning tax strategies, declaring dividends, and performing various correlated functions. Therefore, compensation is only one of the many topics considered in the financial review, and the annual pay increase is only one of several subtopics of compensation for which decisions must be made. Other compensation-related matters might include stock options, discretionary bonuses, profit sharing, collective bargaining trends, group insurance, retirement plan, subsidized eating facilities, and other supplemental benefits which are part of the total compensation package. Of the four company systems listed as having direct impact on compensation, it is apparent that the financial review is the only one dealing with compensation as a subsidiary function; the other three have an impact on compensation directly as a primary function.

MAKING PAY SYSTEMS SUCCEED

Two administrative changes are needed to transform these traditional approaches into systems that will evoke understanding and acceptance. One strategy is to utilize the natural job relationships that exist in all organizations, to involve horizontally and vertically related family groups in the problem-solving–goal-setting approach described on pages 138 to 143.

The other strategy is to form task forces which, while pursuing the goals of specific missions, disregard functional and hierarchical relationships within the task force which might ordinarily impair the goal orientation of the group. Such a strategy is illustrated on pages 195 to 198, in describing the development of a company group insurance program.

The financial review and performance appraisal systems, because they deal with natural work groups, are best administered through the *natural-relationships strategy,* whereas job evaluations and wage and salary surveys, which cut across organizational lines, may be achieved better through emphasis on the *task-force strategy.* These two strategies are not mutually exclusive, as the success of one requires the support of the other, and it is only a matter of emphasis when one strategy is recommended over another.

The financial review, administered through the natural-relationships strategy, begins by broadening the number and depth of individuals who participate in the top management planning and control functions. The planning function, described on pages 151 to 155, illustrates this base-broadening process. Each manager presents to his peers and top management a plan developed through iterative problem-solving relationships within the natural work groups of his organization. The ratification of the plan is the basis for the manager to give feedback to the members of his organization in terms of plans, goals, and problems. This is a unique opportunity for people to comprehend the organization's financial status and plans for utilizing profits or coping with deficits. This feedback is communicated to all members of the manager's unit through periodic (quarterly or monthly) "department meetings" and through the individual goal-setting process of the performance review process.

Hence, individuals at the bottom of the organization, through the problem-solving–goal-setting process, aid their supervisor in solving problems and setting his goals. He, in turn, with his peers, assists his supervisor in the problem-solving–goal-setting process until the president of the organization is ultimately presented with the goals and strategies of the people reporting to him. But the president and his economic researchers and marketing planners have concurrently been providing information downward, giving direction to the problem-solving–goal-setting process of the natural work groups and task forces below. Hence, approved plans and strategies finally converge in the year-end (as well as quarterly) financial review and are melded into the corporate plans and goals. The natural-relationships strategy is neither a top-to-bottom nor a bottom-to-top process but, rather, a multidirectional reciprocative or iterative process with fluid flow of information in all directions and opportunity for purposeful involvement at all levels of the organization.

The performance review is an expression of the natural-relationships strategy. All organizations, and each of their progressively subdivided units, exist, of course, for the purpose of achieving goals. Responsibility inheres only in individuals—not in organizations or groups. However, individuals, working collectively within the perimeters of their respective responsibilities, can set goals and organize manpower and material to achieve them. In the goal-oriented organization (as contrasted to the authority-oriented organization), individuals earn the opportunity to survive and succeed by their ability to achieve their goals without impairing the opportunity for others to do the same.

The key distinction between performance review through goal setting and performance review by authority is the involvement of the job incumbent in the goal-setting system in defining his goals, the strategies for achieving them, and the criteria for measuring his accomplishments. In contrast, in the authority-oriented system, evaluations are often influenced by criteria which may not be predetermined or even known to the job incumbent, except that he senses that he must do whatever his intuition tells him is necessary to win the favor of the boss. Evaluation in the goal-setting system is based more objectively on the comparison of an individual's achievements against ratified goals and the performance of others.

The relating of pay decisions and bonuses to achievements of self-influenced goals and the relating of his contributions to the success of the organization are far more acceptable to the goal-oriented person than the seemingly arbitrary dispensing and withholding of merit pay based on the judgments of authority figures using undefined or inconsistent criteria of merit.

Administration of wage and salary surveys and job-evaluation plans is facilitated by the task-force strategy, following the group insurance process described on page 196. Panels made up of technical experts and peer representatives are briefed, in this case, in the theory and practice of pay administration, in compensation problems and conditions unique to the organization, and in procedures for evaluating jobs and conducting compensation surveys. The key to this process is the open access to any information needed or wanted by members.

Panels bring to these systems broader talent and keener awareness of the perceptions of the employees, including real and imagined inequities, thereby improving the validity of the systems by making them more responsive to the needs of the users. Of equal importance is the panel's role in gaining understanding and acceptance of the systems and their application through the fluid communication process of the grapevine. As was pointed out on page 77, systems' successes and failures are determined largely by the attitudes and perceptions of people influenced by the systems.

Under the foregoing conditions, the remaining systems—cost-of-living index, Federal income tax, and social security—can lose much of their mystery and, hence, much of their oppressiveness. These systems are explained as part of the briefing curriculum for panel task forces involved in job evaluation and wage and salary surveys. Panel members learn, for example, the distinction between merit pay and cost-of-living adjustments, and become aware of the negative impact of deceptive labeling when one is substituted for the other. Company newspapers and bulletins, department meetings, the manager's roundtable, and the grapevine are natural media for explaining these systems and announcing changes in them.

The combined impact of the natural-relationships strategy and the task-force strategy can create a substantially different perception of the paycheck. Though few individuals would be able or have occasion to define all the factors impacting their pay, the networks of formal and informal involvement processes supported by open and fluid communication practices make information available if wanted and do much to minimize the dissatisfactions characteristically inherent in pay systems.

An important guiding principle in the administration of supplemental benefits, whether they be maintenance- or motiviation-oriented, is that they be available to people at all levels of the organization. Though it is customary and sometimes necessary to relate the value of the benefit to the responsibility level of the individual as part of the compensation package, dissatisfactions are minimized if certain rank-related privileges can be abolished or, at least, minimized. For example, wage-roll people with entrepreneurial, sociocentric, and existential values cannot see equity in systems that offer them lower tuition refunds than salaried people receive, or limit the life insurance they can buy through their group insurance plan to some multiple of their annual income.

Nor does providing equal benefits to all members of the work force necessarily make them equitable. If the benefits are jelly beans in the form of a Christmas turkey or free coffee, they may be dissatisfiers because of unequal turkey sizes or the resentment of noncoffee drinkers. But if these jellybeans are replaced by a nonpaternalistic benefit such as an increase in the tuition refund plan or improved stock purchase plan, they are less potent as dissatisfiers. Though these substitute benefits are not "equal" to all, as was the Christmas turkey, they are more "equitable" as they encourage achievement and thrift at all organization levels.

Supplemental benefits, administered in accordance with principles described here are essential ingredients or "grains of sand" in the total network of systems which contribute to the joint stake in the success of the organization.

7
The Changing Roles of Management

Management of change is the key function of the manager, in regard to both human effort and technology. The responsibility is not new, of course, but it is becoming increasingly complicated by the accelerating rate of change in all media. Because change requires adaptation at all levels of the organization, the manager is confronted with the circular problem of encouraging innovation while introducing changes in a manner that will not threaten the innovators. Being human, the manager, too, is vulnerable to the threats of innovation, and he must be able to monitor and evaluate his own effectiveness and take measures to prevent his own obsolescence. Through the media of supervisory style, management systems, and other factors affecting the organization's climate, he must gradually shift the source of influence from official authority to people power so that initiative and freedom at all levels of the organization will find responsible expression.

He is challenged further by the requirement for applying principles of human effectiveness in operations in other cultures. The success of the American abroad is strongly dependent on his ability to develop authentic relationships with indigenous personnel. Just as children entering adolescence sometimes rebel against those who nurtured them, indigenous personnel in developing countries are often hostile toward Americans whose paternalism and aggressiveness threaten their economic and cultural sovereignty.

THE ROLE OF THE SUPERVISOR

Chapter 3 presents a framework to bridge the management–labor gap and give substance to the slogan "Every employee a manager"—a manager being defined as one who manages a job. A self-managed job is one which provides a realistic opportunity for the incumbent to be responsible for the total plan-do-control phases of his job. Though many jobs in their present forms cannot be fully enriched, most can be improved and some can be eliminated or fused with others, or more uniquely matched with incumbent aptitudes. Whether the supervisor's mission is to modify the job or to combine it with the right people, he achieves it best by utilizing the talents of the people he supervises.

The supervisor must be able to understand the conditions which promote and inhibit expression of talent in terms of interpersonal competence, meaningful goals, and helpful systems, as defined in Chapter 2. In satisfying these conditions, he is required to take a soul-searching look at himself in the mirror—to find out what new responsibilities and activities he should be involved with, and which of his traditional roles should be modified or discontinued. As he is human, changes in his role are unsettling or threatening, particularly if they are imposed by authority. His dilemma is ameliorated if he himself is the instigator of his changing role.

Self-Imposed Role Ambiguity

During the early 1960s, when production supervisors in Texas Instruments began applying the problem-solving–goal-setting process, their purpose was to invoke the talent of their groups in achieving difficult production goals. Their efforts were rewarded not only by the attainment of production goals but also by improved quality of workmanship; fewer complaints about maintenance factors; less frequent absenteeism and tardiness; and fewer trips to the health center, restrooms, and personnel department. In some cases, they found commitment so high it became essential to remind employees to take the legally required rest periods in midmorning and midafternoon.

With their increased freedom and involvement in managing their own work, operators began working directly with the engineers in methods improvement, value analysis, and rearranging their work place. Supervisors permitted these new work roles of the operators primarily because they resulted in improved performance. But the operators' activities did not always of necessity involve their supervisors, who became understandably uncomfortable with the resultant ambiguity of their new roles. One supervisor's anxiety reached a new high when a problem-solving group told him that he was free to leave the meeting to attend to other matters and that they would keep him posted on their progress. Consequently, a group of these disenfranchised supervisors, with the assistance of the division training director, undertook the task of defining their new role.

Role Redefinition

The results of this group's efforts are reflected in Figure 7-1. Initial efforts to remove role ambiguity produced the traditional authority-oriented role

Authority–Oriented	Goal–Oriented
Set goals for subordinates, define standards and results expected.	Participate with people in problem solving and goal setting.
Give them information necessary to do their job.	Give them access to information which they want.
Train them how to do the job.	Create situations for optimum learning.
Explain rules and apply discipline to ensure conformity; suppress conflict.	Explain rules and consequences of violations; mediate conflict.
Stimulate subordinates through persuasive leadership.	Allow people to set challenging goals.
Develop and install new methods.	Teach methods improvement techniques to job incumbents.
Develop and free them for promotion.	Enable them to pursue and move into growth opportunities.
Reward achievements and punish failures.	Recognize achievements and help them learn from failures.

FIG. 7-1   The role of supervision.

detailed in the left column. After evaluating and rejecting these traditional descriptors as inaccurate definitions of their emerging role, they redefined their supervisory responsibilities, as stated in the goal-oriented role column.

Though most of the items in the left column are acceptable in the light of tradition, their collective effect tends to reinforce the authority-oriented relationship, depicted in the diagram at the foot of the column, in which people are expected to conform to the plan-lead-control directives from supervision. Items in the goal-oriented column do not differ completely from those in the authority-oriented column, but their net effect offers more opportunity for people to manage the full plan-do-control phases of their work, involving supervision as a resource.

Different groups of supervisors became involved in the role redefinition process. One group concluded that an effective supervisor is one who provides a climate in which people have a sense of working for themselves. In terms of their day-to-day relationships, they defined the supervisor's role as:

- Giving visibility to organizational goals
- Providing resources and defining constraints
- Mediating conflict
- Staying out of the way to let people manage their work

Giving visibility to company goals means sharing information with the members of the group who are to be involved in achieving a specific customer goal. In a production line, for example, it means defining the group's mission to provide a product for a customer, including cost, quality, and schedule requirements. It means detailing the overhead, materiel, and labor costs associated with providing the product or service, showing the percentage each contributes to the total cost, and distinguishing between the fixed and variable costs. All members of the group should be able to see the problem essentially as the supervisor sees it and should have access to any information needed to achieve their goal. The key to this function is emphasizing the facts that everyone has a client or a customer, whether this customer is the ultimate customer or another department or assembly line within the company, and that the group goal is to satisfy the customer's need.

Providing resources and defining constraints does not mean financing every improvement or capital investment suggested by the members of the group. It means arranging for a meeting area, providing budgets, and soliciting the involvement of support personnel. It also means defining constraints—sharing with group members the rationale for managing a budget and, if a capital investment is suggested, explaining the amortization process and exploring with them its application to a suggested expenditure. When the group is involved in assessing a proposed investment in terms of increased efficiency, the duration of the project, change in quality, etc., they can see whether or not it is a sound economic investment, and a decision to buy or not to buy is a matter of logic rather than an arbitrary decision based on authority.

The mediation of conflict is an ongoing and often misunderstood role of supervision. Conflict always exists; however, the nature of conflict varies. In an environment of meaningless work and arbitrary supervision, conflict is often a symptom of displaced aggression or of unbearable monotony. In an environment of interesting work and facilitative supervision, conflict may arise as a result of spirited competition and the challenge of achieving individual and group goals. This type of conflict is not harmful, as long as it is surfaced in a climate which enables group members to cope with it. Facilitative supervisors do not avoid or suppress conflict, but encourage its constructive expression.

Staying out of the way to let people manage their work does not mean abandoning the group and heading for the golf course, but it does mean being sensitive to the needs of individuals in regard to their desire and ability to be responsible for many planning and control functions of their job. When delegation is done successfully, people are not subjected to arbitrary and rigid constraints, but have the freedom to pursue goals which they have helped define. They will seek help from any source to achieve this goal, including the supervisor if he has earned their acceptance and has something to contribute in the nature of needed business information or technical competence. The application of authority to such a team effort tends primarily to quash the goal-oriented spirit of the group.

Goals Replace Conformity

This redefinition of the supervisor's role to provide opportunity for people to manage their own work is portrayed in Figure 7-2. In contrast to the authority-conformity-oriented roles of the supervisor and operator shown in Figure 3-9, each now has a goal-oriented role in which the revised *do* phase of the supervisor and *plan* phase of the operator compose the realm of interface between them. Figures 7-1 and 7-2 both show the goal-oriented supervisor to be a resource person whose involvement is invoked primarily at the initiative of the operator.

This role of the leader, evolved initially to illustrate the relationship between the foreman and operators, is a model representing ideal supervisory relationships at any level of the organization. Furthermore, enriching the operator's job has changed higher-level jobs, in some cases making it possible to reduce the number of levels in the management hierarchy. The foreman, now freed of many detailed maintenance and surveillance functions, has more time to be involved with his supervisor in higher-level planning functions and is also more available to serve as adviser, counselor, and facilitator when needed by the natural work group under his supervision.

The application of meaningful work offers substantial short-range incentive for managers to support it. Judged as they are, periodically, in terms of financial criteria such as profit, cost reduction, cash flow, share of the market, and return-on-investment criteria, job enrichment is valued as a process for achieving success. But it offers even greater rewards on a long-term basis, particularly if criteria of success are broadened to include aspects of human effectiveness such as better utilization of employee tal-

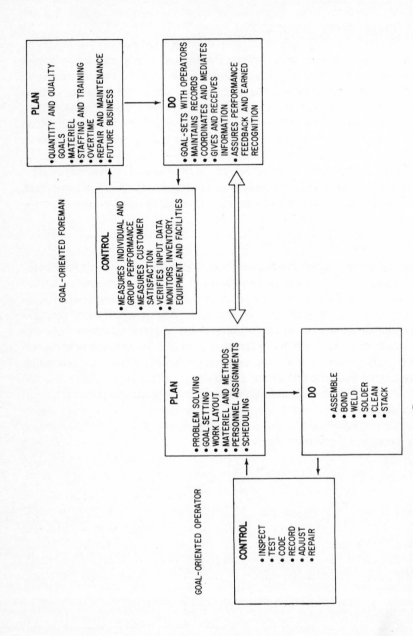

GOAL-ORIENTED FOREMAN

PLAN
- QUANTITY AND QUALITY GOALS
- MATERIEL
- STAFFING AND TRAINING
- OVERTIME
- REPAIR AND MAINTENANCE
- FUTURE BUSINESS

DO
- GOAL-SETS WITH OPERATORS
- MAINTAINS RECORDS
- COORDINATES AND MEDIATES
- GIVES AND RECEIVES INFORMATION
- ASSURES PERFORMANCE FEEDBACK AND EARNED RECOGNITION

CONTROL
- MEASURES INDIVIDUAL AND GROUP PERFORMANCE
- MEASURES CUSTOMER SATISFACTION
- VERIFIES INPUT DATA
- MONITORS INVENTORY, EQUIPMENT AND FACILITIES

GOAL-ORIENTED OPERATOR

PLAN
- PROBLEM SOLVING
- GOAL SETTING
- WORK LAYOUT
- MATERIEL AND METHODS
- PERSONNEL ASSIGNMENTS
- SCHEDULING

DO
- ASSEMBLE
- BOND
- WELD
- SOLDER
- CLEAN
- STACK

CONTROL
- INSPECT
- TEST
- CODE
- RECORD
- ADJUST
- REPAIR

FIG. 7-2 Goal-oriented relationship between foreman and operator.

ent, more responsible civic and home relationships, and the profitable and self-renewing growth of the organization.

Responsibility Replaces Prerogatives

Gone are management prerogatives. Management prerogatives, by definition, are exclusive rights based on authority. The specifying of "management" prerogatives evokes a requirement for "labor" prerogatives. Evaluation of labor prerogatives shows them to be unaligned with, or contradictory to, company goals, as shown in Figure 7-13. Hence, it is self-defeating to articulate and act through the authority of management prerogatives. The divine rights of "King Supervisor" are being relinquished under the self-imposed pressures of enlightenment. The price of management prerogatives in terms of quashed initiative, alienation, and unachieved goals is much too high for all but those seeking satisfaction of pathological needs for power and domination.

Prerogatives have given way to responsibility—to customers, shareholders, employees, and the community. To the *customer* the manager is responsible for delivering a superior product or service at minimum cost. To the *shareholder* or owner he is responsible for maximizing return on investment. To the *employee* he is responsible for providing a meaningful life at work. And the manager's impact is made on the *community* by the emulation in homes of his leadership patterns on the job. Democratic or autocratic managers began the development of their managerial styles in democratic or autocratic homes under parents whose styles of leadership were often influenced by role models in the job situation. Hence, the work place represents the most potent medium for influencing the philosophy of a society.

Competence Replaces Authority

Influence is still needed to satisfy this new leadership role; however, it is not the influence of official supervisory authority but, rather, the unofficial influence or "people power" of all members of the group spontaneously applying their competence and commitment to goals. Both kinds of influence exist in all organizations, and the manager's supervisory style determines and indicates which is predominant. An excessive amount of official authority evokes an excessive amount of people power—as demonstrated in Iran, leading to the deposition of the Shah and the events following thereafter.

For practical purposes, what really matters in industry is not whether the supervisor has official authority or not, but whether he is accepted by the people who depend on his leadership. The supervisor whose behavior has earned the acceptance and respect of his work group has, in effect, transformed his official authority to unofficial acceptance. He is both the formal and the informal leader of the group, and he succeeds as a leader not by virtue of authority from above, but through the willing acceptance of those who are influenced by his behavior.

Leadership is not a psychological trait but a function of the situation and the nature of the group. In a given situation, the effective leader is the person most fitted to take charge. A group leader, officially appointed, will try to see to it that he is accepted, not because of his official authority, but because he is perceived as the appropriate leader in that situation. No matter how technically correct and logically insightful the direction given by a leader, his style of dispensing information and influencing the group will be a key determinant of his success. He avoids the use of official authority and succeeds through the constructive harnessing of his group's competence. He knows how to organize his materiel and manpower in ways that allow free expression of talent in defining problems, in setting goals, and in managing resources for achieving these goals.

The new role of the supervisor is not always accepted easily. For some managers, the involvement of workers in solving management problems is seen as an expression of weakness that is bound to cause loss of respect from subordinates. Such managers oppose worker involvement as capitulation or as relinquishment of managerial prerogatives. Reactions of this type are not uncommon, as authority-oriented relationships fostered in many homes, schools, military organizations, and other institutions find natural expression in most job situations. A supervisor does not switch leadership style as a result of a policy statement or as an immediate consequence of reading a book or hearing an inspiring speech. An intellectual message may sensitize him to his problem, but he must work through the process of self-evaluation, self-acceptance, adjustment of values, and change of behavior at his own pace, in his own way, and only in a climate conducive to change. The pressure of an edict to "be democratic" may only regress him to familiar old authority-oriented patterns, from which stance he will obediently recite the official intellectual message.

Supervisory effectiveness results from job enrichment as a circular phenomenon. In the first instance, job enrichment requires action (or discontinuation of previous action) on the part of the supervisor to provide conditions conducive to human effectiveness. Positive results from this action in turn reinforce it and encourage its emulation by others. Its application brings about subtle changes in the perceptions, practices, habits, and, finally, values of the supervisors, so that in a gradual branching and multiplying process a new way of life at work is put into motion which simultaneously changes and effects changes through the supervisor. Hence, the supervisor is the originator of and the medium for change— providing conditions for the development of others and thereby bringing about his own self-development.

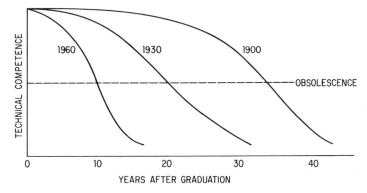

FIG. 7-3 Life span of an engineering degree. (Ernst Weber, President, Polytechnic Institute of Brooklyn, *Electronic News,* Nov. 29, 1965.)

Avoidance of Obsolescence

The manager is both an agent and the potential victim of the accelerated rate of change taking place in society. In industry this accelerated change is shortening the life span of technologies and jobs and placing an unprecedented demand on employees in all functions and levels to adapt to new roles and new job demands. Ernst Weber, as president of the Polytechnic Institute of Brooklyn, illustrated this shortening job life by showing (Figure 7-3) that the engineering graduate of 1900 was able to coast for approximately 35 years before becoming obsolete. The 1930 graduate could go for approximately 20 years before obsolescence. The engineer of today, without ongoing technological training, finds himself obsolete in 10 years or less. This trend suggests that the ever-steepening curve of obsolescence will require the newly graduated engineer to arrange for the continuation of his technological education upon acceptance of his first job as an engineer.

Though criteria for measuring obsolescence are not always as tangible for the manager as they are for the engineer, there is evidence that managerial obsolescence may closely parallel engineering obsolescence. Figure 7-4 presents two management career curves: one for the manager who continues to adapt to, cope with, and effect change, and the other, the "rainbow curve," of an obsolescing manager who experiences progressive disengagement from the realities of changing managerial responsibility. Though actual career curves do not follow such smooth patterns, and seem to have an infinite variety of patterns, these two smoothed curves reflect a common dilemma in industry.

The growth curve reflects an assumption that a manager's effectiveness can continue to improve throughout his career, and that the worst

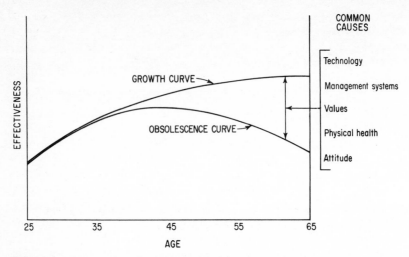

FIG. 7-4   Growth and obsolescence of managers.

thing that need happen to him is a leveling off during the last 10 years before retirement. Some managers seem to follow such a pattern. A few continue to grow at a steep pace up through age sixty-five, departing from the organization to begin new careers.

The obsolescence curve reflects the common plight of people who attain peak effectiveness during the middle years and gradually lose effectiveness, to be put out to pasture at age sixty-five or earlier.

The widening gap between the effective manager and the obsolescing manager usually cannot be attributed to a single cause, but usually can be explained in terms of one or more of five common factors:

1.   Keeping up with technology
2.   Management systems competence
3.   Adapting to changing values
4.   Physical fitness
5.   Overcoming the folklore of aging

Intimate knowledge of *technology* is not seen by many managers as a primary requirement for their success, However, many consider it of at least secondary importance, particularly in research and engineering, if for no other reason than to maintain rapport and credibility within their group. In a world of diminishing management prerogatives, where competence supplants authority as the source of influence, the R&D manager may feel that his credentials as a professional peer enhance his ability to influence his group. However, the pursuit of technological competence may side-track a manager away from his managerial responsibilities. It is sometimes postulated that ignorance of technology, coupled with leadership compe-tence, may result in the better utilization and development of a group's talents.

Management systems technology more appropriately represents the realm of expertise of the professional manager; and like engineers, man-agers are finding it increasingly difficult to keep abreast of their technology. Management systems, as defined here, are not restricted to EDP-based systems, but more broadly are a "process of people interacting to apply resources to achieve goals" as elaborated on pages 69 to 79. The application of constructive group dynamics in a world depersonalized by automation and bureaucratic constraints demands competence in behav-ioral theory as well as EDP technology. The successful manager has learned the futility of imposing masterminded systems and has learned to plan the development and administration of systems in accordance with principles defined in Chapter 2.

Changing values and expectations are natural consequences of the knowledge explosion. The manager who attempts to manage from the foundation of authoritarian values that were tolerated a generation earlier is obsolete. He is obsolete because a manager's values are the foundation for his style of supervision. The value systems described on pages 24 to 33 and the potential for incompatibility reflected in Figures 1-10 and 1-11 portray the dilemma of traditional managers. The manager who sees technical competence and the broadly shared opportunity for prob-lem solving and responsible behavior as the source of influence is attuned to the trends of the times. Adapting to changing values does not, of course, mean capitulation and relinquishment of moral and ethical standards, but does require sensitivity to, and respect for, the increasing need for freedom and independence.

Though managerial effectiveness and obsolescence are largely mental phenomena, they can be influenced by factors associated with *physical fitness.* Busy executives, in their pursuit of organizational success, com-monly overburden themselves, working long hours, eating irregular and unbalanced meals, getting insufficient exercise, and developing the middle-age spread when only halfway through their 40-year careers as managers. As this physical neglect takes its toll through fatigue and health factors, the manager is forcefully hindered and frustrated. He finds himself the unwilling and premature victim of physical obsolescence which forces him to adjust his aspirations and work habits. His usual self-confidence gives way to anxiety and feelings of insecurity. Though preventive mainte-nance in the form of exercise, adequate rest, and balanced diet can avoid this pitfall, most people prior to physical breakdown have little incentive to change well-established living habits. Pritikin[1] and others are showing that physical health can be retrieved and perpetuated by radically changed and rigorously followed living patterns, but few seem willing to make such adaptations.

The manager's *attitudes,* as shaped by tradition, are often the key to his obsolescence or continuing effectiveness. Many managers seem to accept the cliché "You can't teach an old dog new tricks" and abandon hope in the middle years on the assumption that they are too old to learn. Actually, old dogs can be taught new tricks, but not if they think they can't. If a manager is only twenty-five and believes himself incapable of learning, for practical purposes he is on his way to obsolescence.

The attitudinal factor is key for two reasons. First, it is essential that a person see the feasibility of avoiding obsolescence and understand its causes and preventive measures. But perhaps more importantly, a manager must understand that his attitude can influence the obsolescence or growth of people under his supervision. The bypassing of older employees in handing out challenging assignments is a language of action that tells the bypassed individual that his supervisor thinks he is "over the hill," raising his own doubts about his continuing effectiveness. In his anxiety to prove himself in his narrowed responsibility, he strives harder to give visibility to his own achievements. In a circular fashion, his random and ineffective efforts cause his responsibilities to be narrowed further. In a continuing spiral, his anxieties are increased, evoking more random and nonproductive behavior, amplifying and reinforcing his image of ineffectiveness.

But if the aging employee receives a challenging responsibility, it represents a vote of confidence from his supervisor, to bolster his confidence and allay subconscious doubts, providing the opportunity for achievement and continuing growth. Sustained opportunity for success experiences through challenging assignments thus represents a potent antidote to obsolescence.

The causes and correlates of obsolescence enumerated above are not exhaustive, nor can they be assigned relative importance. They tend to be situational to the individual, his job, his organization, or any combination of these and other factors. For one manager, the key may be technology; for another, it may be physical factors; one may need updating in managing systems; for some, all factors may be important. As a generalization, the challenge of continuing human effectiveness in any function or level of the organization is most often satisfied through the opportunities for growth, achievement, responsibility, and recognition afforded by meaningful work.

---

[1]Nathan Pritikin, *The Pritikin Program for Diet and Exercise*, Grosset & Dunlap, New York, 1979.

THE PERSONNEL FUNCTION

Thoughtful students of organization theory sometimes advance the provocative opinion that the ideal organization would have no personnel department—that personnel administration is appropriately the responsibility of the people who manage the mainstream create, make, and market functions of the organization. Their reasoning is buttressed by the viewpoint that attainment of all goals is dependent on concerted human effort; therefore, reliance on the personnel department for personnel administration constitutes managerial dereliction. Such a viewpoint is often a reaction to the perceived existing role of Personnel, which, of course, is not uniformly defined in all organizations nor in all stages of history.

The function of Personnel, as it has evolved over years, has assumed a variety of roles in its relations with the line. Though somewhat evolutionary in the order presented below, all roles tend to persevere and find recurrent expression in contemporary organizations.[2]

1. *Counterbalancing influence.* Personnel counterbalances line management's emphasis on production with emphasis on human relations.

2. *Authority-directed experts.* Personnel experts exercise authority over line on personnel matters.

3. *Bureaucratic control.* Personnel systems and policies guide line management in personnel matters.

4. *Missionaries for participation.* Personnel emphasizes participation as the goal of the organization.

5. *Change agent.* Personnel specialists interact with line managers to define conditions for mutual achievement of organization and individual goals.

The change agent role is gradually evolving as an ideal model for the personnel specialist. However, the other roles are being perpetuated through the conditions and assumptions that brought them into existence. Each of these roles is discussed below in terms of the forces that brought them into existence, and their usual impact on the organization.

The Counterbalancing Influence

The counterbalancing function of Personnel arose from line management's neglect of, or need to unload, certain of its responsibilities. Line managers

---

[2]This historical review of the personnel function is adapted from a working paper by John Paré, written in 1968 when he was vice president for personnel, Steinberg's Limited, Montreal, P.Q., Canada.

typically considered personnel problems as less important than, and not clearly related to, their primary job of getting out production. They appeared to divide management problems into two distinct categories and two separate responsibilities:

1. *Production problems.* Line management is responsible for the planning and controlling of materiel and systems: making the decisions, giving orders, assigning responsibilities, and seeing to it that people get the job done.

2. *People problems.* Personnel is responsible for handling complaints, grievances, and discipline; negotiating labor agreements; administering salary and benefit programs; training supervisors; establishing work rules; and building employee morale.

This split in management responsibilities reflects an assumption that the needs of people and the needs of production are mutually exclusive, and that efficiency in operation results from arranging conditions of work to minimize interference from human factors. The personnel man in turn reacted to the line manager's apparent insensitivity to human factors by emphasizing human relations, often with little regard for production goals.

The Authority-Directed Experts

Traditional organization theory holds that authority must be commensurate with responsibility. When line management relinquished its responsibility for human relations problems, Personnel began asking for, and obtaining, authority over the line in these matters. Since authority was seen as the primary means of influencing behavior, this development was only logical: an individual cannot be held responsible for things he cannot control. Thus, use of authority by the personnel department crept into the line-staff relationship, widening the emerging split between the two management functions. Personnel assumed responsibility for recruiting, hiring, placing, and training line people; handling grievances and labor negotiations; and administering wages, salaries, and supplemental benefits.

This jurisdictional split not only creates a major cleavage in the line-staff relationship but is also impractical, as it is impossible, for example, to separate the function of assigning work from the function of processing grievances that arise from the work assignment.

In the ensuing struggle for power, line managers came to regard the personnel function as a "burden" and a "threat" rather than as a source of help. Rather than cope with this conflict, line managers typically severed contact with Personnel, leaving the staff experts out of touch with operations. As a consequence, personnel specialists became preoccupied with their narrow specialities to the point that they seemed to be talking to themselves and appeared to be unconcerned with the welfare of the business as a whole. Under these conditions, personnel programs and procedures seemed to become more "ivory tower" and less practical as solutions to line problems.

Bureaucratic Control

Line management's reaction to the authority which Personnel was exercising over human relations activities caused management to reconsider the line-staff relationship. It was apparent that another tenet of traditional management theory, the principle of "unity of command," was being violated: every individual must have but one boss.

Line management faced the dilemma of lacking insights and skills to resolve the increasingly complex human relations problem, but finding themselves dependent on the personnel "experts," whose specialities made them essential to the organization.

The solution was to set up the personnel department as a "coordinative" function, replacing the direct control by the staff specialist with standard personnel practices. These practices are expressed through the media of job descriptions and evaluations, organization charts, policies, programs, manuals, rules and regulations, and a variety of formalized procedures for detailing personnel activities. Line management had final authority for adopting or rejecting the policies and programs formulated by Personnel—but Personnel was responsible for obtaining line conformity once the policies and programs had been adopted. In effect, the role of "coordination" proved to be merely camouflaged authority. From the line manager's point of view, the staff man exercises as much authority under the bureaucratic form of personnel administration as he does in the authority-oriented role.

Missionaries for Participation

The "policing" role played by Personnel under the above theories caused the personnel function to be regarded by lower and middle line management as a source of arbitrary, though sometimes candy-coated, authority. Mutual distrust, if not open hostility, characterized line-staff relations, and both groups began to question the use of authority as the exclusive means of managerial control. The influence of partially understood behavioral theory led managers to abandon the principle of authority and to adopt the principle of participation. Based on the assumption that "people support only what they help to create," Personnel sought ways to involve line people more and more in problem-solving activities.

The fundamental error of this approach is in seeing participation as the goal rather than as a means for achieving goals, as decision-making then becomes stalemated by the reluctance on the part of both line and staff to reach any decision until the full support of the line is assured.

Change Agent

The primary purpose of Personnel as a change agent is to maximize the achievement of organizational objectives through the soundest utilization of its human resources. This requires the understanding and support of company goals by all members of the organization. It depends on collaborative commitment of individuals and groups to achieve these goals. It requires that the members of the organization identify and remove those barriers in the culture of the organization which prevent the company from reaching its objectives.

Personnel, in this role, provides specialists, advisers, consultants, trainers, counselors, and researchers to support a goal-oriented philosophy which calls for a reunification of the two categories of management (production and human relations) under the line manager. High concern for quality of decisions and production must be fused with high concern for people on the assumption that maximum efficiency can be best sustained through committed people who recognize a "common stake" in the achievement of organization goals. The proper fusing of these two high concerns brings about not only a better utilization of talent by the line manager, but a significantly different relationship between line management and the personnel function. Many of the responsibilities which Personnel has acquired over the years must now be built back into the line. Personnel's charter is built upon the foundation of "a code for human effectiveness," defined in Figure 7-5, and of course the credentials of the personnel man must be reestablished in the light of his new role as change agent.

Credentials of the Personnel Change Agent

The personnel man's realm of competence is knowledge of the requirements for human effectiveness, as defined in Chapter 2. He acts selectively in the roles of educator, researcher, consultant, adviser, counselor, mediator, coordinator, conference leader, and public relations specialist in implementing personnel philosophy and systems.

- The staffing function, as defined on pages 223 to 231, requires the support of a personnel specialist who not only knows the sources of manpower from employment agencies, universities, technical schools, industry, and community, but more important, can prescribe an appropriate balance between internal and external staffing practices. He prepares line managers by briefing them on sources of personnel and tech-

Organizational effectiveness requires human effectiveness. The effectiveness of the organization is measured in terms of return on investment, and the effectiveness of its members in terms of realized potential. The organization will prosper most when its members accomplish their personal goals through the achievement of organization goals.

Guiding principles:
- People achieve more when their job is worth doing and challenging enough to rouse their interest; when they see the results of their achievements and their impact on group goals; and when their job results in advancement, personal growth and self-respect.

- People act more responsibly when they are involved in setting their own goals, are accountable for their own behavior, and share in the responsibilities and rewards for accomplishing organization goals.

- People work better when there is mutual trust, respect, concern, and integrity among them as human beings, regardless of the level of their job.

These principles are implemented by:
- Creating an organizational climate which enables people at all levels to communicate freely and naturally with each other -- keeping them informed about the organization, their jobs, and their relationships to customer goals.

- Designing jobs that involve people at all levels in planning and controlling their own work, and provide opportunity for individuals to make an impact on, and see how their accomplishments influence, the achievement of organization goals.

- Designing management systems sensitive to the needs of the people influenced by the systems and, where feasible, providing opportunities for persons at all levels to have a hand in developing and managing these systems.

- Providing pay and benefits competitive with the better managed organizations in local communities and comparable industries, and by compensating individuals through a system which places more emphasis on merit than on automatic progression.

- Maintaining equal opportunity practices which meet the spirit as well as the letter of the law in enabling individuals to compete and succeed on the basis of merit.

- Maintaining pleasant, convenient, attractive and safe physical facilities.

FIG. 7-5   A code for human effectiveness.

niques of evaluation, coordinates their recruiting itineraries, and compiles companywide manning tables and recruiting statistics. He instructs line managers in indoctrination procedures, such as anxiety reduction, orientation to physical facilities, supplemental benefits and compensation systems, and company philosophy.

- The personnel specialist provides guidance in the development of performance review systems which place emphasis on the individual's initiative in setting his own goals and measuring his own performance, as described on pages 234 to 244. He instructs supervisors in the use of conference leadership techniques related to problem solving and goal setting, the characteristics of meaningful goals, and the use of feedback rather than criticism as a basis for developing responsible behavior.

- The compensation specialist has expertise in motivation and management systems. He is aware of the piecework incentive trap and the limitations of other traditional pay systems. He chairs panel task forces which conduct and interpret wage and salary surveys, analyze jobs, and develop compensation systems and benefits programs. He briefs supervisors on the multiple roles of pay, as described on pages 177 to 179, and defines the conditions and techniques which optimize the impact of compensation systems.

- Though all personnel specialists are trainers, the training expert has a special role in guiding line managers and other personnel specialists to support a self-development philosophy through appropriate processes for changing knowledge, skills, and attitudes, as defined on pages 157 to 176. He assists line managers in meeting their responsibilities as trainers and makes it possible for them to assess their personal effectiveness by introducing them to "mirror-holding" self-improvement processes such as transactional analysis, the managerial grid, sensitivity training, and attitude surveys.

- The personnel change agent helps managers to understand attitudes as a readiness to respond, to understand that attitudes are learned and provide a basis for predicting behavior. Attitude surveys, as described on pages 143 to 149, afford a means of anticipating and preventing undesirable behavior. Involvement of job incumbents at all levels in the processes of designing, administering, and interpreting surveys contributes to their development and enables them to surface and cope with frustrations. The change agent helps managers to learn that attitudes are not improved by coercion, persuasion, manipulation, or bribery but, rather, from their involvement in authentic relationships, meaningful goals, and facilitative systems.

- The labor relations specialist promotes a philosophy which discourages the application of the traditional strategies for outwitting or fighting unions. Rather, he becomes an interpreter of people's behavior so that managers can take appropriate action in dissipating and constructively harnessing the tensions which might otherwise find expression in adversary relationships.

STAFFING

The purpose of the staffing function is to find, attract, and utilize qualified people in such a way that their talents will find expression in the successful pursuit of organizational and personal goals. Common staffing practice reflects the assumptions that the richest source of talent is outside the organization, that the company is responsible for matching individuals to jobs, and that staffing is a responsibility of the personnel department. The theme of this section is that both organizational and individual goals can be achieved better when staffing is based on a different set of assumptions:

1. The richest source of talent is inside the organization.

2. Individuals should be permitted to pursue and move into growth opportunities.

3. Staffing is a line responsibility.

External versus Internal Staffing

All organizations are, of course, composed of members brought in originally from the outside. However, an organization can be said to be staffed internally when most job openings above the lowest job grades are filled through a process of upward mobility from within. It is staffed externally when job openings above the lowest levels are filled primarily by newly hired employees.

Proponents of external staffing hold that the injection of "new blood" is needed at all levels and that staffing from within is a type of inbreeding that results in excessive conformity and technological obsolescence. Moreover, they reason that hiring in at higher levels attracts stalemated high achievers from other organizations.

Advocates of internal staffing counter with the view that external staffing fills jobs with people who, in a broad sense, failed to make adequate adjustments in other organizations. Hence, managers are often hiring other organizations' rejects. They point out that external staffing, by restricting upward mobility, quashes initiative and results in stagnation, frustration, and higher voluntary separations. Internal staffing, in contrast, stimulates hope and ambition; encourages self-development; and leads to realized potential, personal commitment, and reduced turnover. More important, a sound promotion-from-within practice affords opportunity for retaining the impatient high achiever whose aspirations might otherwise lead him away from the organization in quest of growth opportunities.

External staffing, as a primary strategy, is a costly and wasteful circular process. At a conservatively estimated rate of 20 percent turnover per year, an organization loses the equivalent of 100 percent of its work force in 5 years. These separatees are, of course, replaced by people who (except for first-job applicants) were for many of the same reasons separated from other organizations. Thus organizations are often victims of an insidious and expensive process of exchanging misfits with each other.

Though managers tend to see recruited replacements as superior to the separatees, this is largely selective perception, and the real beneficiaries are the job hoppers. Some, in fact, have found that the only way to improve their job status in their own organization is to move to another organization and return in the status of a newly hired employee. All organizations and, hence, society in general, lose by this escalatory process that accelerates inflation and undermines the organization's competitive ability.

Though the merits of internal staffing generally outweigh those of external staffing, the relative effectiveness of one strategy over another is determined by the policies and practices through which they are implemented. Neither strategy is pure, nor should be, as some promotions and transfers occur in the external staffing strategy; and, of course, replacements are hired to fill lower-level jobs vacated by internal staffing. Moreover, the exceptions which enable outstanding organizations to attract and hire limited numbers of high-level talent do not vitiate the principle of internal staffing, provided most of the openings in middle management and above are filled through promotions.

A company philosophy that supports practices of promotion from within is more likely to retain high achievers on its work force. The hiring of the majority of top management and supervisory people from other companies is no less damaging to the morale and ambition of members of the work force than the sending of managers into multinational subsidiaries to manage indigenous personnel. In both cases, the managers are seen as outsiders, insensitive to the needs of the local people, taking jobs which rightfully belong to them. Hence, an ideal environment for staffing a work force is one that duplicates as nearly as possible the opportunities which people traditionally feel they can find only outside the organization. They must know from the language of action that job openings are visible to them; that they can, without fear of reprisal, apply for the jobs; and that, when they are accepted, they will encounter no difficulty in cutting across job classifications and departmental lines to fill the jobs. Equal-opportunity principles exist not only in regard to the traditional criteria of race, gender, and age, but particularly in regard to their status in the organization.

Staffing Reflects Management Values

An organization's staffing function is implemented by a philosophy of management that attracts and retains individuals who, in a circular fashion, reinforce and perpetuate its philosophy. For example, some persons are attracted to the organization that is guided by a strong central source of authority and detailed procedures. Though conformity is demanded, it is also rewarded by job security and peer acceptance. Others are attracted to the less formal organization where initiative and talent find spontaneous expression. Though freedom can result in failure, it often leads to a sense of achievement and opportunity for high achievers to gain visibility. As each of these two types of persons adapts to his organization and progresses upward to positions of administrative influence, he develops relationships, systems, and policies which reflect his values. Of course, he hires people whose values match or reinforce his own, and promotes and rewards those who most nearly fit his self-image, or who will not interfere with his style of managing.

Though conformists tend to hire conformists, it does not naturally follow that individualists always hire nonconformists. Uncommon men often inadvertently surround themselves with bright but stable personalities who become satisfied with implementing their mentor's innovations. Thus, brilliant or strong individualism may unintentionally quash expressions of individuality in less forceful persons. Hence, all organizations run a greater risk of attracting and developing too many conformists than they do of promoting too much individuality.

An organization's management philosophy and its supportive staffing policies are often reflected by the personnel recruiter. The larger the organization, the more likely the recruiting function is to be delegated to professional recruiters, who tend to select candidates whose values match their own, or match their perception of the requisitioning supervisor's personality. The line manager generally tends to be more goal- or achievement-oriented, but his recruiters from the personnel department tend to be more maintenance-oriented. Though the personnel man's maintenance orientation can be explained in terms of his forced preoccupation with maintenance problems unloaded by line managers, it does, nonetheless, color his strategy for attracting job candidates.

For example, professional recruiters frequently advertise jobs as pleasant and challenging, but emphasize as major attractions, generous pay, supplemental benefits, and a congenial environment. In the screening interview, these factors are customarily stressed, along with detailed descriptions of the compensation system, retirement plan, group insurance, recreation program, and other fringe benefits. The candidate is invited to the company, all expenses paid, where he is taken on a whirlwind tour that steers him away from the less attractive sectors of the organization; he is entertained at an expensive restaurant and is made to feel like "king for a day."

If he accepts the job, he may find that reality differs from the recruiting publicity. Confronted with the ambiguity and pressure of multiple assignments, long hours, the encumberment of bureaucratic systems, and domination by autocratic supervision, he feels deceived. He may rise to such a challenge and thrive, or he may recoil and withdraw in disenchantment. He may leave the organization in search of the nonexistent job described in his employment interview. He is branded by the organization as a "maintenance seeker," though, in fact, it was the organization's recruiting strategy which attracted him by emphasizing maintenance factors.

A far better recruiting strategy would be to advertise the difficulty of the challenge, the opportunity to learn, and the long hours, and perhaps even to understate the value of the maintenance factors. During the company visit, off-site entertainment would be deemphasized, but the candidate would be shown the work place, the goals to be achieved, and the jobs to be done. An informal dinner meeting at the end of the visit with informed company representatives to discuss the company and answer questions could be quite relevant for the achievement-oriented candidate. Although such a strategy might eliminate more candidates, those who were attracted and hired would be prepared for the challenge of reality. Moreover, their first encounter with the organization would not be an act of deception.

Internal staffing not only has more potential than external staffing as a strategy for increasing human effectiveness within the organization, but it also actuates a more achievement-oriented recruiting strategy for supporting that effectiveness. Internally staffed organizations offer growth opportunities where individual talent, effort, and achievements are rewarded, while external staffing tends to lure more persons looking for the ready-made opportunity. However, the success of either staffing strategy depends heavily on the systems through which it is implemented. The key factor here is whether the system is managed by someone above the user (company-managed system) or by the people who use the system to do their job (user-managed system).

Company-Managed System

Company-managed staffing systems which focus on better utilization of talent and the satisfaction of employee needs are unfortunately designed in most cases to keep management in the driver's seat with regard to the application of the systems. Consider, for example, the manpower inventory as a company-managed system.

Manpower inventories are initiated for the purpose of enabling management to match employee talent with job opportunity. They usually utilize EDP-based systems for storage and retrieval of vocational information about employees. Cards are keypunched from forms completed by job incumbents listing their educational achievements, job experience, aspirations, and other special skills or achievements such as foreign language facility, patents, publications, and honors. Job openings are matched against inventory descriptors, and the records of potential candidates are referred to the hiring supervisor.

Though occasionally useful for locating rare skills, manpower inventories are found in practice to have several fundamental shortcomings. For one, they rarely keep pace with the changing skills, aspirations, and membership in the work force. Second, the sensitivity and accuracy of the system are limited by the translation of personnel data to machine language, and the subsequent translation of that machine language when candidates are being considered. Third, qualified candidates are often bypassed because of supervisory reluctance to free them for reassignment. Fourth, the system, particularly when managed through big-company bureaucracy, seldom gives feedback to the members in terms of availability of opportunities, frequency of review, and probability of candidacy. The manpower inventory's impact as a management control system for limiting self-initiated action is perhaps its most harmful characteristic. The system casts the member in a passive, dependent role, waiting for initiative from management to administer the system and "find" them when needed. Systems of this type do little to inspire the initiative of the individual to assume responsibility for his own effectiveness and growth. Misled by an assumption that paternalistic management has his interests at heart and is looking out for his welfare, he may drift into obsolescence or retirement waiting for management to point the way.

User-Managed System

Consider for contrast the consequences of a user-managed, or employee-oriented, system. A system is considered user-managed when it is actuated by the lowest-level user in accordance with the criteria of an effective system, as defined on pages 76 to 78. The user actuates the system to satisfy a personal goal, and it is important to him that he know how to use the system and that he incur no risk in doing so. The job-posting system described on pages 72 to 76 and in the following pages is an example of a user-managed staffing system.

The Texas Instruments job-posting system is based on the company philosophy that individuals are responsible for their own development. However, a philosophy of self-development would be a platitude and an

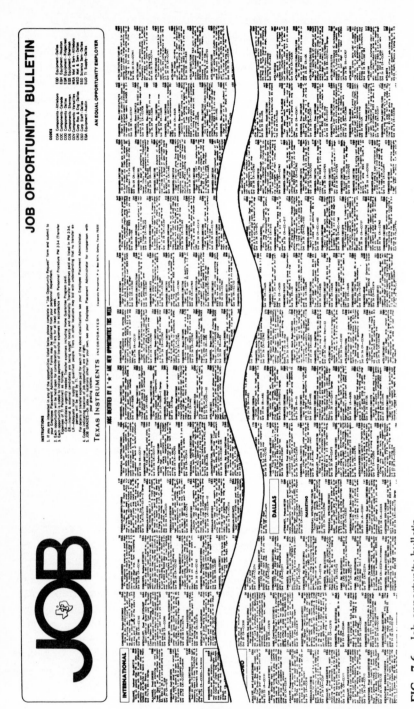

FIG. 7-6 Job opportunity bulletin.

228

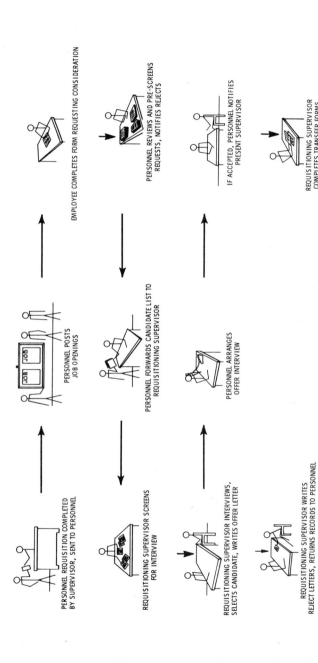

EMPLOYEE COMPLETES FORM REQUESTING CONSIDERATION

PERSONNEL REVIEWS AND PRE-SCREENS REQUESTS, NOTIFIES REJECTS

IF ACCEPTED, PERSONNEL NOTIFIES PRESENT SUPERVISOR

REQUISITIONING SUPERVISOR COMPLETES TRANSFER FORMS

PERSONNEL POSTS JOB OPENINGS

PERSONNEL FORWARDS CANDIDATE LIST TO REQUISITIONING SUPERVISOR

PERSONNEL ARRANGES OFFER INTERVIEW

PERSONNEL REQUISITION COMPLETED BY SUPERVISOR, SENT TO PERSONNEL

REQUISITIONING SUPERVISOR SCREENS FOR INTERVIEW

REQUISITIONING SUPERVISOR INTERVIEWS, SELECTS CANDIDATE, WRITES OFFER LETTER

REQUISITIONING SUPERVISOR WRITES REJECT LETTERS, RETURNS RECORDS TO PERSONNEL

REJECTED APPLICANTS LISTED FOR FUTURE CONSIDERATION

FIG. 7-7 Job posting.

excuse for company dereliction if realistic opportunities were not provided to enable members to meet this responsibility. Job posting is one of the most effective systems for making self-development a realistic expectation.

The system, to support an internal staffing strategy, must give present employees advantage over outsiders. For example, present employees have one week's opportunity before outside applicants are considered. Job requirements are defined in terms of education, skill, and experience requirements; job grade; and location. Biweekly listings of all job openings up to the vice-president level are published, distributed, and posted, and are made accessible to all.

Any employee can actuate the system by completing a form designating his interest in a posted job, and submitting this job bid to his personnel department. Notification of his supervisor at this point is optional with the bidder.

His bid is screened along with others by Personnel and, if not eliminated, is referred to the requesting supervisor who screens, interviews, and selects a candidate (or decides to consider outside applicants). The selected candidate is offered the job by the requesting supervisor, and if he accepts it, he notifies his own supervisor of his acceptance of the new job. The requesting supervisor initiates the personnel transfer paperwork, and the individual is released to his new job within three weeks from the date of acceptance. During this period the releasing supervisor posts the vacated job and attempts to select and train a replacement. In practice, many jobs are filled immediately from a reservoir of qualified bidders on file from previous bids. Hence, several bidders may be released simultaneously for their new assignments.

The job-posting system, appropriately administered, is dramatically successful because the user, as well as the organization, benefits from use of the system. Individuals in quest of growth, responsibility, and change are far more sensitive and perceptive search mechanisms than the programmed computer which performs the search functions for the manpower inventory. More important, the individual is now responsible for growth opportunities and can initiate self-development actions suggested by job-posting specifications and bidding rejects. Participation in Texas Instruments' educational assistance program increased approximately 80 percent after installation of the formal job-posting system.

The system synergistically serves the needs of the user and the organization. Talent now finds more complete and positive expression through promotions, transfers, and reassignments. Though short-term inconvenience is caused by internal personnel displacement, long-term gains are netted by the organization when high-talent transferees find outlets for their competence inside the organization rather than diverting their energy to outside activities or looking for a better job. Job posting also benefits the organization as a system for coping with cutbacks in work force, placing graduates from training programs, upgrading educational assistance participants, placing persons returning from leave, and encouraging the application of equal employment opportunity principles.

Though legally enforced equal employment opportunity programs are commonly monitored and administered by a member of the personnel department, the philosophy of equal opportunity is implemented better when it is included in the organizational responsibility of line management. Hence, job posting is an additional medium through which program quotas can be realized. Other significant, but less tangible, benefits of job posting include a reduced dependency relationship between the job incumbent and his supervisor, higher esprit de corps among the members of the work force, the requirement of excellence on the part of supervision to avoid "escape bidding" by members of his group, and greater community stability.

Other staffing systems which provide interface with job posting become more user-oriented. Training, for example, is more often selected by the job incumbent and keyed to his perceptions of opportunity on the work force rather than being a management-prescribed program which does not always have a realistic relationship to job opportunity or employee aspiration. Training for training's sake gives way to learning as a means for attaining a personal goal.

Similarly, aptitude testing, long perceived as a mysterious tool of management for selecting and rejecting candidates for jobs and training programs, can become an aid to the individual in helping him understand his strong points and limitations. With the insights offered by aptitude tests, he can direct his aspirations and remedial learning activities and thus assume greater responsibility for his own self-development. However, the use of aptitude tests has become complicated by misapplications, absence of uniform professional standards, and legislative restrictions. Despite these limitations, aptitude tests are potentially among the most potent tools available for furthering the philosophy of self-development.

Aptitude Testing

The use of aptitude tests improves the probability of selecting qualified job candidates. However, tests are not perfect predictors of job success, and occasionally they eliminate qualified applicants who perform poorly on tests, or select unqualified applicants who perform well on tests. Unfortunately for the society which stresses equal opportunity as a cornerstone of its philosophy, tests tend to eliminate larger percentages of minority groups. In some cases the selecting out of minority-group candidates is a result of not having included these groups in the test validation studies, in which case the tests are valid predictors of job success only for candidates from within the culture in which they were validated. Even when tests are properly validated as predictors of job success for all groups, it is sometimes reasoned that minority members should be exempt from standardized predictors on the basis that these individuals are innocent victims of social injustice which handicaps them in both test performance and job performance. In any event, aptitude tests, regardless of their validity, are not widely used as a selection device.

Paradoxically, part of the problem of aptitude testing stems from the fact that tests are too potent as predictors. The psychologist's apparent ability to predict behavior from tests often leads to the disregard of interview impressions, biographical data, and job histories. Overreliance on the psychologist stems in part from the esoteric language he uses in describing characteristics, interest patterns, skills, and intelligence of the candidate. Not fully understanding "psychologese," the manager often capitulates and permits the psychologist to make selection decisions. This practice makes him the user of a system he does not fully understand, and aptitude testing becomes a crutch, displacing other proved predictors and common judgment in matters of personnel selection and evaluation.

Much of the mystery can be removed from testing if the user realizes that all tests, regardless of their labels, can be grouped into four families of human characteristics: capacity, achievement, interest, and temperament.

Capacity tests are of two kinds—mental and physical. *Mental* capacity is measured by various intelligence tests in terms of factors such as verbal fluency, numerical facility, space relations, inductive and deductive reasoning, detail perception, reasoning speed, and memory. *Physical* capacity refers to capabilities such as eye-hand coordination, manual dexterity, hand steadiness, sense of balance, visual acuity, depth perception, and color vision.

Achievement tests are measures of knowledge and skill. *Knowledge* achievement tests are typified by measures of knowledge of mathematics, geography, astronomy, EDP machine language, and principles of management or economics. *Skill* achievement tests are typified by measure of ability to type and take shorthand, operate a desk calculator, write a computer program, lead a conference, or operate a lathe.

Interest tests measure vocational or avocational interests, usually through multiple-choice questionnaires or inventories. *Vocational* interest measures may describe a person's preferences for job activities such as computational, persuasive, scientific, or mechanical; or in terms of vocational titles such as mechanical engineer, chemist, clergyman, business manager, or athlete. *Avocational* interest questionnaires measure off-the-job interests in terms of activities or topics such as oil painting, sports, reading, flying, coin collecting, bird watching, historical events, music, politics, or religion.

Temperament tests, depending on their degree of sophistication and the competence of the administrator, measure surface or subconscious personality. *Surface* personality traits are usually described from responses to questions about parents, siblings, friends, enemies, teachers, supervisors, sex, religion, social situations, dishonesty, fears, and aspirations. This kind of test is often transparent and may evoke responses that are deliberately faked or which the individual erroneously believes to be correct or desirable. Even when the respondent attempts to be completely candid or honest, the questionnaire may only tap the respondent's conscious personality. As a measure of surface personality, such a test might be valid. For example, such a test might accurately describe one person as an optimistic extrovert and another as a depressive introvert. In terms of everyday observations, and under normal conditions, these may be valid descriptions. However, a test which measures subconscious personality might reveal quite different personalities. The *subconscious* measure is more subtle, perhaps inducing the respondent to project his personality into the interpretation of ambiguous pictures and patterns, thereby giving surface expression to subconscious feelings. Such a test, coupled with a depth interview by a competent psychologist, might show, for example, that the happy-go-lucky extrovert is really wearing a facade, beneath which is much sadness and despair stemming from alienation and misfortune. The facade makes everyday living bearable to him, and it also becomes the pattern by which his acquaintances may know him. The depressive introvert might harbor a subconscious need to be in the limelight or to be an empire builder, and his behavior might also be a facade imposed by an overdeveloped conscience or a reaction to despair. The paradoxical swing from depression to euphoria, or vice versa, when inhibitions are lowered with alcohol or other drugs, is sometimes an expression of this phenomenon. It does not logically follow, of course, that surface personalities are always in conflict with subconscious personalities; usually they are not.

None of the tests described above should be administered or interpreted by untrained personnel. All are subject to misinterpretation, especially in the hands of the professionally untrained, and particularly the measures of mental capacity and temperament.

When adequate safeguards are provided against the pitfalls noted above, and when tests are properly validated, administered, and interpreted within the balanced context of other predictors, they represent one of the most effective and democratic systems for uncovering hidden talent. People in manual occupations, for example, may have talents untapped by previous roles or submerged by conformity to social norms. Self-discovery through aptitude tests may provide the spark of aspiration and encouragement needed to lift talent from dormancy or to transform it from reactive to constructive expression. Aptitude tests can also perform the merciful mission of redirecting unrealistic aspirations, enabling individuals to recognize and accept reality, and thereby prevent the later trauma of vocational failure.

The application of aptitude tests should not be aimed at labeling people as successes or failures but, rather, should support the concept that all people have aptitude to succeed—but in different roles. Some have a greater variety of aptitudes than others, but opportunities exist for all to succeed. Particularly in the situation of a tight labor market, or in the implementation of a promotion-from-within policy, tests offer a potent key to the location of submerged talent and a stimulus to self-development.

In practice, aptitude tests, as vocational guidance instruments, often represent greater deterrents than catalysts, particularly when they are administered under the direction and control of management authority. No matter how fairly the testing process is administered by management, it increases the dependency relationship of the individual to those above him, and represents one more bureaucratic inhibition to self-discovery and initiative.

However, by transferring the initiative for aptitude testing to the individual, the assessment process can become a developmental personal experience. While it is appropriate for the organization to provide access to, and refund the cost of, aptitude testing, much in the same spirit, and for the same sound business reasons, that educational assistance is offered, the use and control of test scores must be proprietary with the individual. The psychological consultant releases aptitude data only by voluntary authorization of the examinee. Thus test scores become constructive aids to self-development, and are optionally withheld or released, as the examinee chooses, in applying for promotional opportunity.

PERFORMANCE REVIEW

It is customary in some organizations to conduct periodic formal performance appraisals. The avowed purpose of performance appraisal is to assess individual job performance as a basis for making pay determinations and to communicate the results of this evaluation to the individual, along with suggestions for improvement.

During the 1950s, Douglas McGregor took what he called "an uneasy look at performance appraisal,"[3] and noted that the judgmental aspects of ratings, particularly when they appeared to be administered on the basis of theory X assumptions, tended to undermine the developmental potential of the performance review process. As real human development is self-inspired and self-directed, traditional performance appraisals undermine

[3]Douglas McGregor, "An Uneasy Look at Performance Appraisal" (*HBR* Classic), *Harvard Business Review*, May–June 1957 and Sept.–Oct., 1972.

self-development by incurring conformity and resentment, and by fostering dependency relationships. Though some individuals improve their job performance as a result of advice from the supervisor, the value of the improved performance might be outweighed by the conditioned dependency of the individual on the boss for prescriptions for development. Not only is the individual bound to an apron string which relieves him of the responsibility for self-development, but in the process he also acquires a model for development which encourages him, in turn, to meddle with the self-development of the people under his supervision.

This is not to say that performance appraisals are not needed and that supervisors should not have a role in them. Performance appraisals are in process continuously, informally if not formally, in terms of both self-appraisal and evaluations by others. The supervisor, as a member of a natural work group, has a key role in the performance appraisal process. But this role, if it is to result in personal and professional development, is through an Adult-Adult rather than a Parent-Child relationship.

The Parent-Child Approach

The process of appraisal and criticism in industry is a natural extension of authority-controlled relationships learned elsewhere, such as those often existing between parents and children in the home, teachers and students in the schools, or superiors and subordinates in the armed forces. Traditional job performance rating factors, illustrated in Figure 7-8, are similar to school report card criteria, and provide the basis for supervisory judgment

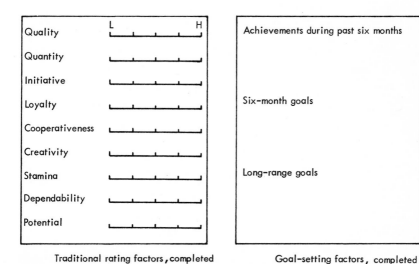

| Traditional rating factors, completed by the supervisor. | Goal-setting factors, completed by the job incumbent. |

FIG. 7-8 Traditional versus goal-setting performance review forms.

and criticism. Studies of the traditional performance review process shows that some people do, in fact, improve as a result of criticism, but most do not change at all, and a few actually perform less well.

Some managers, perceiving the ineffectiveness of criticism, have concluded that the ineffectiveness is not so much to be attributed to criticism itself as to the tactless application of criticism. Hence, much effort has been devoted to the definition and application of "constructive criticism." Attempts to be constructive in applying criticism were usually of the sugar-coated variety, which only tended to make people more wary and defensive. For example, the "sandwich technique" of criticism, which finds recurring expression in various organizations, is based on the assumption that criticism is constructive if sandwiched between two compliments. Though such a process no doubt makes criticism more bearable, repeated applications tend to condition individuals to become wary of compliments.

Interdependence of Goals

Individual goal-setting seldom stands alone. As organizations grow in size and complexity, and interdependence among individuals and functions becomes encumbered by bureaucratic restrictions, individual goal setting becomes more difficult. It is the leader's responsibility to see to it that people with interdependent jobs engage in mutual problem solving and goal setting. This provides the basis for avoiding conflict and overlap, promotes cooperation, and establishes a foundation for setting individual goals.

For example, a manager of a technically oriented manufacturing organization may decide to launch a goal-setting performance review process in the engineering functions on the assumption that well-educated, goal-oriented engineers can establish goal-setting patterns to be emulated by individuals in other functions. But goal setting by individual engineers can find only limited application unless opportunities are created for coordinating the efforts of engineering with other functions. The engineer is a change agent whose success depends on his interface with other functions, such as research, manufacturing, quality assurance, procurement, and sales. Representatives of these functions compose the team that is to develop and implement a strategy for delivering a superior product or service to customers at competitive costs. Hence, group problem solving–goal setting by this natural work group is necessary to obtain consensus on a common goal and the definition of individual roles in supporting the team effort. After the group goal is defined, individual goal setting can be realistically undertaken.

A discussion of short- and long-range goals between the individual and his supervisor enables them to obtain a consensus on priorities and to

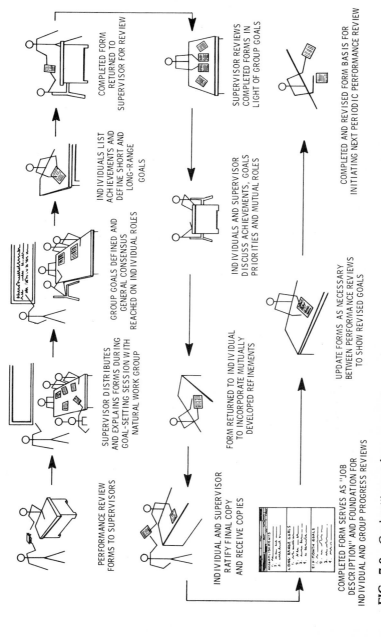

PERFORMANCE REVIEW
FORMS TO SUPERVISORS

SUPERVISOR DISTRIBUTES
AND EXPLAINS FORMS DURING
GOAL-SETTING SESSION WITH
NATURAL WORK GROUP

GROUP GOALS DEFINED AND
GENERAL CONSENSUS
REACHED ON INDIVIDUAL ROLES

INDIVIDUALS LIST
ACHIEVEMENTS AND
DEFINE SHORT AND
LONG-RANGE
GOALS

COMPLETED FORM
RETURNED TO
SUPERVISOR FOR REVIEW

SUPERVISOR REVIEWS
COMPLETED FORMS IN
LIGHT OF GROUP GOALS

INDIVIDUALS AND SUPERVISOR
DISCUSS ACHIEVEMENTS, GOALS
PRIORITIES AND MUTUAL ROLES

COMPLETED AND REVISED FORM BASIS FOR
INITIATING NEXT PERIODIC PERFORMANCE REVIEW

FORM RETURNED TO INDIVIDUAL
TO INCORPORATE MUTUALLY
DEVELOPED REFINEMENTS

UPDATE FORMS AS NECESSARY
BETWEEN PERFORMANCE REVIEWS
TO SHOW REVISED GOALS

INDIVIDUAL AND SUPERVISOR
RATIFY FINAL COPY
AND RECEIVE COPIES

COMPLETED FORM SERVES AS "JOB
DESCRIPTION" AND FOUNDATION FOR
INDIVIDUAL AND GROUP PROGRESS REVIEWS

FIG. 7-9 Goal-setting performance review.

237

jointly plan strategies for achieving them. The involvement of the supervisor is also necessary to enable the individual to dovetail his goals with his peers' goals and the broader departmental objectives. A successful goal-setting performance review experience between the individual and his supervisor will result in mutually acceptable roles for achieving mutually defined goals.

Dimensions of a Goal

An understanding of the characteristics of a goal is vital to this type of performance review. A marketing manager who defined a goal as "increasing his share of the served available market" had not set a goal. However, he had set a goal when he specified that he would progress from 7 to 15 percent of an $80 million served available market with a particular line of products by December of the coming year. Goals have both quantitative dimensions and target dates. Long-range goals also need intermediate checkpoints to enable the individual to know whether he is on schedule and to give progress reports to others who need feedback. When a goal of this type has been set, the performance review is not a mechanism for judging and criticizing the individual. After agreement on the goal, the supervisor's intervention should normally occur only upon request, usually when the job incumbent needs assistance to stay on target. In this context, the performance review is transformed from a system of control by authority to a system for mutual direction and control by the job incumbent and his supervisor.

Feedback versus Criticism

Supervisors who act as self-appointed missionaries for "shaping up the troops" commonly resort to criticism as the basis for bringing about improved performance. The term "criticism," as used here, refers to evaluations, advice, warnings, admonitions, threats, and other judgmental information transmitted by someone of higher authority to someone of lower authority. Criticism among peers, when undertaken as a solicited and deliberate feedback process, may serve a constructive role. However, the same information from a higher authority figure seldom affords the ratee opportunity for candid discussion or uninhibited rebuttal. Hence, the ratee characteristically masks resentment with a veneer of a smile and insincere gratitude for the well-meant criticism.

Successful performance and continuing improvement requires feedback. The term "feedback," as it is used here, refers to an Adult-Adult way of giving help; it is a corrective process through which individuals can learn how well their behavior matches their intentions.[4] Feedback, at its best, is:

1. Timely—usually immediate
2. Descriptive rather than evaluative
3. Specific rather than general
4. Sensitive to the needs of the receiver(s)
5. Directed toward controllable behavior
6. Solicited rather than imposed
7. Tested for accuracy with the receiver(s)

Thus, if a supervisor wishes to convey information to someone in his group relative to his performance, he must decide on timeliness. Should it be immediate, at the next staff meeting, or deferred till the next performance review? In the encounter, the supervisor should describe the incident or circumstances that will enable the receiver to make his own evaluation of the situation. Further, the supervisor will deal with the specifics of the situation rather than generalizing that "the program is a total failure." The supervisor is sensitive to the needs of the receiver by thoughtful choice of time and place for feedback and also by being descriptive and specific rather than evaluative and general. The feedback should deal with information which is within the capability of the receiver to remedy and should be particularly sensitive to limitations governed by equal opportunity guidelines. Though the initial input by the supervisor may not be solicited, the manner in which information is shared should make it easy and natural for the receiver to solicit further information. Finally, the supervisor should test the accuracy of the received message by having the job incumbent repeat it back to the supervisor along with a proposed action program.

Goal-Setting Approach

Because job performance is continuous, performance appraisal must also be continuous. Some critics snipe at periodic performance appraisals on the basis that six-month or annual reviews are not realistically keyed to the continuous and sporadic nature of work. This criticism of periodic reviews is valid if reviews are conducted only periodically. However, periodic performance appraisals and feedback can be a constructive adjunct to, or serve as a mechanism for, continuous and timely feedback. The Adult-Adult periodic review process ideally builds on prework by a natural work

[4]For further information on feedback, see David A. Kolb, Irwin M. Rubin, and James M. McIntyre, *Organizational Psychology—An Experiential Approach*, 2d ed., Prentice Hall, Englewood Cliffs, N.J., 1974.

group. For example, a department head, in planning his charter for the coming year, might lead his natural work group in an off-site, two-day workshop for defining departmental goals and strategies. Having reached consensus on the departmental charter, each member, through choice, negotiation, or assignment, assumes ownership of a chunk of the departmental mission. Responsibilities assumed at this stage are tentative, pending ratification of the proposed departmental charter in the upcoming divisional planning conference.

The individual performance appraisal process is then launched from the ratified departmental charter. The department head activates the performance review process by distributing a review form to each person in his work group to answer three basic questions:

1. What were your major achievements during the past six months?
2. What are your goals for the next 6 months?
3. What are your long-term goals?

Answers to these three questions are usually summarized on a single sheet of paper by each job incumbent, who returns the completed form to his or her immediate supervisor.

After reviewing the completed form, the supervisor consults the person regarding a mutually convenient time to hold the performance review discussion. A supervisor who is sensitive to the symbolism of organizational rank will attempt to hold the meeting away from his own office—perhaps in the job incumbent's office or a nearby conference room. If the supervisor does hold the meeting in his own office, he will avoid the "throne-behind-the-desk" posture, and will also take measures to assure privacy and to prevent interruptions.

The most developmental interviews are conducted by supervisors who approach the performance review discussion with a mental set to do more listening than talking. Supervisors become competent in this role as a result of insights and skills gained through transactional analysis and conference leadership so that the natural use of feedback (rather than criticism) establishes the climate for the discussion. Though constructive discussions are facilitated through the application of these principles, it is important that the supervisor maintain an authentic relationship by not departing too radically from his everyday style.

After opening the discussion—usually with small talk—the supervisor may take his cue from the job incumbent in deciding whether he should open the business discussion by asking a question or whether to follow a course initiated by the other person through a question or comment. If the supervisor begins the discussion, he may acknowledge the enumerated achievements and ask, "In looking over your achievements, Joe, how do you feel about them?" The supervisor is not in a rush to get a response, nor is he afraid of silence. He is prepared to wait to give Joe an opportunity to warm up to the question. He may wish to follow this initial discussion with another question, "Now that this experience is behind you, Joe, if you were doing it over again, is there anything you'd do differently?" Again, the supervisor waits, even if Joe doesn't answer immediately. Or the supervisor might say, "You had a major hand in opening our new production line. I'll bet you learned a lot from that experience?" Again, the necessary pause for Joe's response. Or, "John Smith is going to Charleston to start up operations in our new South Carolina plant. If he asked you for advice, what would you say?"

Joe's answer might be, "It's funny you should ask that question, because if I were doing it over, I'd do three things differently." Joe then proceeds to detail a better approach to his accomplishments of the past six months.

The initial and primary focus of the supervisor's role is to get the job incumbent to assume the responsibility for reviewing and assessing his own accomplishments. If the job incumbent is under the false illusion that he has accomplished his goals adequately, this may be the fault of the supervisor for having failed to give him timely and valid feedback, or it may be a result of the supervisor's failure to help the job incumbent establish well-defined goals and acceptable criteria of achievements through which he could assess his own performance.

Having reviewed achievements and lessons learned through them, they can move on to goals to be accomplished. Jointly they establish short- and long-range goal priorities, strategies for achieving them, and define their individual and mutual roles in attaining and measuring accomplishments. The supervisor does not pull his rank on the job incumbent by overriding his viewpoint with his greater authority. However, the supervisor may have information to share with the job incumbent in terms of constraints imposed by budgets, schedules, policy, laws, and customer commitments. When the job incumbent and supervisor are on the same data base, they can arrive at decisions through consensus in an Adult-Adult style. When agreement is reached, they adjourn, the job incumbent taking the form with him to modify according to their agreement. The individual makes any necessary changes, duplicates the form, gives one to the supervisor, and retains a copy for his six-month charter.

After completing this one-on-one meeting with each individual in his natural work group, the supervisor convenes them for a joint session. Each person reports, in turn, to the total group his or her goals and strategies as a basis for planning collaborative efforts and avoiding conflicts and redundancies.

Though the periodic performance review establishes a six-month charter, it usually needs interim updating. After the forms are completed and discussed, the supervisor may consult the group to choose monthly 2-hour meeting dates for updating their charters. In these monthly meetings, each person reports on his achievements, obstacles, breakthroughs, new assignments, setbacks, problems, and new opportunities. These meetings keep the group updated and provide opportunity for members to help each other, through suggestions and collaborative effort.

Thus, when the next review period arrives, there are no surprises. Under such a system, each person is continuously accountable for his goals and achievements and the measurement of his own performance. If the performance review is the occasion for awarding the discretionary bonus, merit increase, or giving notice of termination, such actions come as no surprise to persons reporting to supervisors who apply the principles of feedback described earlier. To the extent that the individual and the supervisor are on the same data base, allegations of favoritism, unfairness, and arbitrariness are less likely to be made.

When performance reviews are not taken seriously at lower job grade levels, it's usually because they are not appropriately initiated and supported at the higher levels. Vice presidents may protest that their charters are established by the annual planning conference and, hence, they see no need to duplicate it with the performance review procedure used at lower levels. These protestors may fail to realize that the primary purpose of following the performance review process at their level is not to establish charters but, rather, to initiate the system to be used at successively lower levels. The vice president's use of the form with the department heads reporting to him is a language of action which says, in effect, "performance reviews are important." Moreover, successfully conducted performance reviews at the upper levels serve as models to be emulated by persons at lower levels.

Goal-oriented performance appraisals traditionally do not include the hourly paid employees. The reasoning supporting this tradition is that wage-roll people are paid to carry out orders—not to set goals. Moreover, members of the bargaining unit are presumed to have their responsibilities prescribed by a standard job description. Based on such assumptions, performance reviews for the hourly work force tend to be Parent-Child merit rating systems. However, perceptive managers are finding that traditional practice and assumptions provide inappropriate guidelines for dealing with members of the new work ethic, and are beginning to innovate Adult-Adult performance review systems which have equal relevance for salaried and wage-roll people.

The goal-oriented performance review described above can be adapted to hourly workers if it is appropriately keyed to their job constraints. When hourly workers are interdependent members of a work team, it may be appropriate to administer the system on a group basis. In this case, the first-level supervisor may convene his work group in a conference room, distribute the forms to them, and lead them through the goal-setting process. Using a flip chart or chalkboard, he involves them in compiling a list of their group's six-month achievements. Such a list may be narrowed to the most important achievements which each records on his or her performance review form. In a similar manner, he involves the group in defining goals, following the principles of problem solving–goal setting described in Chapter 4. Thus, each person now has a list of the group's achievements and goals on his or her form. This group process has now paved the way for involving each person in a one-on-one discussion.

The supervisor arranges for a private meeting with each member of the group, asking them each to bring the completed form to the meeting. To make the process nonthreatening to the traditional, and worthwhile to the freethinkers, he might say, "Bring this completed form to the meeting, as it will be the basis for much of our discussion. By the way, if any of you wish to add some of your personal achievements or goals to those we have listed as a group, feel free to do so. I'll be glad to discuss them with you."

In the ensuing one-on-one discussions, the supervisor strives to listen more than he talks, to apply the Adult-Adult process of feedback, and to avoid Parent-Child expressions of criticism, condescension, and direction. Also, as in the case of the salaried personnel, the supervisor should schedule interim periodic meetings to keep the group updated and to involve them in the changes which invariably occur in a work place, and to enable them to keep their goals updated.

Controversy continues to rage over the issue of whether or not the performance review discussion of goals and achievements should include a discussion of pay. The traditional Parent-Child viewpoint (Theory X) holds that performance review and pay should be discussed separately on the basis that money is an emotion-arousing subject which would impair the logical and deliberate process of goal setting. The assumption behind this viewpoint is that a disappointing pay adjustment would demotivate people from setting and pursuing challenging goals. The Adult-Adult position (Theory Y) is that people like to understand the relationship between their accomplishments and the reward systems of the organization. Pay, being one of the more tangible forms of feedback from the supervisor, is an integral part of the performance review. Needless to say, the better the individual understands the criteria by which he as an individual is appraised and the better he understands the technicalities of wage and salary administration, the less likely he is to be surprised and disappointed by including compensation in the performance review discussion. To use the analogy of the baseball game, adult players don't blame the umpire when they strike out, nor do they expect the umpire to give them special consideration or tell them how to improve their game. In contrast, immature players more often do try to blame the umpire or others for their failures. A paternalistic umpire who attempted to assume a helping role would perpetuate this immaturity and violate the accepted ground rules in doing so. People are more likely to act like adults when they are treated like adults.

In summary, performance review at its worst tends to incur outrage, intimidation, and disengagement. At its best, it is an Adult feedback process that helps people take charge of their own careers and organizational responsibilities.

ATTITUDE SURVEYS

Attitude surveys were described in Chapters 4 and 5 as media for managing innovation and for developing employees respectively. Following the procedures described in those chapters, and illustrated in Figure 7-10, creates an opportunity for the manager to discover how his administrative burden can be lightened when he involves employees in the diagnosis and solution of organizational problems.

It was pointed out earlier that the primary value of a survey for fostering innovation and development stems from employee involvement in the development and administration of the system—that the survey results themselves usually represent only a small fraction of the value of the survey. In this chapter, it will be illustrated that survey results, if quantified in terms which are acceptable to managers, can represent feedback criteria as meaningful as standardized economic indicators of success.[5]

Businessmen have become quite comfortable using such economic measures as cash flow, return on investment, and earnings per share. Widespread usage has led to their general acceptance by business organizations, financial institutions, and the general investing public, and they have thus become standardized business terms. Though most businesses would agree that employee attitudes might represent assets or liabilities, few have attempted to include them in the review process. Introducing attitude survey results into the matrix of review criteria would not violate or reject traditional criteria of managerial effectiveness, but could add a dimension which could help the manager improve in terms of all criteria.

Attitudes are a mental position toward various life situations and, as such, give direction to a person's knowledge and skills. Job attitudes are intervening variables, which are at once a reflection of the forces brought to bear on people at work and a determinant and predictor of the ultimate criterion, productivity. Therefore, a reliable and quantitative measure of

[5]M. Scott Myers and Vincent S. Flowers, "A Framework for Measuring Human Assets," *California Management Review*, Summer 1974, vol. XVI, no. 4, pp. 5–16.

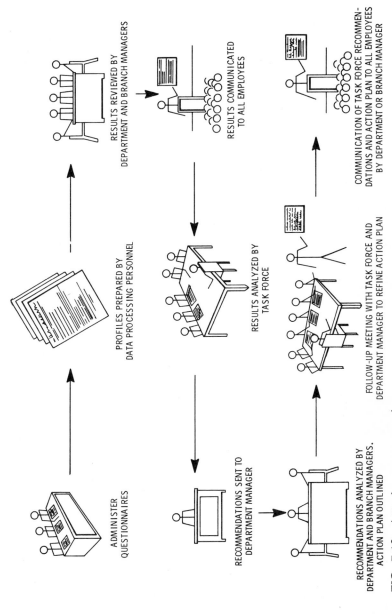

ADMINISTER
QUESTIONNAIRES

PROFILES PREPARED BY
DATA PROCESSING PERSONNEL

RESULTS REVIEWED BY
DEPARTMENT AND BRANCH MANAGERS

RESULTS COMMUNICATED
TO ALL EMPLOYEES

RESULTS ANALYZED BY
TASK FORCE

RECOMMENDATIONS SENT TO
DEPARTMENT MANAGER

RECOMMENDATIONS ANALYZED BY
DEPARTMENT AND BRANCH MANAGERS.
ACTION PLAN OUTLINED

FOLLOW-UP MEETING WITH TASK FORCE AND
DEPARTMENT MANAGER TO REFINE ACTION PLAN

COMMUNICATION OF TASK FORCE RECOMMEN-
DATIONS AND ACTION PLAN TO ALL EMPLOYEES
BY DEPARTMENT OR BRANCH MANAGER

FIG. 7-10 Attitude survey procedure.

	Agree		Disagree
1. My work is satisfying to me.	( )	( )	( )
2. There is not enough cooperation between my work group and others we work with.	( )	( )	( )
3. There are opportunities here for those who want to get ahead.	( )	( )	( )
4. For my kind of job, working conditions are O.K.	( )	( )	( )
5. We don't get enough information about how well our work group is doing.	( )	( )	( )
6. People in my work group work together as a team.	( )	( )	( )
7. I don't understand the objectives of my department.	( )	( )	( )
8. I can be sure of a job here as long as I do good work.	( )	( )	( )
9. There are too many unnecessary rules to follow here.	( )	( )	( )
10. I have as much freedom as I need to plan my own work.	( )	( )	( )
11. I feel free to tell my supervisor what I think.	( )	( )	( )
12. I'm proud to work for this company.	( )	( )	( )
13. I am paid fairly for the kind of work I do.	( )	( )	( )
14. During the past six months I have seriously considered leaving the company for another job.	( )	( )	( )
15. Favoritism is a problem in my area.	( )	( )	( )
16. Most people here are in jobs that make good use of their abilities.	( )	( )	( )
17. My job seems to be leading to the kind of future I want.	( )	( )	( )
18. They expect too much from us around here.	( )	( )	( )
19. I have clear-cut objectives on which to base my work goals.	( )	( )	( )
20. Compared with other companies, our benefits are good.	( )	( )	( )

Years with the company: ( ) 0–2   ( ) 3–5   ( ) 6–10   ( ) 11–20   ( ) 21+

My job grade: _____

FIG. 7-11 Attitude questionnaire (abbreviated). ("Dollarizing Attitudes," *Atlantic Economic Review*, May–June 1974, p. 53. Reprinted with permission.)

job attitudes can serve as a valid index of how well the organization is managing its human resources.

Figure 7-11 is a twenty-item attitude questionnaire, abbreviated here to illustrate the nature of a survey which, in most cases, would be considerably longer. Such a survey may yield misleading results if the attitudes of all respondents are indiscriminately lumped together. For example, a plant manager whose influence can permeate the entire organization obviously has a more influential attitude than the benchworker whose attitudes have a relatively narrow sphere of influence. Further, the 10-year employee's attitude is a more valid reflection of the long-term or real impact of the organization than the 1-year employee whose honeymoon with the company is still not over, or whose attitudes may still be reflecting previous employment experience.

Figure 7-12 is a scheme for weighting attitudes by job grade and company tenure. Thus we see that a newly hired technician in job grade 7 has a weight of 2 applied to his attitude score, while one of his coworkers

JOB GRADES		YEARS TENURE				
Salaried	Hourly	0-2	3-5	7-10	11-20	21+
35+		7	8	9	10	11
33-34		6	7	8	9	10
29-32		5	6	7	8	9
25-28		4	5	6	7	8
22-24	10-12	3	4	5	6	7
	5-9	2	3	4	5	6
	1-4	1	2	3	4	5

FIG. 7-12 Attitude weights.

with 12 years with the company has a weight of 5. His supervisor (JG 26) with 4 years' tenure has an attitude weight of 5, his superintendent (JG 32) with 18 years' tenure has a weight of 8, and his plant manager (JG 36) with 12 years' tenure has a weight of 10.

The administration of attitude questionnaires to large numbers of employees can provide the basis for establishing normative data for differentiating between various levels of motivation. For example, the questionnaire might be administered randomly to several departments to establish a distribution curve of average favorable responses to the 20 statements. The average favorable percentage score of the department falling at the fiftieth percentile could be arbitrarily given a value of 1.00. The average favorable percentage score of the lowest ranked department could be valued at 0.00, and the highest ranked department's score set at 2.00. Therefore, scores significantly lower than 1.00, for example, are more apt to be potential "turnoffs" or "turnovers," and scores above 1.00 are more likely to be "turned-on" high producers.

To the extent that wages and salaries represent investments by the organization to purchase productive skills, attitude scores become meaningful indicators of the extent to which the organization receives an adequate return on this investment. Table 7-1 presents the details of a formula for converting attitude scores into financial returns on payroll investment expressed in terms of gain, breakeven, or deficit. The job grade and tenure would be keypunched along with responses to the attitude survey. A department manager could then receive an attitude index for his department which in itself is a meaningful comparative measure of effectiveness. In addition, he could multiply this index by his annual payroll to determine his dollar gain or deficit per employee. The two indexes which have the greater value for interdepartmental comparisons or for charting trends, are the attitude index and the gain (or deficit) per person.

Tables 7-2 and 7-3 show the same department, but in one hypothetical case with very favorable attitudes, and in the other with very unfavorable attitudes.

In addition to the overall attitude index for the entire work force,

TABLE 7-1   Dollarized Attitudes

Individual	Annual salary	Job grade	Years tenure	Atti-tude weight	Atti-tude score	Weighted attitude score
1. John Doe	$ 28,000	28	5	5	1.05	5.25
2. Mary Brown	14,000	7	11	5	1.12	5.60
3. Harry Smith	18,000	12	22	7	1.21	8.47
4. Bill Jones	13,000	5	3	3	1.26	3.78
5. Jim Johnson	37,000	30	4	6	1.15	6.90
	$110,000			26		30.00

$$\text{Attitude index} = \frac{\text{(weighted A-score)}}{\text{(attitude weight)}} = \frac{30.00}{26} = 1.15$$

Dollarized attitudes = attitude index (annual payroll) = 1.15($110,000) = $126,500

Gain = $126,500 − $110,000 = $16,500

$$\text{Gain per person} = \frac{\$16,500}{5} = \$3,300$$

subgroups (e.g., job grade 2, foremen, clerical, and ethnic groups) may be studied to pinpoint and diagnose problems. Moreover, individual items on the questionnaire may be studied separately to diagnose the causes of attitude index changes and abnormalities.

Though the attitude index or the gain (or deficit) per person may not be seen immediately by managers as a standard index, common usage

TABLE 7-2   Dollarized Attitudes—Very Favorable

Individual	Annual salary	Job grade	Years tenure	Atti-tude weight	Atti-tude score	Weighted attitude score
1. John Doe	$ 28,000	28	5	5	1.50	7.50
2. Mary Brown	14,000	7	11	5	1.45	7.25
3. Harry Smith	18,000	12	22	7	1.68	11.76
4. Bill Jones	13,000	5	3	3	1.55	4.65
5. Jim Johnson	37,000	30	4	6	1.72	10.32
	$110,000			26		41.48

$$\text{Attitude index} = \frac{41.48}{26} = 1.60$$

Dollarized attitudes = 1.60($110,000) = $176,000

Gain = $66,000

Gain per person = $13,200

TABLE 7-3 Dollarized Attitudes—Very Unfavorable

Individual	Annual salary	Job grade	Years tenure	Attitude weight	Attitude score	Weighted attitude score
1. John Doe	$ 28,000	28	5	5	.51	2.55
2. Mary Brown	14,000	7	11	5	.73	3.65
3. Harry Smith	18,000	12	22	7	.65	4.55
4. Bill Jones	13,000	5	3	3	.45	1.35
5. Jim Johnson	37,000	30	4	6	.75	4.50
	$110,000			26		16.60

Attitude index $= \dfrac{16.60}{26} = .64$

Dollarized attitudes $= .64(\$110,000) = \$70,400$

Deficit $= \$39,600$

Deficit per person $= \$7,920$

could make it so, just as they have learned to report in terms of cash flow, return on investment, profit before taxes, earnings per share, and so forth. If included in the criteria of the standard quarterly review, annual plan, or other reports to management, as illustrated in Table 7-4, attitudinal measures would assume the importance accorded to them by organization leaders.

The partial summary of annual planning data shown in Table 7-4 reflects asset-effectiveness information for the current and prior years and planned data for the coming year. Concentrating exclusively on the traditional economic criteria of sales, costs, and profits can yield a misleading representation of what is really going on. For example, the 1980 profit for Department 128 increased significantly compared to 1979, return on nonhuman investment increased from 8.3 to 13.9 percent, and turnover was reduced from 25 to 12 percent. The 1981 planned data indicate that these favorable trends should continue. Using only economic measurements leads to the conclusion that this manager has been, and will continue to be, "successful," He would have little trouble winning financial and management support because, under traditional assumptions, profit making, even when short-range, is considered the best evidence of efficient and effective use of resources.

However, incorporating a measure of employee attitudes into the reported data suggests that although the manager may be winning the annual profit battle, he may be on the verge of losing the war. The department attitude index dropped from 1.21 in 1979 to .91 in 1980, resulting in an attitude loss per person of $720. Coupling this unfavorable trend in

TABLE 7-4 Annual Planning Data: Asset Effectiveness Statement, Department 128

	Actual		Plan
	1979	1980	1981
Sales	$1,500,000	$2,000,000	$2,200,000
Cost of sales	800,000	1,000,000	1,050,000
Gross margin	$ 700,000	$1,000,000	$1,150,000
Sales, percent	47.0%	50.0%	52.2%
Other department costs	$ 319,000	$ 334,000	$ 350,000
Department profit	$ 381,000	$ 666,000	$ 800,000
Sales, percent	25.4%	33.3%	36.4%
Asset effectiveness measures			
Total assets	$4,500,000	$4,800,000	$5,000,000
Sales/assets	33.3%	41.7%	44.4%
Profits/assets	8.3%	13.9%	16.0%
People effectiveness measures			
Number of people	80	75	86
Attitude index	**1.21**	**.91**	**1.10**
Total payroll	$ 640,000	$ 600,000	$ 700,000
Turnover, percent	25%	12%	10%
Sales/person	$ 18,500	$ 26,667	$ 25,581
Profit/person	$ 4,762	$ 8,890	$ 9,302
Attitude gain/person	**$ 1,680**	**($ 720)**	**$ 895**

attitudes with the apparently favorable trend in turnover suggests that employees are becoming dissatisfied.

Getting timely feedback through the attitude index and coupling this information with turnover and economic figures could alert this manager to the need for human resource investments *before* a crisis occurs. This department manager might have skimped on concern with, or expenditures for, motivation and morale with little or no immediate unfavorable effect on economic measures. However, his managerial strategy may be alienating a significant portion of his work force. Strategies for improving motivation and morale may yield a high return on investment and ward off a potential disaster.

When only short-term economic criteria are used on managerial appraisal, managers are sometimes rewarded for reductive behavior. The economic results of Department 128 indicate that the manager's behavior has been "good," and he will probably be financially rewarded accordingly. The financial reward will act as a positive reinforcer for continuing his present management style. Indeed, he might be promoted before the ultimate criteria of his failure become apparent, and he may duplicate his dereliction at a higher level.

Only when managers perceive attitudinal criteria to be as important as financial criteria will they accord it the same attention and effort. The annual planning data summary in Table 7-4 reflects balanced concern for the end-result criteria of sales, costs, and profits and the intervening variables of people-effectiveness measures. These intervening variables are the bridge which leads the manager from end-results back to causal factors.

Authoritarian or manipulative managers may try initially, by trial and error, to improve attitudes through traditional strategies of fear, persuasion, paternalism, and manipulation. Finally, they must learn that attitude improvements can result only through the practice of good management. Only when they are able to understand the relationship between employee attitudes and organizational effectiveness will managers' talents be directed toward changing their own managerial strategies.

LABOR RELATIONS

The administration of labor relations is traditionally based on the assumption that the goals of the organization, as represented by upper-level managers, are naturally in conflict with the needs of its "workers" or "labor" at the lower levels of the organization. The labor portion of the work force is usually made up of hourly paid personnel in production, maintenance, and administrative jobs who are not exempt from the restrictions of the Fair Labor Standards Act. They compose more than 80 percent of the work force in United States business and industry.

In contrast, people in the top layers of the organization are usually identified with the organization, by themselves as well as by others, and bear the label of "management." People in the middle ranks are often uncertain about their identity as management or labor, though most of them are exempt from the requirements of the Fair Labor Standards Act. Though they are usually assured they are members of management, they feel at times as though they are being treated like labor. In many unionized organizations, management and labor have come to represent two enemy camps whose conflicting goals and philosophies are the basis for the ongoing warfare moderated through collective bargaining. The basis for the management-labor dichotomy is illustrated in Figure 3-5 and described in greater detail as the "win-lose adversary" relationship on pages 89 to 91.

Rights of management

The management of the plant and the direction of the working force is vested exclusively in the Company. This shall include and not be limited to the right to hire, classify, promote, transfer, suspend, discipline, discharge for cause, layoff, or release employees for lack of work, provided these rights shall not conflict with this Agreement.

Rights of labor

1 – The Company recognizes the Union as the exclusive representative of all employees.

2 – The Company agrees to deduct the initiation fee and monthly Union dues from the pay of employees who authorize such deductions.

3 – Stewards are privileged to handle grievances in the plant during working hours without loss of compensation.

4 – The Company will maintain a bulletin board for the use of the Union.

5 – The Company shall provide the Group Insurance Program as outlined in Appendix "B" of this Agreement.

6 – The Retirement Plan shall remain in effect as specified in this Agreement.

7 – Overtime records shall be kept by the Company for the purpose of distributing overtime work as equally as possible.

8 – When terminating employment, an employee shall be paid for each day of earned sick leave not used.

9 – An employee who works on a day considered a holiday shall receive holiday pay plus double his regular rate for all hours worked on the holiday.

10 – The Maintenance Electrician job includes installation and maintenance of electrical systems and equipment; electronic controls and tape making equipment used on machine tools; and installation, maintenance, repair, servicing and alteration of air conditioning and refrigeration systems.

11 – The Maintenance Electrician job excludes electrical assembly and maintenance work on airplanes and their component parts.

12 – All job classifications and their descriptions as listed in Appendix "A" shall remain in effect for the duration of this Agreement.

*Excerpts from a 1966 Agreement between an aerospace firm in the Southwest and the IBEW.

FIG. 7-13   Examples of traditional prerogatives of management and labor.

Formalizing the Management-Labor Gap

Most formal agreements between management and labor reflect an implied conflict of interest between the two parties. Figure 7-13, excerpted from an agreement between a large aerospace firm and the International Brotherhood of Electrical Workers (IBEW), illustrates some typical prerogatives of management and labor. Though the term "prerogative" is traditionally used in this context to denote management rights, labor rights by definition and comparison are no less prerogatives. The rights of management define time-honored prerogatives stemming from authority vested by ownership. Implicit in this statement is the assumption that these rights are needed to protect the plant from the insatiable and irresponsible demands of labor. In a climate of mistrust, the average member of the organization could understandably see this array of management rights—to hire, classify, promote, transfer, suspend, discipline, discharge, lay off, release employees—as threatening. Certainly the specification of these management prerogatives would seem to require the need for a counterbalancing array of labor prerogatives.

To a manager accustomed to his role in a nonunion plant, the rights of the union may represent a startling degree of capitulation by management, and a serious limitation on the manager's freedom to manage. However, these rights are protected, or even required, by law in union plants, where they are also perpetuated as unquestioned long-standing tradition. Nevertheless, recognizing the union as the exclusive representative of employees does reflect the assumptions that people need a protector against management, and that the goals of the employees are different from the goals of the organization. Moreover, the union's initiative in defining the terms for providing bulletin boards, group insurance, retirement plan, equitable distribution of overtime, and other conditions suggests that these programs were opposed or neglected by management. When the union has established itself as the people's protector, enlightened as well as unsophisticated managers often find themselves on the defensive. The union, with single-minded determination, directs more effort to wresting rights from management than to supporting the health of the company, and pressures management unremittingly to relinquish profits for distribution to its members.

Though management may be only trying to keep the organization in financial equilibrium, it often acquires the image of the penurious exploiter. The union, in its unrelenting drive to support its membership, unwittingly impairs management's ability to invest in the future and remain competitive, and simultaneously plants the seeds of indolence, dependency, and disaffection. Now, for example, sick leave has become more than a cushion against the burden of unanticipated illness; it is time off with pay to be used as the job incumbent sees fit or to be exchanged for unearned income. Triple pay for holidays makes holiday work attractive to the worker and undesirable to management, but either alternative—holiday pay or holiday closing—is harmful to the organization and ultimately to its members. The circumscribed definition of jobs reduces the flexibility, versatility, and job satisfaction generally required for a creative and viable work force. Union leadership, while paying lip service to the long-range growth needs of the organization, usually applies pressure for a share of any short-term gain, thereby undermining long-range growth strategies and encouraging defensive financial reporting by the company.

Symptoms of Management Failure

Management brought the problem of unions on itself by earlier exploitation, paternalism, and manipulation. Much of management's failure was incurred innocently by promoting people into supervision whose primary credentials were unrelated to leadership. Though managers trained in human management are infiltrating organizations in increasing numbers, they are plagued by two obstacles.

One obstacle is a work force of maintenance seekers, the older ones jaded by long confinement to meaningless work and the younger ones rebelling against conformity pressures imposed by the company, the union, and work itself. Initial or cursory attempts to treat people as responsible adults typically evoke at least temporary suspicion, hostility, or disengagement; and few managers have the courage, capability, and perseverance to undertake the reprogramming of such a work force.

The second, and often the greater, obstacle is top management, conditioned to act with authority vested by management prerogative. The boss, when conditioned to mistrust the enemy below, seldom affords innovative managers the freedom necessary to effect significant changes in relationships and work roles. The development of responsibility and commitment in the work force is a long-range strategy involving the risk of short-run setbacks. Idealism in the face of unbending authority incurs discouragement and capitulation—and the aspiring innovator may understandably elect to survive by perpetuating the status quo. He may justify his capitulation with the rationale that it is better to survive today in order to win the grand battle tomorrow. Hence, all but the very courageous take on the protective coloring of the world about them, and become inadvertent perpetuators of a philosophy they know intellectually and feel intuitively to be destructive. "But," they rationalize, "all organizations are equally handicapped by the same bad management practices and at least we're not as bad as most of them."

Union-company stalemates and win-lose strategies are understandable in the light of history. Nineteenth-century management flagrantly, though often innocently, exercised assumed prerogatives in motivating people through fear, threats, manipulation, and paternalism. Wage earners living at the bare subsistence levels responded well to the security of uninterrupted employment. When Henry Ford opened an automated assembly line in 1914 and doubled his workers pay to $5 a day, his plant prospered and the workers were both happy and motivated. Though his management innovations satisfied many needs of that era, they embraced two characteristics which became the foundation for latter-day labor problems. One innovation was the simplification of tasks, forerunner of a trend resulting in a situation described in one sociological study,[6] in which 83 percent of the jobs in an automobile assembly plant had fewer than ten operations and 32 percent had but a single operation. The average time cycle for these jobs was 3 minutes, and the learning time was a few hours to a week.

As jobs became more impoverished, pay rates continued upward, maintaining the automotive industry's leadership in providing higher-than-average wages and supplemental benefits. Hence, people's maintenance needs were satisfied better, but their talents were utilized no better, or even less well. In the era of thwarted maintenance needs, the automotive worker with a steady job counted his blessings, taking the monotony of the automated assembly line in stride. But as the total culture achieved greater affluence, improved maintenance factors lost their relative importance in the wage earner's hierarchy of needs. Furthermore, opportunities abounded elsewhere for satisfying maintenance needs, and his security was not jeopardized by changing jobs. The union had successfully protected him against the arbitrariness of management and given him discretionary income to buy goods and services previously beyond his aspirations, and more time to enjoy them. The source of his frustration was thus gradually transferred from inadequate maintenance needs to thwarted higher-order needs, or the motivation needs shown in the inner circle of Figure 1-2.

Attacking the Symptoms

The individual who experiences need frustration is not always able to pinpoint the cause. This was true for the factory worker who was culturally conditioned to gain satisfaction by improving wages, hours and working conditions. But union-led victories came to have less value for the benefits they yielded than for the sense of achievement or successful conquest they represented. The opposing teams of management and labor have some of the characteristics of team sports such as baseball, football, or hockey. They are competitively matched by the terms of their agreement and are refereed by the National Labor Relations Board. Workers are vicariously aligned with the union team, and supervisors with the management team. The issues are of relatively less importance than the satisfaction of winning the battle, and the more bitter the relationship between parties, the sweeter the victory. Hence, the vicarious winning and losing of battles provides outlets for frustrations that otherwise have little opportunity for dissipation.

Rebellion against the *status quo,* particularly after World War II, became more frequent and demanding. Whole industries were paralyzed by

[6]Charles R. Walker and Robert H. Guest, *The Man on the Assembly Line*, Harvard University Press, Cambridge, Mass., 1952.

strikes and other forms of reactive behavior, some of which were directed toward the union leadership which, in some cases, had become no less a source of oppression to its members than the company management. In frantic attempts to perpetuate their jurisdiction and to demonstrate their clout, unions bargained indiscriminately for continuing improvements in wages, hours, and working conditions, baffled by their members' unconcern for interrupted incomes and lack of gratitude for hard-won battles. Hence, the worker, the union, and the company were all victims of their mutual failure to understand the real causes of worker frustration and alienation.

A Gradual Awakening

Allegations of deterioration of worker loyalty and loss of pride in work reached consensus proportions. Only gradually, and among an enlightened few, was an awareness developed of the real causes of disaffection. Discovery of the key to revived human effectiveness stimulated enthusiastic, though often misdirected, efforts to return responsibility and challenge to the job. As the concepts and techniques of job enrichment led to the redefinition of the supervisor's role as discussed early in this chapter, labor relations specialists became aware of their dilemma. They found themselves administering a strategy based on the use of power, authority, and cunning to satisfy maintenance needs, in the face of an emerging philosophy based on the influence of mutual respect and competence and the pursuit of self-actualization. The "labor skate" or "labor hack," accustomed to the use of compromise, deception, and coercion, began to realize he had been dealing primarily with symptoms of problems—and that real and lasting peace could be obtained only by curing the causes. The insights of the behavioral sciences were needed, and the labor relations specialist had a choice of acquiring these insights, becoming vocationally obsolete, or changing vocations.

Strategies for reorienting labor relations must adapt to the uniqueness of each organization. Certainly the nonunion organization requires a different approach than the union plant. In the unionized organization, the intermediate goal may be to make peace with the union—to reach a condition of détente as described on pages 91 to 94. This is not easy, of course, because in most union-management relationships any act initiated by one party arouses the suspicion and resistance of the other. The first goal is to prepare both parties to listen to each other.

Grappling with the Cause

One approach to this first step is through some form of training. Sensitivity training, as noted on pages 167 and 168, is a process used alone or in combination with problem-solving–goal-setting exercises to enable people to see themselves as others see them, to understand the assumptions which motivate their behavior, and to gain some insights into their own styles of management. Skills of interpersonal competence are developed through this process. A major retail food chain in Canada exposed their managers to various instrumented forms of sensitivity training.

When managers in this food chain first acquired the skills of candor and leveling, they were frustrated by their continuing inability to develop authentic relationships with union leaders. Union spokesmen continued to be on guard and to maintain at least a facade of mistrust in response to management's overtures of openness. Finally the ice was broken when union officers, at their request, were permitted to participate in the company's instrumented sensitivity training program, which at that time was the managerial grid.[7] When the union leaders had completed the one-week course, they agreed to participate in an intergroup confrontation with management for the purpose of surfacing some of the causes of mistrust and conflict. In the initial meeting the parties agreed to undertake separately the task of defining what they thought would constitute a sound relationship between them. Each defined their own and the other party's role in this ideal relationship, and then they convened for comparisons and discussion. Though their lists were different, there were no basic points of contradiction. Avoiding the customary win-lose traps, they carried on candid discussions of their respective roles and images. These working sessions were the basis for reconciling or accepting most of their differences and misunderstandings. Though culturally conditioned by three decades of traditional labor-management relationships, the ice was broken in the mid-1960s, and the two parties began working together with common goals, developing compatible strategies to satisfy the mutual needs of the organization and its members.

Learning to talk to each other is not the ultimate goal, but it is a necessary beginning toward implementation of a philosophy based on mutual respect. Nor is this first goal achieved easily or quickly. The values of labor leaders and company managers are deep-seated, having been conditioned throughout the professional careers of both. Hence, change requires initiative and time, and follows an evolutionary process which will continue only in a climate of mutual trust. Mutual trust cannot be developed by the language of words, but only through the language of trustworthy behavior by both parties.

The Intermediate Goal

The intermediate, and sometimes the ultimate, goal of labor relations is the harmonious coexistence and active cooperation of the company and the

[7]Robert R. Blake and Jane S. Mouton, *Corporate Excellence through Grid Organization Development*, Gulf Publishing, Houston, Tex., 1968.

union in the attainment of their mutual goals. For some, of course, the ultimate goal is the synergizing of individual and organizational goals to the point that union intervention is unneeded. However, pursuit of the intermediate goal of constructive coexistence offers the best platform for launching a program of constructive union-company confrontation.

Charles A. Myers listed some conditions for constructive coexistence of companies and unions, based on a review of thirteen case studies sponsored by the National Planning Association.[8] Though there were variations among case studies, the following characteristics of the union-management relationship were found in most situations:

1. There is full acceptance by management of the collective bargaining process and of unionism as an institution. The company considers a strong union an asset to management.

2. The union fully accepts private ownership and operation of the industry; it recognizes that the welfare of its members depends upon the successful operation of the business.

3. The union is strong, responsible, and democratic.

4. The company stays out of the union's internal affairs; it does not seek to change the workers' allegiance to their union.

5. Mutual trust and confidence exists between the parties. There have been no serious ideological incompatibilities.

6. Neither party to bargaining has adopted a legalistic approach to the solution of problems in the relationship.

7. Negotiations are problem-centered: More time is spent on day-to-day problems than on defining abstract principles.

8. There is widespread union-management consultation and highly developed information sharing.

9. Grievances are settled promptly, in the local plant whenever possible. There is flexibility and informality within the procedure.

The "collaborative adversary" and "organizational democracy" relationships described on pages 91 to 95 illustrate the evolutionary consequences of satisfying the conditions in the foregoing list. Through intervention processes described more fully in *Managing with Unions*,[9] union and management people participate in joint educational experiences which become the foundation and building blocks for converting adversary to collaborative relationships. The development of collaborative relationships

[8] Clinton S. Golden and Virginia D. Parker, *Causes of Industrial Peace*, Harper, New York, 1955, p. 47.

[9] M. Scott Myers, *Managing With Unions*, Addison-Wesley, Reading, Mass., 1978.

has become more feasible as a result of four changing conditions:

1.   Contemporary union members are more enlightened than their counterparts of earlier eras and are more responsive to opportunity for self-actualization and less tolerant of domination by company and union authority figures.

2.   Union leaders are also more enlightened and recognize the limitations of wages, hours, and working conditions for satisfying the needs of their more enlightened constituency. Though somewhat uneasy about the increasing ambiguity of their time-honored adversary charter, more union officers are willing to explore their changing role in the pursuit of industrial democracy.

3.   Company managers are more sophisticated in principles of motivation and are encouraging the constructive expression of talent as the only viable alternative to counterproductive rebellion. Today's managers have fewer hangups than their predecessors with needs for managerial prerogatives and rank-oriented status symbols.

4.   Trends in legislation and corporate innovations are encouraging the broader implementation of total systems sharing plans such as employee stock ownership, profit sharing, and Scanlon-type plans. Such systems, in combination with improved work-life processes, tend to depolarize the management-labor dichotomy.

Unions came into existence primarily as protectors of the less privileged at the lower levels of the organization, and usually continued as a counterbalancing influence against arbitrary management authority. Hence, survival of a union would seem to require continuing conflict between management and labor. However, when a company and its local unions learn to achieve industrial peace through cooperative pursuit of common goals, this attainment alone will not automatically cause the dissolution of the unions. The inertia of traditional management practices, legal restrictions, and conditioned dependency relationships with the union, coupled with active resistance by the parent (usually international) union, make the decertification of a union dependent on extraordinary initiative on the part of both parties. Thus, unions may continue functioning long after they achieve a level of mutual trust that would have prevented their initial formation. Their continuity, of course, depends on their ability to redefine their role under conditions of industrial harmony.

The Ultimate Goal

The ultimate goal of labor relations is the same in both the nonunion and the union groups: namely, building a climate of mutual trust through goal-directed individual and group relationships throughout the organization. These conditions are described as "organizational democracy" on pages 94 and 95, and are illustrated in Figure 5-1. The strategy for building such an environment is the theme of this entire book, particularly Chapters 3, 4, and 5. In essence, it is a philosophy of involving the talent of people at all levels of the organization in the pursuit of visible, desirable, challenging, and attainable goals through involvement processes in which the influence of competence rather than the application of authority provides direction.

If nonunion organizations are to withstand organization attempts, their members must have economic conditions comparable with those of their unionized counterparts. However, the traditional maintenance factors of wages, hours, and working conditions are of secondary importance if employees have better opportunities to develop and use their talents in the performance of meaningful work. Their managers are not practitioners of coercive and manipulative techniques but, rather, they follow practices which satisfy the conditions of interpersonal competence, meaningful goals, and helpful systems as defined in Chapter 2. They must defend the rights of the people to exercise their legitimate roles in the organization with the fervor of union stewards, but as supervisors, they must make the relationship of individual and organizational goals synergistic, or at least compatible.

Handling Grievances

Grievance procedures in nonunion organizations cannot be patterned after the procedures in the union plant, for this would imply and incur the assumptions that precipitated the intervention of unions. In a typical union plant, the grievance procedure moves upward through dual chains of command, engaging the contestants in win-lose conflicts to be resolved sooner or later in fact finding, power pressures, compromise, and mediation. As noted earlier, this process is based on the premise that management and labor have conflicting goals and hence are incapable of voluntary or natural problem resolution. Such a strategy in the nonunion plant would fail to surface grievances because of the intuitive recognition by the individual that his supervisor has the trump card of authority and that there are no safeguards against the subtle reprisals that might occur if the "management-labor" style of grievance procedure were applied. Hence, simply introducing a traditional union grievance procedure into the nonunion plant not only fails to surface and resolve grievances, but more damagingly, it precipitates and broadens the "management-labor" cleavage associated with alienation.

Grievances rarely spring full blown into existence as a consequence of a single recent event or cause. More often a grievance is an eruption that releases tensions built up from sustained subjection to petty injustices, oppressive restrictions, monotonous and demeaning work, economic pressures, and particularly in the large organizations, frustrations arising from the lack of opportunity to be heard or to obtain wanted information. Emotions displayed in connection with a grievance often seem disproportionate to the stated reason for the grievance. However, taken in the context of the backlog of culminating factors, the grievance is understandable for what it usually is—the final straw which pushed the individual temporarily beyond his threshold of self-restraint. Many grievances are filed by persons who would normally seek more rational resolutions for their problems. However, having locked themselves into a win-lose conflict during a moment of high emotion, their pride and the lingering pressure of previous frustrations formalize the grievance for official processing.

Psychologists in the Los Angeles school system, recognizing that teenager rebellion often has its roots in frustrations arising from the absence of someone trustworthy to talk to about their problems, established a "hotline" telephone number to call for help. Counselors receiving their calls listened and gave advice, often referring them to others; but most importantly, they were immediately available and did not require identifying information. Most of 7000 calls received during the first year dealt with boy-girl relationships and conflict with authority, problems not considered "important" by many adults. The availability of an understanding ear when they needed it was a key factor for many in reducing tensions which might otherwise have found harmful expression.

Many grievances in industry are precipitated by the absence of someone who cares enough to listen to employees' problems and give them information or advice when they need it. Their frustrations, like those of teenagers, often result from an accumulation of unresolved minor problems and unanswered questions about such matters as supplemental benefits, job opportunities, interpersonal conflict, and home problems. The large organization needs an "information line" to give immediate and anonymous response to requests for information and complaints about real or imagined injustices. This immediate dissipation of emotion would prevent the ground swell of alienation which infiltrates the organization and ultimately contaminates the vast majority whose attitudes are otherwise characteristically neutral or uninvolved.

The first step in a grievance procedure for the nonunion plant grants the individual complete freedom to use his judgment in whatever way seems appropriate to *him*. It cannot force him, as a first step, even informally, to take the matter up with his supervisor, because the supervisor may be his problem. He should be able to consult an anonymous information line, his peers, a personnel representative, a technical specialist, or someone above his supervisor. In other words, he must have the freedom of a citizen in a democracy to appeal his case in whatever manner seems appropriate, with confidence that he is not violating rules by doing so and that he will receive a fair hearing. At the same time, sustained circumvention of supervision deprives the supervisor of feedback necessary for his job effectiveness. The anonymous information line could provide constructive suggestions to supervisors without jeopardizing the anonymity of the complaint system.

If the grievance is not resolved through the informal first-step procedures, the second step of the grievance procedure should allow the supervisor opportunity for involvement, perhaps through the "neutral-third-person" intervention of a mutually acceptable member of the organization who informally assists in clarifying the problem and working out a satisfactory resolution. Should the grievance become more formalized, the third person and/or the supervisor may assist the complainant in writing the formal grievance. Grievances not resolved at this level to the satisfaction of the individual and his supervisor may be appealed upward to successively higher levels of management. If not resolved through the management hierarchy, the services of a mutually acceptable outsider serving an ombudsman role might be needed to mediate an impartial and acceptable resolution.

A large machine tool company has managed to defuse grievances through what they call their "24-hour turnaround" policy. Any person who presents a grievance to his or her supervisor can expect an answer in 24 hours. If the problem is not satisfactorily resolved in the 24-hour period, the supervisor gives a progress report by the end of the period, along with another 24-hour commitment to resolve the problem.

Discipline

In traditional organizations, the infractions of rules call for punitive discipline in the form of a finger-pointing admonition called "oral warning." If violations are repeated, the additional steps of "written warning," "disciplinary layoff," and "termination" may ensue. The underlying assumption supporting this four-step "progressive disciplinary" procedure is that people will eventually shape up if the discipline becomes harsh enough. In practice, particularly with today's enlightened work force, it is found that such a Parent-Child approach is not appropriate as a behavior modification process. Moreover, it often incurs costly litigation.

Richard Grote[10] defines more constructive methods for handling discipline through a four-step progression that on the surface appears similar to

---

[10]Richard C. Grote, *Positive Discipline*, McGraw-Hill, New York, 1979.

the traditional steps mentioned above. However, their implementation is based on theory Y assumptions which are more likely to evoke commitment than resentment. The four steps of positive discipline are:

1. Oral reminder
2. Written reminder
3. Decision-making leave
4. Discharge

The oral reminder is an Adult-Adult discussion of the problem rather than an attack on, or criticism of, the offender. The aim is to evoke a voluntary commitment and plan to prevent recurrence of the problem. In the Eaton Corporation described in Chapter 3, this first step is labeled disciplinary counseling. The written reminder is a description of the problem, written by the supervisor, in phraseology which both persons agree is fair and accurate. The violator receives a copy of the statement, and a copy is placed in the personnel file with the understanding that it will be removed at some mutually agreed-upon time, appropriate to the seriousness of the offense, when the violator has demonstrated success in solving the problem. Decision-making leave with pay is given an offender who has not successfully responded to previous corrective attempts. The leave period, which may range from a half-day to a week or more, allows a period of deliberation to enable the violator to decide whether he will follow the rules and stay with the organization, or resign. The fourth step is termination from the work force as a result of failure of the preceding steps to correct the problem. Discharge can also take place for very serious offenses without going through the previous three steps.

Anecdotal testimonials from companies employing positive discipline show it to be effective in modifying behavior and also not costly to the organization. Needless to say, responsible reaction to decision-making leave could not be expected if introduced into win-lose adversary circumstances. However, in a climate of evolving collaborative commitment, where it is understood that the price of freedom is responsibility, positive discipline could serve both a cause and an effect role in creating and maintaining a harmonious work place.

Role of the Labor Relations Specialist

The labor relations specialist's responsibility must be focused increasingly on preventive maintenance and less on the fire-fighting or counterbalancing role of dealing with problems spun out by inept supervision. Though he must, of course, continue to handle these problems as they are surfaced, his talents are better applied in reorienting supervision to prevent their recurrence. The reorientation problem is not restricted to the lower levels of supervision, but perhaps is even more applicable to middle and upper-middle management's nonverbal communications. The labor relations person is prepared to orient supervisors to understand behavior as a response to the restrictions and opportunities represented by the job and supervision. In an advisory or educative role he reinforces them as they relinquish outmoded supervisory tactics and gradually internalize the definition of supervision defined earlier. He is succeeding in his new role when supervisors are able to surface and cope with conflict within their own natural work groups with diminishing reliance on personnel specialists to bail them out.

In addition to his educative role, the effective labor relations specialist is qualified by his combination of professional competence and responsibility to serve the following ongoing functions:

1. Pulse taking within the work force and the community to anticipate, and prepare strategies against, irresponsible actions of labor unions.

2. Imparting legal advice to supervisors, systems designers, and procedure writers to prevent innocent infractions of rules.

3. Provision of information to local, state, and Federal lawmakers to promote the enactment of sound industrial relations laws.

The nonunion plant offers the most immediate opportunity for the labor relations expert to serve his new role, and the qualified specialist can phase naturally into this new role with few transitional changes. In the unionized plant, the strategy is more complex and long-range. He must, of course, continue his fire-fighting functions during the early process of building interpersonal competence between management and union leadership, but 5 years of sustained effort by the company and union may be required before they feel they are working from a foundation of common goals. Having promoted interpersonal competence and compatible goals, the labor relations specialist can enter more fully into his new educative role of supporting the efforts of natural work groups to manage their own conflict.

THE TRANSPLANTED MANAGER

The widespread infiltration of American business into the divergent cultures of the world has given prominence to the problem of defining the roles of American managers and technicians who find themselves transported into new and strange cultural settings. Though many cultures are becoming "Westernized," most cling to certain vestiges of their unique cultural characteristics—some with unbending determination. Hence, the manager in the multinational organization must acquire greater competence in dealing with problems of intercultural conflict.

The hostile demonstrations against Americans concomitant with the overthrow of the Shah of Iran are testimonial to the failure of three decades of American advisors for educational, governmental, agricultural, and military programs in Iran to develop a persevering friendship with the people they were attempting to help. Nor is the hostility toward Americans restricted to Iran. Americans visiting other developing cultures in which billions of dollars of technical aid have been provided continue to encounter resentment. United States tourists abroad sometimes find it expedient to lead host-country citizens to believe they are Canadians. Not that Canadians have different personality traits; rather, Canada has not subjected other countries to the indignity of feeling inferior to, and dependent upon, a paternalistic benefactor. Within Canada, however, some of this same hostility is observed between the French- and English-speaking citizens whose only "crime" was being born into the "wrong" culture.

Detailed guidelines are needed for each culture, of course, and principles outlined herein are intended only as general guidelines for people on assignment in cultures whose social and economic status and values are different from their own. The desire that inheres in all individuals to manage their own lives is not, of course, restricted to Americans. "Every employee a manager" is a meaningful concept in every culture. However, one additional condition must be satisfied if indigenous people are to be led by an expatriate. Not only must the conditions for self-management as defined throughout this book be satisfied, but additionally special sensitivity must be shown to their need to preserve their cultural uniqueness and national pride.

Though this section is illustrated largely with examples of Americans on foreign assignments, the principles herein apply equally to managers and advisers who are simply adapting to the different cultures within their own country, community, or organization. For example, in joint union-management seminars it is apparent that the two parties bring different cultural values and perceptions to the confrontations. The mission of the joint seminar is to develop collaborative effort built on a shared data base.

Principles defined herein are based on the author's experience of almost 5 years in Iran and on visitations to the international operations of Texas Instruments. The text incorporates suggestions from Iraj Ayman, Franco Bertagnolio, Stewart Carrell, Pierre Clavier, Bill Dees, Manuchehr Derakhshani, Derek Lawrence, Gernot Mueller, Herman Peusens, Robert Pierson, Louis Pierson, John Powell, Homayoun Sahba, Ben Schranil, Don Wass, and Stephen Wilcock, most of whom are, or were, citizens of countries outside the United States. Though many American managers also agree with these principles, this section does not include the dissenting views of American managers whose managerial styles abroad and at home inspired its writing.

Managers and technicians on location outside the United States are presumed to be on transitory assignment with the primary mission of developing their local counterparts to take over operating responsibilities. In the balance of this book, the term "adviser" connotes the expatriate on duty outside his country, whether he be a professional manager or a technical expert, and the term "counterpart" refers to the local nationals) to whom he must transfer his managerial or technical competence.

Other-Culture Characteristics

Many of the factors in the foreign culture also exist at home, of course, and in this sense they are not new. However, in the amplified form in which they are sometimes encountered, they present new challenges to the adviser; and it may be the first time that his success has been so strongly dependent upon an understanding of these factors.

The Welcoming Facade   Americans arriving in a foreign country usually receive courteous and respectful treatment. The businessman and the appropriately dressed and behaved tourist are typically received with sincere friendliness. However, when the visitor takes up temporary residence in an extended business relationship with the local citizens, he may find that some of this behavior is a facade.

People in certain host countries seem to have developed a propensity for "rolling with the punches." This trait is an understandable consequence of a long history of hosting occupational troops and foreign advisers, many of whom were regarded as necessary evils to be tolerated for the sake of satisfying international agreements, protecting sovereignty, appeasing home-office officials, receiving financial or technical assistance, or stimulating commerce. Host-country officials tend to give advisers polite and courteous treatment, provide them with pleasant facilities, and avoid open disagreements, but they may show little initiative in implementing recommendations. It is easy for an adviser to be lulled into thinking he is receiving wholehearted support and understanding when, upon his departure, the most tangible evidence of his visit is an English-language report which is routed dutifully to selected readers and finally filed in the archives with earlier foreign advisers' reports.

The National Inferiority Complex   A "national inferiority complex" is one of the common self-ascribed traits in developing countries. However, inferiority feelings are sometimes disguised under a facade of "superiority." National inferiority feelings may have several roots. A common factor is the forced dependence of developing countries upon foreign capital, leadership, and political support. Another factor may be a country's minor role in world affairs, particularly for its foreign-educated citizens, whose sojourns abroad have sensitized them to their country's oblivion to the rest of the world. Unscrupulous and inept local leadership, with their consequential intellectual, social, economic, and moral impoverishment, may be key factors.

Americans abroad in key industrial roles may perpetuate inferiority feelings by their failure to respect local customs and values, to delegate responsibility to local personnel, to provide equitable compensation structures, to provide realistic opportunity for multinational assignments, or to develop indigenous personnel for key positions. Even when granted official autonomy, local managers in American international operations often feel they are being deprived by home-office authority of opportunity to succeed through their own initiative and competence. Though they may believe their association with the parent organization offers rich opportunity for realizing their personal and professional goals, they often feel subjected to unnecessary amounts of arbitrary and overbearing behavior by American bosses. They welcome and acknowledge the technical competence of the American adviser, but his manner of dispensing it may unintentionally reinforce their feelings of inferiority.

Fatalism   "Outer-directedness" and "fatalism" are terms to describe the feeling that life is controlled by forces outside one's influence. Though less common in Western cultures, many citizens in the Middle East, for example, preface statements of plans or aspirations with *ensha 'allah* (God willing). It is felt that plans come to fruition through chance factors or the influence of supernatural powers. Religion plays an ambiguous role, ranging from unquestioning acceptance of orthodox religion by the illiterate villager to agnosticism by many educated leaders and urban residents. Outer-directedness or fatalism, if not understood, can be a source of frustration to the adviser whose personal philosophy is more often based on self-reliance.

In some cultures (and in some organizations in all cultures), the selection and placement of persons for desired positions, particularly government offices, is said to be based more on nepotism and political alignment than on merit. In such cases, organizations are believed to be dominated by powerful networks of friends and relatives who protect and advance each other to the exclusion of outsiders. Regardless of the validity of this allegation, the presumed influence of nepotism in itself breeds fatalism and stifles initiative. Exceptions to this generalization are seen in "obligation cultures" of the Far East where networks of family, social, and political relationships are the media through which achievement needs are satisfied, and which have at least temporarily fostered successfully competitive organizations.

Other factors contributing to fatalism and despair include lack of confidence in management, the nearness of militant and unstable neighboring countries, lack of deep faith or common values, lack of vocational opportunities, health hazards, and unemployment.

Little evidence of realistic long-range planning exists in many of the developing countries. This is apparent in the personal life of the citizens, in business enterprise, and in public administration. Few seem willing or able to prepare for the inexorable realities of old age and death by subscribing to life insurance or financial security programs, or to budget living expenses in accordance with a realistic appraisal of personal incomes. Business and government planning more often reflects attempts to justify expenditures of funds rather than to achieve defined long-range goals. Workable plans for 5- and 10-year programs and strategies in business and government are virtually nonexistent.

Education for Status and Conformity The low status of manual vocations in many developing countries is a hindrance to industrial progress. Unwillingness to "get one's hands dirty" is one manifestation of a class-consciousness syndrome. Those who can afford education usually aspire to government office positions or professions with established high-status levels. It is difficult to attract talented people into blue-collar vocations, and thus skilled and semiskilled workers must come from the ranks of other craftsmen, laborers, and minority groups. However, recent progress in literacy and vocational training, plus accelerated acceptance of modern consumer products, is bringing into prominence new classes of craftsmen. The increasing need for mechanics, plumbers, electricians, machinists, and radio and television repairmen has raised the income of craftsmen, enabling them to buy the symbols of status. Their increasing affluence and sheer numbers are forming a new middle class which is giving its members, as individuals and as a class, more social acceptance and favorable recognition in their society.

Some of the educational processes in many cultures, including the United States, seem more suited to the development of followership than leadership qualities. Success in school is often based more on memory work than on logical and analytical reasoning, grades being influenced strongly by the student's ability to quote the instructor and memorize textbooks. Little opportunity is provided for students to begin bridging the gap between theory and practice by solving relevant problems, participating in laboratory experiments, and conducting original research. Heavy emphasis has been placed on perpetuating classical curricula. Students learn to "second-guess" the instructor, giving him the answer they think he wants, thereby establishing a survival pattern that naturally perseveres into relationships with supervisors in business and government.

Requisites for Intercultural Competence

The adviser's professional role is influenced by the fact that he is also a guest in a foreign country. It is easy for the visiting expert, particularly if he has had little foreign service experience, to be misled by the ingratiating behavior often encountered in host countries. The politeness, flattery, ceremony, hospitality, and generosity of his hosts may make it easy for the naïve adviser to assume an authoritarian order-giving role, or a passive and capitulatory role. He may fail to see beneath the expressions of humility and servility what is sometimes a deep-rooted hostility but more often an underlying and normal desire for recognition, reciprocity, equality, and independence.

Competence of Advisers   The American's success is determined by his successful fulfillment of two roles—his role as a competent technician and his role as an acceptable personality. His spoken word has little impact if his "language of action," on and off the job, conveys a conflicting message. He is seldom judged by the standards of his fellow countrymen, or even by the standards by which the local citizens evaluate each other, but rather by standards which fit their conceptual image of what the American should be.

The ideal adviser is a cosmopolitan—willing and able to adapt himself to the local culture. His job success is considerably enhanced by his tolerance for and readiness to adapt to local values, living patterns, foods, and social customs. He should be able to identify with people of various socioeconomic levels and participate in their local events, and nothing in his behavior or remarks should reflect disapproval or disparagement. His behavior should reflect acceptance of, respect for, and confidence in the country and its citizens.

The adviser's competence in the local language is an asset, perhaps more for the attitude it conveys than for the actual language facility. No matter how broken his grammar or thick his accent, if his use of the local language represents attempts to learn more about and adapt to the culture, it is usually well received. Language facility does not, of course, assure success, as some advisers, assigned because of language facility, have failed because of undesirable personality traits or technical incompetence. Hence, sensitive regard for the feelings of others is more important than language fluency per se.

The adviser's behavior should reflect the staff man's philosophy of staying out of the limelight. He must make his abilities known and available in a manner that will encourage the local people to use them, and will result in progress, recognition, and a sense of achievement and security for having done so.

The above characteristics of the American adviser are listed as ideals, recognizing that they exceed the qualifications that can be realistically imposed on all persons who must serve as advisers. Many advisers are appointed or requested because of their technical competence and availability, and to insist on their meeting all the above qualifications would leave their positions unfilled. However, the above qualifications, coupled with the total content of this paper, can serve as guidelines in selecting and training American advisers.

Competence of Counterparts   The counterpart's freedom to act independently and responsibly in behalf of his organization has a direct bearing on his ultimate success in carrying on in an executive or technical capacity after the departure of the adviser. If the adviser has influence in selecting his counterpart, care should be exercised that the candidate is not in any way disqualified for full support by local people. "Un-American" as these criteria may be, socioeconomic status, minority group membership, personality, his role during the adviser's visit, as well as technical competence are factors that may have a bearing on the counterpart's acceptance and support by local people, particularly after the departure of the adviser when the counterpart is left to his own resources.

Ideally, the counterpart's experience and education should have some relationship to his work. In the case of complex technologies, experience and education are, of course, highly relevant. However, a high correlation between the person's past experience and his ultimate administrative responsibility is not always necessary or even desirable. Nor is level of education a reliable predictor of success, other than the support it incurs through local values. James Lee[11] found that high school graduates in developing countries tend to display a higher degree of motivation than college graduates—perhaps due to the absence of the degree laurel on which to rest.

The prospective counterpart's motives are important considerations. Does he see his job as an opportunity to qualify himself for a meaningful role in a local organization, is he simply seeking to improve his English language facility, or is the job a steppingstone to emigration or a job in another company? Scarce as candidates are in most countries, compromises in selection standards are not the answer. The aspirations of the candidate should be aligned with company interest and in balance with his potential achievement level. He should have enough intelligence and language facility to be trainable, but not vastly more than is required for the ultimate job.

[11]James Lee, "Developing Managers in Developing Countries," *Harvard Business Review*, Nov.–Dec. 1968, pp. 55–65.

A source of talent often overlooked may be found in the ranks of host-country personnel in the United States enrolled in universities, on extended business assignments, or recent immigrants who would welcome opportunities to return to their home country in meaningful roles. Many find such assignments attractive, particularly under the condition of more liberal compensation plans and the diplomatic protection of American citizenship. However, the Americanized returnee, who becomes known as the "150 percent American" because of his tendency to use invidious comparisons, may be poorly qualified for native country assignment.

The assessment of aptitudes of multilingual people often presents a unique problem which can mislead the inexperienced test interpreter. Nationals who have received much of their education and other language facility in other countries tend to be handicapped in both languages. Their second-language competence seldom qualifies them to compete on mental ability tests on an equal basis with people of the other culture. At the same time, their educational leave from their country often arrests the development of their native-language facility. Hence, lacking complete facility in either language, their aptitude test scores in either language usually underestimate their true talent. Apart from the aptitude test handicaps, a local citizen with a "foreign" accent or substandard fluency in his own language may not be fully effective in business relationships.

Importance of the Host-Country Language   The host country's language is the everyday language of the people in which school textbooks and newspapers are printed and through which local business is transacted. However, in some countries the problem is complicated by the existence of various dialects. Though an "official" language may be prescribed, legislation seldom succeeds in effecting the countrywide adoption of a common language. American management in this situation must secure agreement with the indigenous work force on their "company language of business" which will respect governmental policy, be sensitive to local sentiment, and serve the long-range needs of the organization and its members. Too often English is automatically presumed to be the official language without giving adequate concern to factors that might alter this presumption.

Use of the local business language in the definition of management systems and programs contributes in several ways to the development of the counterpart, the organization, and the country:

- The writing or translation process tests the counterpart's knowledge of the subject and gives him an opportunity to clarify questions in conference with the adviser.
- Use of the local business language results in the development and standardization of a technical vocabulary.

- Use of the local business language prepares the counterpart to communicate more fluently with his countrymen.
- Use of the local business language assures the message of a wider and more understanding readership in the local setting.
- Nationals are able to take a more active role in discussing, evaluating, modifying, and implementing a system defined in their own language.

The conference room or classroom is a special situation involving the adviser and counterpart for which the above principles also apply. It is a common practice for foreign advisers to give presentations or lectures with the assistance of interpreters. The local participants themselves frequently request this method of instruction to improve their foreign-language facility. But hearing the message in the foreign language may contribute little to their understanding of the subject matter, and because much technical terminology has no ready-made translations, it may actually interfere with their ability to apply the subject in their own culture. Since a culture is circumscribed by its language, there are many technical subjects which cannot be learned until terms are translated, coined, defined, or transliterated for use in the local language. The technical aid missionary innocently perpetuates the problem by teaching classes in the local setting in his own language. The local citizen who has returned with a new degree acquired abroad is ultimately required to make his effectiveness felt locally through his own language, and he may find his language inadequate to convey ideas learned in the foreign language. Hence, much can be gained by going through the tedious procedure of preparing presentations in the local language, developing the necessary vocabulary, and preparing indigenous people to present the information.

The language barrier sometimes works to the disadvantage of the counterpart despite the conscientious efforts of a competent adviser. For example, when advisers are not fluent in the local language, it is necessary to develop all ideas, programs, and correspondence first in the adviser's language and then translate them into the local language. Even if the counterpart contributed most of the ideas in developing a program, the very fact that it appeared first in English and then was translated into the local language creates an impression that the nationals are borrowing a foreign idea. The mechanics of translation are such that a local reader can usually discern that the style is not spontaneous or natural and that it is a translation of a foreign proposal. The counterpart's success in writing a meaningful and intelligent proposal or system in his own language is, of course, a direct function of his technical competence and often a measure of the success of the adviser.

Relationships that Fail The counterpart-adviser relationship is a subtle and crucial one which, if properly developed, takes the counterpart through a process of training and personal development which enables him to carry on independently after the departure of the adviser. It is not a static relationship, but one that undergoes continuous and progressive change. In the beginning, it may have many characteristics of the instructor-student or supervisor-subordinate relationship. But the adviser must avoid crystallizing and prolonging this dependency relationship, however appropriate it may have seemed initially, if the counterpart is ultimately to step into a leadership role.

Sometimes the adviser-counterpart relationship is destined to at least initial failure by the manner in which the adviser is introduced to his assignment. Consider, for example, the impact of the following note sent to a manager of a European subsidiary by his supervisor in the States:

> To: Hans F. Wilhelm
> From: J. T. Johnson
>
> Dear Hans,
> Herewith I am asking you to list the problems you have in running your business and send this list to Jim Smith so that he will be able to plan a program for himself and you. Jim will visit you two weeks from now and will stay for approximately six months to help you increase your personal effectiveness.
>
> Regards,
> J. T. Johnson

The understandable defensiveness of the recipient naturally failed to evoke the cooperation essential to the counterpart-adviser relationship. The alienation of the counterpart (behind a facade of tight-lipped courtesy and respect) put the adviser in a position of taking unilateral actions which were neither as appropriate nor as well accepted as they could have been through a jointly initiated and developed strategy.

Advisers, even when appropriately introduced to their mission, are sometimes insensitive to the benefits of participation, and launch a program of their own creation without "wasting time" by explaining it to their counterparts or involving them in the development of the proposal. Consequently, many counterparts never fully understand their adviser's program, or if they do finally understand it, the time lag between the adviser's conception and their understanding of it deprives them of the opportunity to contribute to its development. Thus the counterpart role in developing a program is often confined to the translation of words and partially understood or unintegrated ideas for which he feels no commitment. Not only does this type of relationship fail to develop the national into an able associate, but it actually develops and reinforces conformity behavior and feelings of subordination and inferiority.

Many counterparts never get beyond the interpreter-translator role. Retention of the counterpart in such a role reflects an assumption that the counterpart has no ideas of his own, thereby contributing to his feelings of incompetence and dependency. The adviser commonly concludes after a few cursory and unsatisfactory trials that his counterpart can have no ideas of his own, not realizing that this innovative impoverishment has been reinforced by his own behavior.

The typical role of the counterpart manager is one that rarely affords him opportunity to acquire the abilities of his in-residence American adviser. From the time he meets the adviser at the airport, as instructed by the home office, the local manager may find himself serving as a "detail kid" or office boy for the American, becoming his echo through his translating and interpreting activities. He arranges appointments and transportation, and performs many other routine administrative and clerical duties. This self-perpetuating pattern of servility and desire to please sometimes even extends to the performance of personal services for the visiting manager after working hours. Through this gradual conditioning process, his personality becomes submerged and dominated to the extent that his creativity and initiative are replaced by blind conformity.

The Development of Counterparts

When the American adviser completes his tour of duty, the program he has initiated or rejuvenated sometimes deteriorates or collapses. This failure is not intentional, of course, but usually stems from the expert's lack of familiarity with principles and techniques for developing the people who are to perpetuate and support it.

The Counterpart as a Peer   The richest opportunities to develop local managers, and at the same time to develop sounder programs, are frequently overlooked. For example, it is not unusual to find a group of home-office managers in conference on location developing policies and programs without the participation of local personnel. Not only does this practice deprive the planners of the type of guidance that only indigenous personnel can provide regarding laws, practices, resources, customs, and other cultural factors, but it also results in the development of programs not fully understood by the people who are to implement them. On occasions when counterparts are included in meetings, the adviser usually dominates the conversation and decision making, the counterpart merely parroting him in the local language. The counterpart's prestige and self-respect are undermined by this pattern.

The counterpart's role in business meetings is critical to his development. Generally speaking, local personnel should outnumber expatriates in planning meetings and financial reviews, and the local language should be the primary medium of communication. With little preparation, the counterpart's role in a meeting can be changed from what appears to be that of a mere assistant or interpreter to that of a responsible and qualified executive or technician. The counterpart himself can assume the major role in the meeting, if he is coauthor of the subject matter for the meeting, or at least is thoroughly briefed prior to the meeting. The following advantages result from this approach:

1.   The counterpart acquires essential knowledge in the process of preparing for the meeting.

2.   His commitment to the program, resulting from his role in developing it, enhances its chances of success.

3.   His use of his own language enables him to evoke more participation and commitment from local personnel.

4.   His initiative and freedom from dependence on the adviser enhance his status in the eyes of his countrymen.

5.   The relegation of foreign advisers to a more appropriate "adviser" role tends to bolster the self-confidence of local managers and their willingness to accept responsibility.

The adviser's conduct at all times should reflect a sincere conviction that his counterpart is socially his equal and organizationally his superior. From the beginning of the relationship, the adviser must show respect to his counterpart as ultimate administrator of their developing program. Though the initiative is in the hands of the counterpart, he must, of course, be preconditioned to integrate the goals of the local plant with the needs of the total corporation. The adviser and counterpart must finally agree on the objectives of the program through candid and continuous interchange of ideas between them. Agreement should not be obtained by authority from any source, but rather from consensus gained through open exchange of information among all participants. Ideally, plans, programs, and proposals are developed first in the local language, and are translated into the adviser's language only as an expedient for involving him or for transmitting plans and reports to the home office.

The Adviser as a Trainer   If the primary role of the American adviser is to develop nationals to meet their responsibilities, he is first and foremost a trainer with full awareness of the principles of training outlined on pages 162 to 176. His ability to train others requires competence both in his field of specialization and in knowledge of learning processes. Though learning takes place naturally as a consequence of involvement in the managing process, the training process defined by the professional trainer—prepare, present, perform, and follow up—can be a helpful frame of reference.

The *preparation* phase of the long-term relationship is one in which the adviser and his local counterpart get acquainted, become adjusted to each other's idiosyncrasies, assess physical and human resources, and jointly develop appropriate plans. In the *presentation* stage, the adviser develops a peer relationship with his counterpart, while instructing or assisting him in various skills, knowledge, and procedures. He will participate with the counterpart, for example, in balancing a production line, designing a system, planning a financial review, conducting a market survey, setting up a cost accounting system, and preparing a proposal. It may be appropriate for the adviser and counterpart to visit an effective operation together, in the United States or in other international operations. The adviser should realize that his style in giving instructions or leading conferences is usually emulated by the counterpart. In the *performance* stage of the relationship, the counterpart begins to take the lead in managing, calling on the adviser when he elects to do so. If the adviser-counterpart relationship is based on authentic relationships developed early, the adviser can help the counterpart to benefit from successes and failures through feedback and discussion. This critique is effective only if it is a candid and informal, but mutually respectful, two-way process. The final or *follow-up* step begins with the phase-out of the adviser. An adviser on a 2-year assignment should aim to begin his phase-out 3 to 6 months before departure—to be on hand if needed and to participate in or monitor periodic progress reports. Ideally, the follow-up relationship is continued after the adviser's return home by occasional exchanges of information by mail and, when requested by the counterpart, return consultation trips.

Opening New Plants   The foregoing principles are guidelines for advisers serving already established plants. However, they are equally valid when planning the establishment of new plants. Presumably the opening of new operations provides opportunity to start off with a clean slate, with the advantage of forward planning. In practice, the opening of new plants often occurs as a crash effort with little benefit from advance planning. As a consequence, the advantage presumed to be gained by the hasty implementation of a decision is often lost in the costs of coping with unanticipated problems and administering inappropriate systems, and in the alienation of nationals through inept supervision by transplanted Americans. The appointment of an expatriate manager, particularly for a sustained period, not only undermines the initiative of the subordinate indigenous manager but also handicaps the organization with a leader unacquainted with the host country's culture. It also sometimes leads to the local manager's emulation of American habits or styles of management which are unnatural to him and, hence, tend to alienate him from his countrymen.

Ideally, the opening of a new plant should be preceded by the recruitment of several high-potential managers from the host country for assignment in at least one of the company's successful operations for a period of from 6 to 24 months, to serve in one or more broad operating roles. During their assignment with the parent organization, they should have opportunity to participate with officers and high-level managers in long-range planning activities and in planning the mission, location, and layout of the plant they are destined to manage, and to visit other international operations. Also, during this home-office assignment they should be able to recruit additional personnel from their home country to be given technical training in the parent organization. This strategy would enable managers, in opening and managing new operations, to establish long- and short-range charters compatible with the long-range goals of the parent organization, would prepare them to cope with technological problems, and would help free them from overdependence on American managers.

In practice, the ideal lead time usually does not exist to select and prepare indigenous managers to open and manage plants. The American typically moves in on the assumption that it is too late to find local leadership on short notice, and that this problem can be deferred until the plant is operating successfully. The survival and apparent financial success of operations initiated through this crash strategy would seem to defend it. However, the development of a competent and committed indigenous work force, necessary for sustained organizational effectiveness, is deferred until local leadership and ego involvement find expression.

When an American manager or specialist is sent abroad, he should be a winner by usual home-office standards. He should have distinguished himself by his achievements as a comptroller, manufacturing manager, sales manager, systems analyst, etc., in terms of his technological competence in his area of specialty and his knowledge of company procedures and philosophy. The marginal performer who is sent abroad because he has exhausted home-office opportunities cannot be expected to overcome his characteristic shortcomings and, in addition, to display the skills of an international diplomat.

An organization reflects the personality and management style of the top executive and the people reporting directly to him. Organizations tend to attract and develop, through a multiplier process, individuals whose values and style of management match those of the organization's leaders. Hence, selection of the manager to head up a new organization is tantamount to programming the management style and effectiveness of the organization.

Protecting the Local Manager's Autonomy   Once a manager is established in charge of an operation with self-influenced goals and criteria for evaluation, and opportunities to update his charter through involvement in company and division planning activities, he is much better prepared professionally and emotionally to manage his operation. Every effort should be made to grant organizational status to managers of autonomous operations, with titles reflecting appropriate status in the local culture. Criteria based on factors such as gross sales, return on investment, share of the market, profitability, and growth rate could be a basis for elevating an operation to a group or division status and for promoting a plant manager to officer status (e.g., president of a Swedish subsidiary, or assistant vice president or vice president for Italian operations). This increased status would then be both a measure of, and an incentive for, his effectiveness as a manager.

Having succeeded in granting autonomy and opportunity for responsibility to the plant manager, the role of the adviser becomes more appropriately centered on dispensing technical advice rather than authority, and he acts in this consultant role at the request and under the direction of his client, the local manager. The local manager has the freedom to terminate the adviser's assignment without fear of reprisal. The key point here is that the adviser is seen less as a threatening authority figure and more as a source of help to be utilized as defined by the local line manager in achieving his organizational goals. Since the operating manager is measured against company standards through a philosophy of self-direction and self-control, he will naturally seek to utilize technical assistance, from whatever source, in a manner which will best achieve his organizational goals.

Index

Index